"This is a solid work of biblical exposition. I would expect nothing less from the pen of Al Mohler. This is a welcomed addition to the Christ-Centered Exposition series and will serve well all who dive into the wonderful epistle to the Hebrews."

Daniel L. Akin, president, Southeastern Baptist Theological Seminary

"Albert Mohler is to be commended for providing readers with a theologically focused, exegetically faithful, and Christ-honoring exposition of the book of Hebrews. This insightful and impressive commentary on one of the most challenging books in the New Testament simultaneously points readers to the superiority of Christ while wrestling with the historical meaning and contemporary significance of the book's structure, as well as the serious warning passages scattered throughout the epistle. In doing so, Mohler has given us more than a cogent and clearly written theological commentary for preachers and teachers, he has also provided his readers with an immensely helpful, warm-hearted resource for all who wish to understand the truth of God's Word. It is a joy to recommend this marvelous book for pastors, church leaders, and students alike."

David S. Dockery, president, Trinity International University

"Albert Mohler is, by any measure, among the most important Christian leaders of the century. He consistently calls the church and the world to the authority and sufficiency of God's Word. This commentary demonstrates keen exegetical insight, sharp personal application, and deep worldview analysis. This commentary brilliantly equips the Christian to see and proclaim the glory of Christ from a biblical book that ties together the whole story of redemption."

Russell Moore, president, Ethics & Religious Liberty Commission of the Southern Baptist Convention

"When Dr. Al Mohler is involved, I always have a difficult time knowing whether I had rather read his philosophy and worldview insights or to peruse his keen exposition of Scripture. This volume on Hebrews may solve the equation. Polymath extraordinaire, Mohler mixes that intellectual attainment with a tender heart for God's Word and a love for the auditor in a rare style of commentary for preaching to the man on the street. A man who plans to preach the Bible cannot afford to miss this commentary on Hebrews."

Paige Patterson, president, Southwestern Baptist Theological Seminary, Fort Worth, Texas

"Readers will be grateful for Mohler's biblically faithful and theologically rich exposition of Hebrews. Hebrews is often difficult for readers to understand. Mohler helps us comprehend the letter in its historical context but also applies it powerfully to today's world."

Thomas R. Schreiner, James Buchanan Harrison Professor of New Testament Interpretation and associate dean, The Southern Baptist Theological Seminay

"With this commendable commentary on Hebrews, Al Mohler has done preachers and teachers a great service. Readers will find that the book is thorough, informative, and profitable, and that it will stir up the coals and fan the flames of preaching passion and fire. Take up and read!"

Terry L. Wilder, Wesley Harrison Chair and professor of New Testament and associate dean, PhD Program, Southwestern Baptist Theological Seminary, Fort Worth, Texas

"No one navigates the stream of thought and flow of biblical revelation in Hebrews quite like R. Albert Mohler. With the focus of a careful exegete, the heart of a pastor, and a mind saturated in the redemptive history of its Old Testament background, Dr. Mohler makes the epistle to the Hebrews breathe and live for anyone who will walk with him across these pages. This commentary is like having one of the greatest contemporary preachers and theologians in the study with you, patiently helping you to understand, explain, and apply the text of Scripture."

Hershael W. York, Victor and Louise Lester Professor of Christian Preaching, Southwestern Baptist Theological Seminary, and pastor, Buck Run Baptist Church, Frankfort, Kentucky

NT / COMMENTARY

AUTHOR R. Albert Mohler Jr.
SERIES EDITORS David Platt, Daniel L. Akin, and Tony Merida

CHRIST-CENTERED
Exposition

EXALTING JESUS IN

HEBREWS

HOLMAN
REFERENCE

NASHVILLE, TENNESSEE

Christ-Centered Exposition Commentary: Exalting Jesus in Hebrews
© Copyright 2017 by R. Albert Mohler Jr.

B&H Publishing Group
Nashville, Tennessee
All rights reserved.

ISBN: 978-0-8054-9647-5

Dewey Decimal Classification: 220.7
Subject Heading: BIBLE. N.T. HEBREWS—
COMMENTARIES\JESUS CHRIST

Printed in the United States of America
1 2 3 4 5 6 7 8 9 10 • 22 21 20 19 18 17
V

SERIES DEDICATION

Dedicated to Adrian Rogers and John Piper. They have taught us to love the gospel of Jesus Christ, to preach the Bible as the inerrant Word of God, to pastor the church for which our Savior died, and to have a passion to see all nations gladly worship the Lamb.

—David Platt, Tony Merida, and Danny Akin
March 2013

TABLE OF CONTENTS

Acknowledgments   ix
Series Introduction   xi

Hebrews

Jesus: The Glorious King Who Speaks	1:1-3	3
Jesus: The Praiseworthy King Who Created	1:4-14	16
Jesus: Do Not Neglect His Salvation	2:1-9	23
Jesus: Our Tempted and Tried Savior and Priest	2:10-18	31
Jesus Is Greater Than Moses	3:1-6	41
Exhort and Encourage for the Sake of Faith	3:7-19	48
Let Us Enter His Rest!	4:1-13	55
Jesus: Our Tempted Yet Sinless High Priest	4:14-16	64
The Chosen High Priest	5:1-10	70
Warning against Stagnation	5:11-14	78
Warning against Apostasy	6:1-8	86
God's Certain Promise	6:9-20	93
Melchizedek the King-Priest	7:1-10	98
Jesus the Priest-King	7:11-22	105
Jesus the Superior Priest	7:23-28	112
The Great High Priest of the New Covenant	8:1-13	119
The Tabernacle and the New Covenant	9:1-10	126
The Superiority of Redemption in Christ	9:11-22	133
The Sufficient and Final Sacrifice of Christ	9:23-28	140
The Sufficiency of Christ's Once-for-All-Time Sacrifice	10:1-18	145
A Confident Confession of Christ	10:19-25	154
The Obedience of the Faithful	10:26-39	161

The Hall of Faith   11:1-10   169
The Faith of Abraham, Sarah, and Those
        Who Died in Faith   11:11-19   181
Faith in the Faithfulness of God   11:20-40   187
Run the Race   12:1-11   194
Running to Finish the Race   12:12-17   201
An Unshakable Kingdom   12:18-24   207
God's Impending Judgment   12:25-29   214
Final Instructions: Love, Marriage,
        and Money   13:1-6   219
Final Instructions   13:7-14   225
A Fitting Conclusion   13:15-25   231

Works Cited   237
Scripture Index   239

ACKNOWLEDGMENTS

The assignment of writing a commentary on the book of Hebrews is no small undertaking. This commentary began in the privilege of teaching and preaching the book of Hebrews, line by line, to members of Highview Baptist Church in Louisville, Kentucky, where my wife Mary and I were members for more than twenty years and where I gladly served as a teaching pastor. We remain so very thankful for this warm and faithful congregation. My expositional teaching on Hebrews lasted more than two years, and there is no way to exhaust the riches of any text of Scripture—and that was certainly clear as we studied Hebrews together.

Along the way, many others contributed to this project and to my ministry. Among these were an excellent team of interns in the Office of the President. They included Jeremiah Greever, Duncan Collins, Forrest Strickland, Chris Winegar, Andres Vera, John Pendleton, and Timothy Kleiser. These interns were a tremendous team, and I am thankful for every one of them. Matt Tyler and Jon Swan served as my personal librarians during this project, and they also contributed tremendous assistance. Jon Pentecost served as my media producer during this period, and I am very thankful for him. J. T. English and Thomas Hellams served as executive assistant and chief of staff in my office during these years, and both of them made a dedicated contribution to this effort—believing in it with patience and understanding.

Two others deserve special commendation. Sam Emadi, director of research, is simply the indispensable man in organizing, supervising, and orchestrating the flow of all the books, writing projects, lectures, speeches, sermons, essays, and other projects I commit myself to do. A man of great scholarship and even greater heart—to him I owe a great debt of gratitude.

Similarly, I want to thank Ryan Troglin, who really assumed responsibility for the management of this project and helped me to transform the content from sermon and teaching to a commentary that would serve the church for years to come. Without him, this project would have remained incomplete.

I am thankful for all the faithful preachers and scholars who have added to my understanding of the book of Hebrews and to the teaching faculty of The Southern Baptist Theological Seminary, with whom I have been privileged to teach and lead for almost twenty-five years.

Finally, as always, my greatest debt in this life is to my wife, Mary, who has so sweetly and perceptively encouraged me in every good work, who listened to me preach and teach almost every word, who encouraged me beyond all measure, and who adds more to my life than any words can express.

SERIES INTRODUCTION

Augustine said, "Where Scripture speaks, God speaks." The editors of the Christ-Centered Exposition Commentary series believe that where God speaks, the pastor must speak. God speaks through his written Word. We must speak from that Word. We believe the Bible is God breathed, authoritative, inerrant, sufficient, understandable, necessary, and timeless. We also affirm that the Bible is a Christ-centered book; that is, it contains a unified story of redemptive history of which Jesus is the hero. Because of this Christ-centered trajectory that runs from Genesis 1 through Revelation 22, we believe the Bible has a corresponding global-missions thrust. From beginning to end, we see God's mission as one of making worshipers of Christ from every tribe and tongue worked out through this redemptive drama in Scripture. To that end we must preach the Word.

In addition to these distinct convictions, the Christ-Centered Exposition Commentary series has some distinguishing characteristics. First, this series seeks to display exegetical accuracy. What the Bible says is what we want to say. While not every volume in the series will be a verse-by-verse commentary, we nevertheless desire to handle the text carefully and explain it rightly. Those who teach and preach bear the heavy responsibility of saying what God has said in his Word and declaring what God has done in Christ. We desire to handle God's Word faithfully, knowing that we must give an account for how we have fulfilled this holy calling (Jas 3:1).

Second, the Christ-Centered Exposition Commentary series has pastors in view. While we hope others, such as parents, teachers, small-group leaders, and student ministers, will read this series, we desire to provide a commentary busy pastors will use for weekly preparation of biblically faithful and gospel-saturated sermons. This series is not academic in nature. Our aim is to present a readable and pastoral style of commentaries. We believe this aim will serve the church of the Lord Jesus Christ.

Third, we want the Christ-Centered Exposition Commentary series to be known for the inclusion of helpful illustrations and theologically driven applications. Many commentaries offer no help in illustrations, and few offer any kind of help in application. Often those that do offer illustrative material and application unfortunately give little serious attention to the text. While giving ourselves primarily to explanation, we also hope to serve readers by providing inspiring and illuminating illustrations coupled with timely and timeless application.

Finally, as the series name suggests, the editors seek to exalt Jesus from every book of the Bible. In saying this we are not commending wild allegory or fanciful typology. We certainly believe we must be constrained to the meaning intended by the divine Author himself, the Holy Spirit of God. However, we also believe the Bible has a messianic focus, and our hope is that the individual authors will exalt Christ from particular texts. Luke 24:25-27,44-47 and John 5:39,46 inform both our hermeneutics and our homiletics. Not every author will do this the same way or have the same degree of Christ-centered emphasis. That is fine with us. We believe faithful exposition that is Christ centered is not monolithic. We also believe, however, that we must read the whole Bible as Christian Scripture. Therefore, our aim is both to honor the historical particularity of each biblical passage and to highlight its intrinsic connection to the Redeemer.

The editors are indebted to the contributors of each volume. The reader will detect a unique style from each writer, and we celebrate these unique gifts and traits. While distinctive in their approaches, the authors share a common characteristic in that they are pastoral theologians. They love the church, and they regularly preach and teach God's Word to God's people. Further, many of these contributors are younger voices. We think these new, fresh voices can serve the church well, especially among a rising generation that has the task of proclaiming the Word of Christ and the Christ of the Word to the lost world.

We hope and pray this series will serve the body of Christ well in these ways until our Savior returns in glory. If it does, we will have succeeded in our assignment.

David Platt
Daniel L. Akin
Tony Merida
Series Editors
February 2013

Hebrews

Jesus: The Glorious King Who Speaks

HEBREWS 1:1-3

Main Idea: God has spoken to his people in many ways, but he has now spoken to us by his Son, Jesus Christ, who is the exact imprint of his Father's glory, the agent of creation, the purifying sacrifice for our sins, and the King who rules the cosmos from his rightful place at the right hand of his Father.

I. **Introduction**
   A. Title
   B. Original audience
   C. Date of composition
   D. Author
   E. Prolegomena: keeping our Old Testament open
II. **Hearing God's Revelation from Long Ago (1:1)**
III. **Listening to God's Revelation in the Last Days (1:2)**
IV. **Seeing the Supremacy of God's Final Revelation (1:3)**

Introduction

Hebrews is certainly one of the most intriguing books of the New Testament. It poses unique challenges, particularly when it comes to answering introductory questions regarding its author and original audience. Hebrews is peculiar in this sense. For example, the letters of Paul not only explicitly state that Paul was the author of each epistle, they also often explicitly or implicitly indicate the historical context, the audience, and the situation surrounding the origin of the letter. Of course, similar statements could be made about the epistles of Peter, Acts, Revelation, and even the Gospels.

Yet the book of Hebrews—so rich in its biblical theological exploration of the work of Christ and the gospel—provides very little information about its own origin. In fact, we know almost nothing about who wrote it, its original audience, or the context behind it. In order to set the stage, we will examine the following introductory issues:

- Title
- Original Audience

- Date of Composition
- Author

Title

We typically refer to this book simply as "Hebrews." The title found in most ancient manuscripts reads, "to the Hebrews," thus identifying this book as a letter or an epistle. Hebrews, however, is unique in that it does not begin with a salutation, as in the case of Paul's epistles. Yet, while the book does not have a typical epistolary salutation, other features of this book (particularly its end) share similarities with other epistles in Scripture.

Original Audience

Who were the original recipients of this letter? As already stated, in ancient manuscripts the epistle is addressed "to the Hebrews." The tone of the book assumes that the readers were Christians. This indicates that the book must have been meant for a Jewish community that had converted to Christianity. But this does not necessarily answer every question about the original audience. Some in the early church suggested that the letter might have been intended for converts who were formerly Jewish priests, since Hebrews assumes a great deal of knowledge about the Old Testament Scriptures and the Levitical priesthood. As intriguing as this suggestion may be, there is no evidence that the letter is intended for such a specific group.

The most detailed description we can give of the overall audience is that they were converted Jews. Other clues in Hebrews also reveal some traits of the original recipients. Hebrews is obviously written to people who have a significant amount of knowledge of the Old Testament. At the same time, the author of Hebrews frequently quotes from the Septuagint (the Greek translation of the Hebrew Old Testament), demonstrating that this is the version of the Scriptures most familiar to the original audience. Since they were depending on the Septuagint, it is likely that the audience was made up of Hellenistic Jews. They composed part of the cosmopolitan areas in the Greco-Roman Empire outside of Palestine. Their primary language was Greek, and they mainly resided in Alexandria and Rome.

Ultimately, we must exercise a certain reluctance to be dogmatic in our historical reconstructions. Three things we do know about the

Epistle to the Hebrews are that it was written to the church of the Lord Jesus Christ (2 Tim 3:16-17), it plays a unique role in the canon, and it instructs all Christians on how to read the Old Testament in proper relation to Christ.

Date of Composition

Hebrews was probably written prior to AD 70 and the destruction of the Jewish temple. The epistle was almost certainly penned prior to this date because the book mentions the sacrificial system in Jerusalem as if it were still in place (7:27-28; 8:3-5; 10:1-3). Furthermore, the book mentions Timothy (13:23), who we know from elsewhere in Scripture was a contemporary of the apostle Paul. These clues point to the fact that Hebrews was written sometime before the Romans destroyed the Jerusalem temple in AD 70.

Author

Who wrote Hebrews? Ultimately we do not know. Biblical authority and inerrancy require that we affirm the authorship of every book as it is attributed within the Scriptures. Therefore, we must contend for the fact that Peter wrote 1 and 2 Peter because that claim is made within the inerrant text itself. The same applies for the epistles of Paul. When it comes to anonymous authors of New Testament books (e.g., Matthew, Mark, Luke, Acts), we have good historical and textual reasons to continue to affirm the traditionally proposed authors. Hebrews, however, does not give any hints as to who wrote it. Furthermore, there is no unanimous historical tradition that testifies to a specific author. In fact, scholars have posited several possible authors for the letter.

Many in the history of the church have proposed that Paul wrote Hebrews, but there is no evidence that Paul wrote this letter. As a matter of fact, the grammar, syntax, and phraseology found in Hebrews are not characteristic of Paul's writing. What is characteristic of Paul's writings, however, is a salutation in which Paul makes clear that he is the author! Moreover, Paul often indicates that he writes as one with apostolic authority. The author of Hebrews, however, never makes such claims. Instead, the author of Hebrews communicates as one who is affirming the truth of what was revealed to the church through the apostles.

Other suggestions as to who wrote the book include Apollos, Barnabas, and Luke. The reason these names crop up is because the author of Hebrews seems to have known Timothy intimately, thus linking him with the apostolic circle. There are, however, problems with each of these proposals. Luke, for example, comes from a Gentile background—a background that has obviously influenced the way he wrote both his Gospel and the book of Acts. Hebrews, on the other hand, seems more likely to have been written by someone immersed in Judaism. Barnabas is an attractive choice since he was a Levite. His Levitical status would explain the book's attention to priestly issues, but there still remains a lack of evidence for assigning authorship to Barnabas. The eloquence of the letter could point to Apollos as the author, but again, there is insufficient evidence to ascribe Hebrews to Apollos. Proposed authors for the book of Hebrews are simply appealing guesses.

Ultimately, we need to limit our imaginations and trust that the Holy Spirit has given us all that we need. God, in his providence, did not reveal to us the human author or the original recipients. Evidently we are not meant to know these things and can still understand this book. Perhaps God did not reveal that data because with it we might read the book differently from the way the Holy Spirit has intended for us to read it. What is clear is that the Holy Spirit desires for us to read this book— along with all of Scripture—as written to "the church." Therefore, we must approach the book of Hebrews understanding that it is God's word to all Christians, and we must allow the book to shape how we read the Old Testament after the reality of Christ's sacrificial work on the cross.

Prolegomena: Keeping Our Old Testaments Open

Many Christians find Hebrews a very challenging book to understand. This is most likely because Hebrews assumes a certain amount of knowledge of the Old Testament. Hebrews discusses most of the major figures, covenants, and biblical-theological themes found there. The book even spends a significant amount of time discussing minor characters in the Old Testament such as Melchizedek. Therefore, in order to understand this New Testament letter we must become familiar with the history, themes, and theology of the Old Testament. Hebrews will guide us along this journey, but it is important that we keep our Old Testaments open as we read this epistle.

Hearing God's Revelation from Long Ago
HEBREWS 1:1

Hebrews 1:1 begins with the words "long ago." Just like Genesis and the Gospel of John, Hebrews opens with a chronological reference taking readers back to the beginning of creation. This is a remarkable feature of Hebrews, one that sets a trajectory for how the book needs to be interpreted. These introductory verses set the context for how the author of Hebrews will explain the gospel. It is significant that he begins his retelling of the gospel not with Jesus's birth in Bethlehem, but with the creation narrative and the covenants in the Old Testament. Why is this so weighty? Because the Holy Spirit, through the author of Hebrews, is placing the story of Christ within the context of God's entire redemptive plan—a redemptive plan that spans from creation to new creation. The person and work of Christ can only be rightly understood when given proper place at the center of history's metanarrative. The story of God's saving work in Jesus Christ begins not just during the age of the Roman Empire but "long ago" in the narratives of the Old Testament. The account of God's saving work in Jesus Christ begins at the very beginning of creation.

The writer also highlights that understanding the story of Jesus and his work on the cross means grasping that the incarnation of Christ was not the first time God intervened in history. The incarnation is certainly unique among God's acts in history, but God has been active in unfolding the drama of redemption and setting the stage for the incarnation of his Son since the dawn of creation. Specifically, God has been active in speaking. The gospel comes to us in the context of a revelation that has already been delivered to us by God. The gospel is not God's first word to humanity, nor does it arrive in a vacuum. For centuries Yahweh "spoke to the fathers by the prophets." This revelation came "at different times and in different ways." Sometimes God spoke through dreams, in visions, by inspiring Scripture, and even through a donkey (Num 22:28-30)! In all this, what has been preserved for us in the Old Testament is the inerrant record of God's word and its faithful transmission to his people.

The use of the phrase *the fathers by the prophets* not only establishes the theological and redemptive-historical context for the epistle but also subtly introduces the author's apologetic argument for the superiority of Christ over the old covenant. The fathers and the prophets were the reference point for any type of theological argumentation for the Jewish community. The ultimate authority was God's revelation found in Israel's Scriptures. In fact, as early as the very next verse (1:2), the author will begin demonstrating how Jesus has fulfilled (not abolished, see Matt 5:17) God's revelation given in the Old Testament.

Obviously, the author of Hebrews carefully crafted this introductory verse. He affirms the authenticity and authority of the Old Testament. The Old Testament continues to function authoritatively for God's people. Yet at the same time, as the next verse will show, there is something more. The Old Testament is a story in need of a conclusion—a messianic conclusion. The fathers and the prophets indeed spoke the word of God, but that word was not the final word.

Excursus: The God Who Speaks

One of the most important assertions made by the author of Hebrews in these initial verses is that God is a speaking God. The Bible regularly affirms this fact, and Hebrews 1:1-3 reminds us that few things are more important than the notion that God has spoken throughout history and has now given his final revelation in Jesus Christ. The Bible also regularly reminds us that God's revelation is part and parcel of his amazing grace to us. We regularly think of God's grace in the context of salvation, but we must also think about God's grace in the context of revelation.

If God did not reveal himself to us in his Word, we would have no knowledge of the meaning of the cross and resurrection of Christ, nor would we have any knowledge of the appropriate response to the gospel. In other words, we could not know God without revelation. Carl F. H. Henry describes this beautifully when he speaks of revelation as God's willful disclosure, through which he forfeits his own personal privacy so that his creatures might know Him (*God Who Speaks*, 405). We have no claim on God. There is no necessity for him to forfeit his own personal privacy. More simply, in the words of Francis Schaeffer's book title, "he is there and he is not silent." It is nothing but pure grace on God's part for him to speak to us. We do not deserve his life-giving words. If God could not or did not speak, we would be left in darkness and ignorance.

The Bible also clearly indicates that there are two types of revelation. First, God has spoken to us in nature. This is called *general* revelation. Psalm 19:1-2 clearly affirms this reality:

> *The heavens declare the glory of God,*
>   *and the expanse proclaims the work of his hands.*
> *Day after day they pour out speech;*
>   *night after night they communicate knowledge.*

Romans 1 also clarifies the nature, extent, and purpose of general revelation. In general revelation, God's "invisible attributes, that is, his eternal power and divine nature, have been clearly seen . . . through what he has made" (Rom 1:20). Yet at the same time, general revelation is not sufficient to give us any understanding of salvation available in Christ.

The second type of revelation spoken of in Scripture is *special* revelation. This is the type of revelation referred to by Hebrews 1:1-3. This type of revelation is direct, verbal revelation that comes from the very mouth of God. Special revelation is what we have in Scripture: when Scripture speaks, God speaks.

Listening to God's Revelation in the Last Days
HEBREWS 1:2

In this verse the author is contrasting two different periods of time: what took place "long ago" among the fathers and prophets (in the former days), and what has now taken place in Christ Jesus ("in these last days"). Verses like this help shape our biblical theology and remind us that the overarching schema of reading the Old and New Testaments in relation to one another is one of promise and fulfillment. As the writer of Hebrews will meticulously demonstrate in the coming chapters, the New Testament fulfills the Old Testament. The climax of God's redemption is found only in Jesus Christ.

In one sense, the fact that God has spoken is not new. As we already discussed, the gospel must be understood within the context of the revelation already provided by God. Jesus is the conclusion to an already existing story found in the Old Testament. Yet, in another sense, God's revelation through his Son is new. The gospel story is the long-awaited conclusion that fulfills all promises and realizes all types and shadows of the Old Testament.

A clear qualitative difference exists between a prophet and a son. Further, this Son is defined in Hebrews in a way that demands that readers recognize the divine character of the Son. God is no longer merely speaking through the prophets; he is now speaking through a son—*his* Son. The Son is the fullest, most complete revelation of the Father possible since he shares the Father's divine nature as the second member of the Trinity.

This Son is designated as the "heir of all things." The writer of Hebrews is using traditional categories of Hellenistic Judaism that his audience would have understood. To be an "heir" was to be invested with everything. The son is given full authority. To do business with the son means to do business with the father. Moreover, if you are going to know this Father, you can only do so through his Son (John 14:6-7).

The next phrase, he "made the universe through him," recalls the language of John's prologue:

> *In the beginning was the Word, and the Word was with God, and the Word was God. He was with God in the beginning. All things were created through him, and apart from him not one thing was created that has been created.* (John 1:1-3)

The Son is not only the fulfillment of the Old Testament and the pinnacle of God's saving works in history, he is also the agent of creation. Jesus is, thus, the beginning and the end. He is the *Creator* and the *telos* of creation. It is significant that the author of Hebrews connects the doctrines of redemption and creation. This is because the God who creates is the God who redeems. As followers of Jesus Christ, we must recognize that if we do not have the right doctrine of creation, we will not have the right doctrine of redemption. Creation and the gospel are inextricably linked.

Seeing the Supremacy of God's Final Revelation
HEBREWS 1:3

Verse 3 is an exposition of how the Son reveals the Father to us. The idea of "radiance" goes back to the notion of the *shekinah* glory in the Old Testament. The *shekinah* was a shining, visible glory that demonstrated the majesty of God, as in the exodus (Exod 13:21; 40:34-35) and at the dedication of Solomon's temple (1 Kgs 8:10-11). Looking at Christ is the way we see most fully the glory of God. More than that, Christ is the exact expression of the Father's nature. Christ shares the divine nature with the Father as the Second Person of the Trinity. This is where the divine Son is different from a human son. No human son is the exact representation of his father. There is a close relation, but not an exact representation. Christ, however, is an "*exact representation.*" He and God are of the same divine essence.

There are almost innumerable applications to the doctrine of the Trinity as expressed here in Hebrews 1. For example, this is one of the reasons Protestants have been opposed to the use of icons. There is no need to hang icons on a wall when you believe in the One who was hung on a cross. A Trinitarian Christology is of vital importance to the health of the church. The author of Hebrews is clear: we only understand Christ rightly when we see him in a redemptive-historical context as the climax of God's revelation, and in a theological context as the Second Person of the Trinity.

As this important divine figure, the Son is not only the active agent of creation, but he is also active in the preservation of creation. He sustains "all things by his powerful word." If the Son ever ceased to will the universe to remain, then the universe would cease to exist. The power to create is also the power to preserve, the power to control, and the power to bring to an end. Hebrews tells us the Son possesses this kind of power.

These are deep waters. The inner workings of the Trinity are indeed a profound and glorious mystery. Martin Luther, the great Reformer of the sixteenth century, was once asked by a young theology student a speculative question about the nature of God. Luther responded, "I think an angel would be scared to ask that question." Similar reverence should accompany our own study of the doctrine of the Trinity. There are certain questions we simply cannot ask since God has not revealed an answer to us. What is revealed, however, is that the Father through the Son accomplished creation and continues to sustain it.

The transition to "purification for sins" happens rather suddenly. Yet we must see in this how tightly the Bible intertwines the person and work of Christ. The word *purification* is not one we typically use to summarize the gospel. This word encapsulates the priestly work of Christ and recalls the sacrificial system of the Old Testament. The rest of Hebrews, particularly Hebrews 9–10, will further expound on the significance of purification. The author introduces the term here in order to prepare readers for the trajectory of the rest of his argument.

The final statement highlights the kingly authority of Christ. To be at someone's "right hand" is to be in a place of favor and authority. For Christ to be at the right hand of the heavenly "Majesty" means he is above all powers and he rules over the cosmos. The place of Christ in heaven at God's right hand also alludes to his work of intercession for us (Rom 8:34).

In short, the first three verses of the Epistle to the Hebrews are some of the most remarkable in all of Scripture. Consider the doctrines embedded in them:

- Revelation
- Creation
- The Trinity
- The Relationship of the Old and New Testaments
- Christology
- Atonement

Even more, consider the wonderfully high Christology that the author has presented in just a few words. Christ is the . . .

- Son of God
- Revelation of God
- Fulfillment of God's Revelation in the Old Testament
- Heir of All Things
- Agent of Creation
- Radiance of God's Glory
- Expression of God's Nature
- Preserver of All Creation
- Purifier of God's People
- Mediator for God's People

Hebrews is not for the theologically faint of heart. Hebrews is for those whose endurance will be richly rewarded with a remarkable portrait of Christ. Let us treasure him, our Creator and Redeemer. He is worthy, for he is supreme over all things.

Excursus: Reading the Old Testament as Christians

Christians have often been troubled by the question, How do we rightly read the Old Testament? Thankfully, the book of Hebrews provides us with important directions on how to interpret the Old Testament rightly, now that Christ has fulfilled all things. However, the history of theology and the history of the church demonstrate that there are disastrously wrong ways to read the Old Testament.

The first major error made in approaching the Old Testament comes down to reading it as if it is a book that does not belong to the church. This way of reading the Bible assumes that the Old Testament belongs to the Jews, whereas the New Testament belongs to the church. Sometimes the way we describe our congregations can unintentionally lend to this type of understanding. For example, Protestants (and Baptists in particular) are very concerned about ordering their church life so that they are legitimately a "New Testament church." By this we mean that we are seeking to follow the ecclesiology modeled in the New Testament by the apostles of the Lord Jesus. Of course, this is certainly right and good, but we must be careful that when we describe ourselves as a "New Testament church" we do not give the impression that our Bibles begin in Matthew as opposed to Genesis. Instead, the Old Testament Scriptures belong to the church because they bear witness to and provide the redemptive-historical context of the gospel of Christ (Rom 3:21).

Marcion, a famous heretic in the days of the early church, epitomized the worst form of this type of Old Testament interpretation. He posited that the God of the Old Testament was not the same as the God of the New Testament. He ultimately tried to do away with the Old Testament and almost everything in the New Testament that was in any way favorable toward Judaism. The early church quickly smelled the scent of heresy in Marcion's teachings—the stench of deadly error. Many of Marcion's heresies, however, are perpetuated in modern liberal theology, which asserts that the Old Testament portrait of God is crude and rudimentary. Regrettably, this way of thinking often sinks into certain sections of evangelical churches as well.

A similar though less pernicious version of this error, perhaps more common within evangelicalism, is simply to ignore the Old Testament. The temptation to ignore it is quite strong for many Christians. Many simply do not understand the Old Testament because it seems so alien to our culture and difficult to comprehend. Anchoring our quiet times in Philippians is easier than trying to focus them on Leviticus. Yet, as we will discover in the rest of Hebrews, the Old Testament cannot be ignored, for it provides us with the theological and redemptive-historical context for understanding the gospel.

The second major error associated with reading the Old Testament is equal and opposite to the first. This erroneous hermeneutic assumes that Christian theology is primarily grounded in the Old Testament without recognizing the significant redemptive-historical transitions that have occurred because Christ has inaugurated God's eschatological kingdom. To be certain, there is continuity between the Old and New Testaments, but there is also significant discontinuity. We are a New Testament people and a new covenant people. Therefore, when we read the Old Testament, we must read it in light of its fulfillment in Christ; that is to say, we must employ a distinctively Christological hermeneutic.

Christians, therefore, must not resent, ignore, dismiss, or uncritically exalt the Old Testament. Christ did not come to abolish the Old Testament but to fulfill it (Matt 5:17). His followers must always remember that our Bible begins with Genesis, not Matthew. The Old Testament was written for our instruction and is profitable even now in the new covenant era "for teaching, for rebuking, for correcting, for training in righteousness" (2 Tim 3:16). Further, in Romans 15:4, Paul writes,

> For whatever was written in the past was written for our instruction, so that we may have hope through endurance and through the encouragement from the Scriptures.

The Old Testament, which was "written in the past," is for our "instruction," "hope," and "encouragement." In order to live faithfully before God, we must not only read the Old Testament, but also learn to read it rightly in relation to Christ. Hebrews will help us to that end.

Reflect and Discuss

1. Why is it so important to remember that the gospel message begins with the creation narrative and the covenants of the Old Testament? Do you think it is necessary to incorporate the Old Testament into presentations of the gospel? Why or why not?
2. How does the Old Testament set the context for how we should share the gospel? How do the first few verses of Hebrews help us in considering the relationship between the Old Testament and the gospel? Do these verses change the way you think about presenting the gospel? Explain.
3. In what significant ways did God speak to his people in the Old Testament? How do those ways relate to the way God has spoken to us in Jesus Christ?

4. In what ways does the author of Hebrews present Jesus Christ as superior to the old covenant in the first three verses of the letter? What does Christ's superiority over the old covenant mean for the old covenant?

5. How does the fact that God speaks to us fuel our complete confidence in Scripture and serve our knowledge of God and our understanding of his character? What does it say about his relationship to us?

6. How does the doctrine of creation affect the doctrine of redemption? In what ways are the two doctrines inextricably linked?

7. Why is the doctrine of the Trinity such an essential doctrine for the health of the church? How do these verses help inform our understanding of Christ's sonship?

8. How do the theologically rich contents of Hebrews 1:1-3 impact the way you view Christ? Does your everyday life and theology reflect the worth of Christ? Explain your response.

9. Which of the two major errors we discussed concerning reading the Old Testament do you think is most prevalent in our churches and our culture today? How can you combat and prevent the spread of these errors in your church?

10. Why is it so essential that we be students of the Old Testament just as much as we are of the New Testament? What is the danger of being students of the New Testament alone? In what ways does the New Testament give us tools for reading the Old Testament rightly?

Jesus: The Praiseworthy King Who Created

HEBREWS 1:4-14

Main Idea: God the Father has given Jesus Christ the Son a name greater than all names and the throne to a kingdom that has no end. All things have been created by the Son and through the Son—including angels— for the worship and service of the Son.

I.   **The Superior Name of the Son (1:4)**
II. **The Superior Worship of the Son (1:5-6)**
III. **The Superior Throne of the Son (1:7-12)**
  A. Seeing the Son as Yahweh
  B. Enjoying the eternal kingdom of the Son
IV. **The Superior Reign of the Son (1:13-14)**
  A. Worshiping the Son as King
  B. Knowing the angels as his servants

From its very first words, the book of Hebrews focuses squarely on Jesus Christ. Theologically speaking, the book is Christocentric. The reason is obvious. The gospel ultimately boils down to three questions:

- Who is Jesus Christ?
- What has he done?
- What is the significance for us?

Similar to the way Paul begins his epistle to the Colossians (Col 1:15-20), the author of Hebrews begins by introducing his readers to the person of Christ *before* teaching them about the work of Christ. These two categories—person and work—help us theologically navigate the richness of the Bible's Christology. While it is impossible to divorce Christ's identity from his actions, dividing Christ's person and work into individual theological categories helps us better articulate a comprehensive picture of what Scripture teaches us about Jesus.

One of the problems Christians have when we talk about Christ is that we often jump straight to the *work* of Christ before talking about the *person* of Christ. This is particularly true with evangelistic conversations. We typically start by talking about what Christ has done for us without first giving a clear testimony of who Christ is. Hebrews, however, reminds us to keep first things first. "Who is this Christ?" is the first question we must address when we talk about Jesus.

Hebrews also reminds us that we know Christ in the context of a narrative. His identity is revealed to us in the Holy Scriptures as part of the biblical storyline. He is the climax of the drama that moves from Old Testament promise to New Testament fulfillment. This means we cannot fully understand Christ's identity without first seeing him in the context of the story of Israel and the story of the old covenant—an old covenant rendered obsolete by Christ's inauguration and mediation of the new covenant.

The Superior Name of the Son
HEBREWS 1:4

As we have already seen, Hebrews 1:1-3 is a narrative within a narrative. The larger grand narrative of these verses is summarized in the major plot developments of creation, fall, redemption, and consummation. Yet within this larger narrative storyline is the story of Christ himself—the Creator, Redeemer, and ascended King. It is difficult to imagine a better distillation of the entire gospel story than these first three verses.

Hebrews 1:4 transitions readers into an extended section arguing for the superiority of Christ in relation to the angelic host. For many readers this may seem strange: Why would the author of Hebrews spend such a significant amount of time demonstrating that Christ is superior to angels? Isn't this obvious? Yet, when we look at the historical background of Hebrews, we find that this section is absolutely necessary for the author's overall argument. Why? Literature from the intertestamental period—the time between the Old Testament and the New Testament, often called Second Temple Judaism—demonstrates an intense focus on angels. Some of this theological reflection was good, but it was also mixed with error. Many people in Israel considered angels to be both God's messengers and Israel's protectors. Many Jews looked at angels as those who would come as the army of God to rescue and vindicate the nation. Second Temple literature also attests to the rise of the notion of "personal angels," or what we might call "guardian angels." Due to this fascination with angels, the author of Hebrews, writing to a Jewish audience who was familiar with Second Temple literature, needed to recalibrate the theological understanding of his audience—particularly concerning Christ's relationship to angels.

The author of Hebrews thus answers a number of important questions for a potentially theologically confused first-century audience: How does Christ "fit" with the angels? Is he an angel? Is he the servant of angels? Of course, one of the benefits of this section of Hebrews is that we not only learn a great deal about angels, but, even more importantly, we learn a great deal about the glory of Christ. Hebrews 1:4 explicitly indicates that Christ is superior to angels. The writer indicates that one of the reasons why is because "the name he inherited is more excellent than theirs." What name has Christ inherited? One option is to follow the logic of Philippians 2, where Paul tells us that Christ has now been given the title of "Lord"—a title belonging to God himself. This does not mean that there was a time when Jesus was not divine; he has been fully God from eternity. In fact, Hebrews has already indicated that he was the agent of creation (Heb 1:2; cf. John 1:1), and as Hebrews will later indicate, Christ could only accomplish our salvation as the agent of redemption if he was the eternal Son of God. Inheriting the more excellent "name" of "Lord" means instead that Jesus Christ has been appointed as the reigning Lord.

However, the context of Hebrews indicates that the name Jesus inherited is the name "Son." Again, this does not mean that Jesus was adopted into divine sonship. He has always been the eternal Son of God. Hebrews 1:2 makes this clear. Instead, as verse 5 tells us, it points to that messianic element of sonship that fulfills the promises of the Davidic covenant (Rom 1:4).

The Superior Worship of the Son
HEBREWS 1:5-6

It is important to remember that we are not merely reading the author's random devotional reflections when he references different sections of the Old Testament. Through the author of Hebrews, the Holy Spirit is providing his own inerrant, infallible commentary on the Old Testament. In other words, we are learning from the author of Hebrews himself the importance of reading Scripture in the light of the rest of Scripture, specifically in the light of the New Testament. We have here the Holy Spirit's own commentary on the very Old Testament Scriptures he inspired.

The Old Testament passages quoted are each taken from one of the major divisions in the Hebrew Scriptures: Psalm 2:7 from the Writings, 2 Samuel 7:14 from the Prophets, and Deuteronomy 32:43 from the Law. Through a rhetorical question, the author makes the point that God never makes any claim of sonship for any of the angels. An angel may serve as God's agent, messenger, and witness, but not as God's Son. The quotation from 2 Samuel 7 shows this sonship refers not only to Jesus as the eternal Son of God, but to Jesus as the messianic Son—the fulfillment of the Davidic promises.

The final quotation, from Deuteronomy 32:43, is particularly interesting. In its original context, the statement about the angels bowing down in worship is in reference to Yahweh, whom the writer of Hebrews now identifies as Jesus! The argument is clear. The angels worship Christ; it is not Christ who worships the angels. The angels declare the birth of Christ; it is not Christ who declares the ministry of angels. The angels are not called sons, but that is the very name that Christ himself, the Davidic Messiah, has inherited.

The Superior Throne of the Son
HEBREWS 1:7-12

The Old Testament quotation in verse 7 comes from Psalm 104:4. The psalmist uses exalted language to describe the angelic host. They are a flame of fire; they enjoy God's presence and carry out his purposes. However, they are only "servants" in God's court. The contrast is made even more explicit in verses 8-11. Yahweh says that the angels are only servants, but the Son is divine (1:8)! The words in verses 8-9 are from Psalm 45:6-7. Angels may surround the throne of God, but the Son sits on the throne. Angels may be sent, but Christ is the Anointed One.

The quotation in verses 10-12 comes from Psalm 102:25-27. Again, in their Old Testament context these verses are about Yahweh. Yet the Holy Spirit, through the author of Hebrews, identifies the Son with Yahweh. The only explanation for this logic is a Trinitarian theology beneath the surface of the text. The notion that the Son laid the foundation of the earth revisits the fact that it was "through" the Son that God created the world.

This passage also highlights the distinction that exists between the creature and the Creator. The contrast is specifically between things permanent and things temporal. Creation will perish. It will "wear out like clothing." The Son, on the other hand, will not. The Son is eternal and permanent. Whereas the created order is subject to change, decay, and ultimate destruction, the person of Christ is unending and unchanging. His years have no end. He knows no change.

The Superior Reign of the Son
HEBREWS 1:13-14

The final Old Testament citation comes from Psalm 110:1. The author ends his argument the same way he started it: with the rhetorical question, "to which of the angels has he ever said . . . ?" (cf. 1:5). Psalm 110 communicates that Yahweh promised the Messiah utter dominion over the world. He is the *singular* Son of God. He is *the* agent of creation and redemption.

Again, verse 14 draws a contrast between the reigning Christ and angelic servants. Yet it also speaks of the role of angels in the lives of God's people. They are "ministering spirits" who are sent out for our good. What is this ministry that they have among God's people? A good short course in "angelology" might be helpful here, especially since American Christianity is often confused by the unbiblical, pop culture portrayal of angels. The commercialized, cute, chubby, cupid-like angels seen in get-well cards could not be further from the biblical portrait of angelic beings. When an angel shows up in Scripture, people fall down in sheer terror. Just think about the response of the shepherds to the angelic visitation in Luke 2:9. Clearly we need to recover a biblical doctrine of angels.

Both the Old and the New Testament make clear that angels are creations of God. While they may have distinct privileges and even extraordinary powers, they are by no means divine. Angels reside in the heavenly assembly and are part of the throng worshiping before the throne of God. The Bible also indicates that angels are messengers of God and that they carry out his purposes. The angels function as witnesses of major redemptive-historical events, such as the birth of Christ. They are also agents of God's justice. After the fall, God placed an angel with a flaming sword at the border of the garden of Eden to exact vengeance on anyone who would try to eat from the tree of life (Gen 3:25). Revelation indicates that Christ will lead an angelic army in the last day to execute his just judgment on the world. Hebrews 1:14 underscores the glorious reality that for those of us who believe in

Christ, angels are sent from God's throne room to work for the good of the church. We may not know exactly how angels are engaged in spiritual warfare on behalf of the church, but we can be confident that these agents of God's throne are sent out for that very purpose. God works all things for the good of his church (Rom 8:28). This includes the ministry of angels.

Yet while this passage gives us a clearer understanding of the function of angels in God's purposes of redemption, we must not miss the main point. Angels are spirits that minister to the body of Christ and are thus sent out by Christ himself. Angels are indeed remarkable. But they pale in comparison to the glory of the Redeemer, the Son of God, Jesus Christ. He is superior to every angel—indeed to the entire angelic host.

Reflect and Discuss

1. What is the difference between the person of Christ and the work of Christ?

2. How does the author of the book of Hebrews aid us in our understanding of the person and work of Christ, particularly in terms of our evangelistic conversations? What are some of the ways we can incorporate both the person of Christ and the work of Christ into our gospel conversations?

3. How might developing a deeper understanding of the person and work of Christ help you better articulate a comprehensive picture of what Scripture teaches about Jesus?

4. Based on what you've learned so far, what are some ways the author of Hebrews answers the three questions introduced earlier: Who is Jesus Christ? What has he done? What is the significance for us?

5. In what ways is Jesus Christ superior to the angels? What is his relationship to angels?

6. The author of Hebrews used the Old Testament fluidly. How might this help us as we read the Old Testament in light of Christ and the New Testament?

7. What are some of the ways that the portrait of angels presented in this passage differs from the portrait of angels presented in pop culture? How can we critique culture's angelology with the angelology provided in this passage?

8. How do angels serve the Son? How do they serve and minister to the church?

9. What things in your life do you consider supreme? How does the reality of Christ's superiority over all things change the way you view those things? How does Christ's supremacy affect the way you live your life day to day?
10. How does the ministry and spiritual warfare of angels on behalf of the church serve as an encouragement to your faith in Christ?

Jesus: Do Not Neglect His Salvation

HEBREWS 2:1-9

Main Idea: If God exacted retribution against those who broke the old covenant, how much more should we heed the message of the new covenant delivered to us by the last Adam, Jesus Christ?

I. **Heeding the Warning Signs of Spiritual Drift (2:1-3a)**
    A. The potential of spiritual drift
    B. The danger of spiritual drift
II. **Hearing the Witnesses of God (2:3b-4)**
III. **Honoring the Coronation of the Last Adam (2:4-9)**
    A. Read as biblical theologians.
    B. Rest in the already; hope in the not yet.
    C. Rely on the One who tasted death.

In today's world we are virtually drowning in an ocean of communication, media, and advertisement. At all times, somebody somewhere is trying to get our attention and deliver a message to us. Commercials, billboards, Twitter feeds, political campaign ads, television preachers, entertainment, conversations, and a thousand other things flood our eyes and ears. The key to navigating these treacherous waters is deciphering which messages are worthy of our focus.

This section of Hebrews urges us to pay the utmost attention to the most worthy of messages. In short, God has spoken. He has spoken in his Son. The most important message we can hear is the message that comes from the Father through the Son in the incarnation of the Lord Jesus Christ. That God has revealed himself and made a way for us to be saved through faith in the person and work of his Son is the most earth-shattering news we will ever hear. God has spoken to us in Jesus Christ. What could possibly be better news than that?

Heeding the Warning Signs of Spiritual Drift
HEBREWS 2:1-3a

The Potential for Spiritual Drift

Words like "*therefore*" and "*for this reason*" help us come to the right conclusions when reading Scripture. Hebrews 1 establishes the superiority of Christ over the angels in a breathtaking display of Old Testament biblical theology. But what was the point of this display? What should we take away from the author's argument? The words *for this reason* direct us to the appropriate application. Given the superiority of Christ over the angels and his identity as the divine Son of God, Jesus both demands and deserves to be heard. In the Old Testament, messages from angels (cf. Heb 2:2) came with such authority and power that their recipients were often nearly frightened to death. How much more then should we lend our ears to God's words now that "he has spoken to us by his Son" (Heb 1:2)! We must "pay attention"—we must *listen*—to the God who speaks. How foolish to ignore him!

We do not listen to the Son so that we can puff ourselves up theologically. Doctrine is not for bludgeoning our brothers and sisters in Christ, nor is it for impressing our neighbors. We engage the Bible with the utmost seriousness in order to commune with God himself and thereby not "drift away." The language of drifting conveys nautical imagery. In the ocean, those who row in the wrong direction are not the only ones who fail to reach their desired destination; it is also those who do not row at all. There are only two options in the Christian life: we can either sail forward in fidelity or we can drift backward in faithlessness. There is no such thing as standing still in the Christian life.

Spiritual drift is often imperceptible when it starts. But just like boats at sea, our souls can veer almost entirely off course in moments. You do not need to be far off course to end up a very long way from where you initially intended to be. The writer of Hebrews indicates that there is only one way to fight against the danger of spiritual drift: we must pay attention to and obey the Word of God. Orthodoxy and obedience are the oars we must use for fighting against the straying current of spiritual drift. Theology and practice will keep us sailing forward in fidelity. The fight of sanctification is a fight against the tides of the world, the flesh, and the devil. Either we are listening to the Son and walking in his

Word, or we are drifting away from biblical thinking and getting carried away by the cultural confusion of our day.

Sadly, we witness theological and spiritual drift all too often. It is the story of many denominations, churches, families, and individuals. Even the most cursory knowledge of church history demonstrates that heresy and theological liberalism do not capsize denominations and churches with one revolutionary wave. Instead, churches and individuals end up on the wrong side of the doctrinal equation by drifting a little at a time. Churches once orthodox in their theology slowly minimize and relax their theological convictions until they become unwilling to draw boundaries or speak clearly on issues essential to orthodox Christianity and the evangelical gospel.

So how do we avoid the danger of spiritual drift? The answer is the beginning of Hebrews 2:1. We must "pay attention all the more to what we have heard." The importance of "hearing" God's Word pervades Scripture. Paul reminds us, "Faith comes from what is heard, and what is heard comes through the message about Christ" (Rom 10:17). Of course, when Scripture talks about "hearing," it means more than just audibly perceiving God's Word. For example, concerning those who did not believe him, Jesus said, "looking they do not see, and hearing they do not listen or understand" (Matt 13:13). "Hearing" the Word of God rightly is a spiritual hearing—one that involves believing, obeying, and submitting to what is heard. Right hearing is more a matter of the heart than a function of the ear. We must hear with our hearts.

Christian faithfulness has no secret formula. God sanctifies us through his Word (John 17:17). We avoid the danger of spiritual drift by reading, hearing, meditating on, and obeying Scripture. As B. B. Warfield said, "When Scripture speaks, God speaks" (*Inspiration and Authority of the Bible*, 119). We avoid spiritual drift by dropping the anchor of our souls in the deep waters of the Word of God.

The Danger of Spiritual Drift

Verse 2 further explains this point (notice the connecting word "*for*," which provides the grounds of the author's argument). Verses 2-3 confuse many readers because the passage is comprised of is quite a long sentence and is a little complicated. Therefore, we will look at each phrase individually so that we can understand the sense of the whole verse.

What is the "message spoken through angels"? A quick survey of the Old Testament reveals that angels delivered many messages on behalf of Yahweh and that each of these messages was "legally binding" and reliable. The New Testament also records several angelic messages in the gospels, such as the announcement of Christ's birth in Luke 2:10-11, or the announcement to Cornelius in Acts 10:1-8. However, as the following phrase makes clear, the message mentioned in Hebrews 2:2 is probably referring to the Mosaic covenant that the Bible indicates was delivered "through angels" (Acts 7:53; cf. Deut 33:2; Gal 3:19).

The next phrase is, in a sense, a summary of the old covenant as delivered through angels: every sin justly deserves punishment. That's the logic of Torah. Deuteronomy 30:19 summarizes this principle:

> *I call heaven and earth as witnesses against you today that I have set*
> *before you life and death, blessing and curse. Choose life so that you*
> *and your descendants may live.*

The message is simple: You obey, you live; you disobey, you die. Under the old covenant, every transgression of the law demanded a just penalty.

The point of the author's argument is now a little more obvious when he writes, "How will we escape if we neglect such a great salvation?" He has moved from the lesser (angels/old covenant) to the greater (Jesus/new covenant). If the old covenant that came from God and was delivered by mere angels demanded retribution for sin, how much more will God judge those who have spurned the gospel now delivered to us by his own Son! This judgment is explicitly portrayed in Revelation 19 as Christ returns to "trample the winepress of the fierce anger of God, the Almighty" (Rev 19:15). The danger of spiritual drift is not only that we might miss out on a spiritually flourishing life; the true danger of spiritual drift is that we abandon the gospel itself and find ourselves under the judgment of God.

The gospel is good news. The good news is only good, though, when it is accepted in place of the bad news. The bad news is we are truly deserving of hell for our transgression of God's righteous requirement. The really bad news is we will be even more accountable to God if we reject Christ. The seriousness of the gospel cannot be overstated. The gospel is good news for those who repent of their sin and trust in Christ. It is terrible news for those who do not.

Hearing the Witnesses of God
HEBREWS 2:3b-4

Hebrews 2:3-4 further shows how Christ's superiority over angels relates to the danger of spiritual drift. Again, the contrast is clear: failure to heed the reliable message brought by angels brings retribution and death. How much more guilty, then, are those who reject the "great salvation" declared by the incarnate Lord himself? This new stage in redemptive history brings great privileges, but also great responsibilities.

The author indicates that the message of the new covenant inaugurated by Christ (this "great salvation") is superior to the message delivered by angels in at least four ways. First, it was "spoken of by the Lord." Once again, the author leans heavily on his previous declaration that God has now spoken to us "by his Son" (Heb 1:2). These words are essential for understanding the logic of the theology of Hebrews.

Second, this message was "confirmed to us by those who heard him." Though we may not often think of it, the New Testament consistently teaches the profound theological importance of the testimony of the apostles to the person and work of Jesus Christ. After all, Christ set apart the apostles and commissioned them to function as the foundation of the church (Eph 2:20). We do not believe myths and legends about Jesus. The message of the gospel has come down to us from the credible eyewitness testimony of the apostles.

Third, God himself "testified" to the veracity of the gospel "by signs and wonders" and "various miracles." Many Christians, while rightly affirming the historicity of God's miraculous works, misunderstand their purpose. The author of Hebrews reminds us that miracles do not exist for their own sake. They do not ultimately point to themselves. Instead, miracles attest and validate God's major works in redemptive history. In the New Testament, miracles attest and confirm the truth about the identity and work of Christ.

Finally, the "gifts from the Holy Spirit" attest to the truthfulness of the gospel and its superiority over the message delivered by angels. Again, the author of Hebrews helps us strip away our misconceptions about why spiritual gifts exist. Spiritual gifts are not an end to themselves to be used for our personal, private enjoyment. Spiritual gifts edify the church (1 Cor 14:3-5; Eph 4:11-12) and testify that Jesus Christ is Lord. As Paul explains in Ephesians 4:8, Christ has ascended on high, and now, with all authority in heaven, showers gifts on his church. Gifts within the church, therefore, bear witness to Jesus Christ as the resurrected Lord and to the superiority of the new covenant over the old.

Honoring the Coronation of the Last Adam
HEBREWS 2:5-9

Read as Biblical Theologians

The author of Hebrews continues his argument about Christ's superiority over the angels. This time, however, he requires his readers to do a little bit of biblical theology. That is to say, the author of Hebrews wants us to read Scripture according to its own internal storyline and then see Christ as the fulfillment and climax of that story. Hebrews 2:5 communicates that God never promised angels dominion over the created order. The Genesis narrative communicates that the earth was subjected to Adam and Eve—to humanity: "Then God said, 'Let us make man in our image, according to our likeness. They will rule the fish of the sea, the birds of the sky, the livestock, the whole earth, and the creatures that crawl on the earth'" (Gen 1:26).

The subsequent verses in Hebrews (vv. 6-8) show us how the Bible itself theologically develops the dominion mandate given to Adam. The author quotes from Psalm 8:4-6, in which David provides his own biblical theological commentary on Genesis 1–2. David marvels that though man is made "less than God" (Ps 8:5), man is also made "ruler" over the world (Ps 8:6)—a dominion that is now exercised through the Davidic king. The author of Hebrews interprets this text as ultimately pointing toward the ideal image bearer and Davidic king, Jesus Christ. The theology of these verses mirrors the theology of Paul: Christ is the "last Adam" (1 Cor 15:45-47), the first man of the new creation (1 Cor 15:20). Whereas the first Adam failed to carry out the duties of image-bearing, the last Adam has succeeded.

Rest in the Already; Hope in the Not Yet

At the same time, the author of Hebrews recognizes a tension between the reality of the ascended and reigning Christ and the continuing presence of sin in the world. For the last Adam, there is "nothing that is not subject to him," and yet, "As it is, we do not yet see everything subjected to him" (v. 8). Many theologians refer to this tension as the already-not yet aspect of the kingdom of God. The kingdom of God and the reign of Christ are in some senses already *inaugurated*, yet we are still waiting for the kingdom's *consummation*.

However, this perceived chaos in the world around us should not cause us to doubt the veracity of the gospel message or the work of the last Adam. We may not see all things subjected to him, but "we do see Jesus" who has fulfilled every aspect of the Old Testament and secured his regal throne in glory. The progression of events in verse 9 is profoundly important. "For a short time"—during the incarnation—Jesus appeared to be "lower than the angels." The eternal Son of God became a man named "Jesus." This is the first reference to the name "*Jesus*" in Hebrews. Up to this point, the author refers to him as the "Son." Now, specifically in the context of the Son's humiliation and incarnation, the author chooses to remind his audience that the eternal Son became a man: Jesus Christ.

Rely on the One Who Tasted Death

Even more, this last Adam has now been "crowned with glory and honor." He is not crowned simply because he is the God-man and therefore worthy of all divine prerogatives. Instead, the author mentions that he has been crowned with glory and honor because he has fulfilled his messianic task of suffering and death. The result of his suffering is redemptive. Christ has "[tasted] death for everyone." The first Adam plunged humanity into sin and death; the last Adam was plunged into death for the sake of humanity. The work of the last Adam undoes the work of the first Adam. As the One who fulfills the task originally given to Adam, Jesus represents the ideal man who bears God's image rightly and exercises dominion over the cosmos. He has inherited the place of dominion spoken of in Psalm 8. He is superior to all things, *including the angels*.

As we will see, the following verses more fully explain the work of Christ in our redemption. Again, the contours of the book of Hebrews (indeed the contours of the entire canon) must shape our theology. We must articulate and celebrate the work of Christ on our behalf, but we must do so understanding his work in the context of his identity. As Hebrews 2:9 reminds us, the person and work of Christ are intimately intertwined. He is the eternal Son who comes to glory through suffering. As the glorious God-man, he is superior to all things, *including the angels*.

Reflect and Discuss

1. What are some things in your own life that make it difficult to hear God's message? What do you frequently entertain that distracts you from hearing his Word and tempts you to drift?

2. What role does doctrine have in helping us fight spiritual drift? How do the spiritual disciplines—prayer, daily Scripture reading, Scripture memorization, fasting, journaling, and evangelism—help?

3. How does the local church help us fight spiritual drift? Think about this in the context of your own church. How can you incorporate your church into the fight against spiritual drift?

4. How do you see culture tempting the church to make concessions and drift spiritually?

5. What is the purpose of signs and wonders, spiritual gifts, and miracles? How have you seen spiritual gifts in your church bear witness to Christ in the life of the church? In your own life?

6. In what ways do you feel the tension of the already-not yet playing out in your own life? How do you see this tension manifest itself in the world?

7. What things cause you to doubt the veracity of the gospel and the work of the last Adam? How does this passage help you overcome those fears and doubts?

8. How do you understand the work of Christ in the context of his identity? How would you articulate the person and work of Christ to someone who has never heard of Jesus?

9. How can Christ's superiority in all things help us avoid spiritual drift?

10. Describe in your own words Christ as the last Adam. How does Christ as the last Adam change how you relate to him?

Jesus: Our Tempted and Tried Savior and Priest

HEBREWS 2:10-18

Main Idea: By becoming a man and experiencing the trials of temptation and the agony of death, Jesus Christ, our faithful high priest, destroys the power of Satan, helps those being tempted, and provides full propitiation for the sins of his people.

I. **The Source of Our Salvation (2:10-13)**
   A. Preaching the gospel with prepositional phrases
   B. The fittingness of the Father's plan
   C. The messianic message of the Old Testament
II. **The Incursion of the Incarnate Son (2:14-16)**
   A. Knowing our enemies
   B. Defeating our enemies
III. **Priesthood and Propitiation (2:17-18)**

The first half of Hebrews 2 concludes with the astounding claim that Christ tasted death for everyone. In doing so, Christ not only secures our salvation but also demonstrates his superiority to the angels. The rest of Hebrews 2 further explains what it means for Christ to "taste death for everyone." Exactly how does Christ accomplish this feat? What are the results? How do God's people benefit? Hebrews 2:10-18 helps answer these questions.

The Source of Our Salvation
HEBREWS 2:10-13

In the previous section the author of Hebrews demonstrated the superiority of Christ over the angels in his glory-achieving death as the last Adam. Further, his suffering unto death was not indiscriminate or pointless. Jesus "tasted death for everyone" (2:9). In other words, his suffering was *substitutionary*.

While continuing the argument of Jesus's superiority over the angels, verse 10 shifts the focus to God the Father's role in our salvation and in the mission of Christ. This is important for us to remember.

Christianity, at its heart, is Trinitarian. We worship and serve a triune God, who as Father, Son, and Spirit has acted for our salvation. There is no division between the Father's will to save and the Son's will to save. Just as the Father is determined to save, so also the Son and the Spirit are determined to save. Each carries out separate functions in the economy of salvation, but their mission to save sinful humanity is unified.

Preaching the Gospel with Prepositional Phrases

Before moving to the main point of this verse, we should linger over the author's two prepositional phrases, which describe two facets of the Father's work in the history of redemption. First, God is the One "for whom and through whom all things exist." The Father creates for his glory. He is both the beginning and end of the creation. The words are reminiscent of Isaiah 43:6-7:

> I will say to the north, "Give them up!" and to the south, "Do not hold them back!" Bring my sons from far away, and my daughters from the ends of the earth—everyone who bears my name and is created for my glory. I have formed them; indeed, I have made them.

Second, the phrase "in bringing many sons and daughters to glory" is a remarkable summary of the gospel. Few gospel summaries in Scripture so beautifully capture the work and ministry of Jesus than this prepositional phrase in Hebrews 2:10. Christ came to do many things. He came to redeem sinners; he came to save sinful humanity; he came to forgive sin; and he even came to provide us with righteousness. But more, he came to adopt us as "sons and daughters to glory." These words provide a gospel summary that focuses on the relational and familial aspects of the gospel. The gospel transforms believers into children of God and siblings of the Lord Jesus (cf. Heb 2:11).

We see then, in both of these prepositional phrases, that God has both created and redeemed us for his glory. Our purpose is to bring the glory of God into greater visibility—to be the public display of the glory of God both now and for all eternity. Thus, we become "sons and daughters to glory" in order to magnify the glory of God for all to see.

The Fittingness of the Father's Plan

The main point of verse 10 is the fittingness of the Father's plan to redeem humanity through a perfect and suffering Savior. The justice of God demanded a substitutionary atonement for the forgiveness of sins. This verse hints at the need (it was "appropriate") of the active and passive obedience of Christ in order to secure our redemption and to atone for our sins.

That Christ became "perfect through sufferings" does not imply that Jesus was somehow sinful prior to the crucifixion. The author of Hebrews regularly emphasizes the sinlessness of Christ during his incarnation (cf. 4:15). Instead, the phrase *made perfect* refers to Jesus's unflinching submission to the Father in the face of escalating difficulties. In the words of Paul, Jesus was obedient to the point of death—even death on a cross (Phil 2:8). Because of Christ's perfect obedience to the Father, Jesus has become the "source" of salvation.

The Messianic Message of the Old Testament

Hebrews 2:11 and the Old Testament citations that follow in verses 12 and 13 further explain the activity of the Father and the Son in "bringing many sons and daughters to glory." Both "the one who sanctifies" (Jesus) and "those who are sanctified" (believers) come from one source: the initiative and plan of the Father. Since Christ (the Father's commissioned Redeemer) and the church (those elected by the Father to redemption) are united in the plan and purposes of God for the history of redemption, Jesus is not ashamed to call us his "brothers and sisters." As the Old Testament citations in verses 12 and 13 confirm, the accent in this phrase is rooted in the reality that because believers are Christ's "brothers and sisters," we are also "children" of God.

The first citation is from Psalm 22:22, whereas the two that follow come from Isaiah 8:17-18. Psalm 22, when read in the context of the entire Psalter, is clearly messianic and points forward to the death and resurrection of Christ. After the Messiah undergoes tremendous suffering, he is vindicated in receiving life from the dead (Ps 22:19-24). Yet, as the author of Hebrews highlights, this risen Messiah invites his brothers (his disciples; Matt 28:10) to join in the celebration of the finished work of salvation. Similarly, the quotation from Isaiah 8 shows that the Old Testament already hinted that those who trusted in the Lord were children of God.

These Old Testament citations remind readers that there is a distinctively Christian way to read the Old Testament. The Law and the Prophets bear witness to Christ. He is their *telos*. In some instances this is obvious, such as in the messianic psalms and prophetic predictions about the coming Messiah. In other instances, the Old Testament more subtly points to Christ through typological patterns and redemptive historical themes. Whatever the case may be, the author of Hebrews reminds us that the message of the Old Testament is fundamentally messianic. The Old Testament must be read in light of its fulfillment in Christ.

The Incursion of the Incarnate Son
HEBREWS 2:14-16

Each new section in the book of Hebrews takes us to brand new depths. The previous passage demonstrated the activity of the Father, the accomplishment of our redemption, and the role of Christ as our perfect mediator and the securer of our adoption. This next section explains the logic of the redeeming work of Christ. In other words, these verses show us *how* Christ brings sinners into a position of sonship with the Creator.

Christianity stands or falls on the incarnation of Jesus Christ. To save those who were "flesh and blood," Christ himself had to become flesh and blood. To save the race of Adam, Jesus became the last Adam. In the incarnation, the eternal Son of God assumed a human nature. He was made of the same flesh we are made of and shared in our same experiences, yet he remained without sin. Though he was the Creator of all, he became hungry. He grew tired. He ate, drank, slept, ached, and "shared in these" things that all humanity knows and experiences. This is the first and one of the most fundamental truths of the gospel story. God became a man. He became like us.

Yet the incarnation itself is not enough to secure our redemption. As the latter half of verse 14 and verse 15 make clear, Jesus, as the God-man, had to accomplish a specific work—the destruction of death and the devil.

Knowing Our Enemies

Christ came to defeat two great enemies: death and the devil. Let's look at each in turn.

Death is a harsh reality, yet I am continually amazed how rarely most people consider their own impending deaths. One thing that always strikes me in the midst of the hustle and bustle of an airport is how busy folks seem in getting from one gate to another. Newspapers must be read, coffees must be bought and consumed, and phone calls must be made. In some ways, the airport is a metaphor for the remainder of our lives. We are constantly running around, so tirelessly consumed with day-to-day tasks that we seldom stop to meditate on some of the more sobering aspects of life—like death. In fact, many of us use busyness to avoid thinking about our mortality.

Yet no matter how much we try to ignore the reality of death, it is inevitable. In fact, a colleague once told me that as he was on a long flight back home, the man sitting next to him died of a heart attack. Given that the flight attendants had nowhere to put the body, they simply left the man buckled in his seat. Whether or not you are ever forced to sit that close to death before your own end, the reality of death's inevitability remains. Honesty compels us to admit that if the gospel is not true, then death is a horrifying reality we should fear. Death is the most frightening thing we can ever face without the gospel.

The second enemy Christ overcomes for us is the devil. Christians have never been sure what to do with the devil. We certainly should not blame the devil for every sin or envision him hiding in every closet and lurking behind every corner. At the same time, we certainly should not trivialize the devil and turn him into nothing more than a cartoon character. We should also reject a theological dualism that imagines a good God and an evil god (the devil) in a cosmic power struggle between two equals. God's power far exceeds Satan's.

Christians must take the devil seriously. Scripture testifies that Satan is our enemy. In fact, 1 Peter 5:8 says that the devil prowls around like a roaring lion seeking someone to devour. He delights in perverting the gospel and preventing it from being preached. He is a liar (John 8:44); he is a deceiver (2 Cor 2:10-11; 11:14; Eph 6:11); he is a destroyer (John 10:10); and he is a tempter (Matt 4:1-11; 1 Cor 7:5). In short, the devil is maliciously and comprehensively opposed to God's being, God's character, God's purposes, God's people, and God's glory.

This does not always mean that Satan pursues public wickedness as we typically envision. Donald Grey Barnhouse once asked the question, "What would a city look like that was completely ruled by the devil?" While many of us might picutre a city like Sodom and Gomorrah or Babylon, Barnhouse said a city completely ruled by Satan might look like something we never imagined: Every lawn would be mowed and every bridge would be clean of graffiti. No one would drive over the speed limit, children would be obedient to parents, marriages would remain intact, and every church would have a beautiful building. However, the gospel would not be preached at any place or in any pulpit because the devil's primary ambition is to prevent the gospel from being preached. The devil's aim is to keep people from believing the gospel. He will even use moralism and the appearance of perfection to accomplish that end (Horton, *Christless Christianity*, 15).

Defeating Our Enemies

Christ gives us victory over both of these adversaries. First, the gospel provides hope in the face of death. As John Owen's famous book title so poignantly phrases it, the gospel tells the story of "the death of death in the death of Christ" (*Death of Death*). As Jesus said in Matthew 16, the power of the gospel is such that the gates of Hades (death) would not prevail against the church (v. 18). Christ offers us the hope of life from the dead. In fact, Jesus parallels receiving salvation with receiving "eternal life" (John 3:16). Eschatologically, the gospel message culminates with resurrection hope. Verse 15 indicates that Christ achieves victory over death so that he can "free those who were held in slavery all their lives by the fear of death." The looming prospect of death should *rightly* cause those outside of the gospel to fear. Death not only brings the end of this life, but the beginning of God's retributive justice against sinners. Christ, however, saves those who turn to him in faith and repentance and delivers them from holy wrath. Christians no longer need to be paralyzed by the fear of death. It is simply one more step toward resurrection. Moreover, after death we have the blessed hope of being absent from the body but present with the Lord (2 Cor 5:8).

These verses also reveal that Christ has destroyed the devil, "the one holding the power of death." Of course, this destruction does not refer to Satan's ultimate, eschatological destruction. As we have already seen, Satan remains a real and active enemy of the church. Instead, Christ destroyed the devil in such a way that Satan can no longer do any ultimate spiritual damage to God's people. Christ's penal and substitutionary atonement completely exhausts Satan's powers of accusation. Thus, while the devil may continue to prowl about, he prowls with a limp. He has been stripped of his most destructive weapons. His accusations against God's people do not stick.

Before leaving verses 14 and 15, the author of Hebrews demonstrates *how* Jesus defeats death and the devil. His victory comes "through his death." Jesus overcomes death and the one who has the power of death by dying himself. The echoes of Genesis 3 and the curse are difficult to miss. Christ has overcome the curse by undergoing the curse in our place. He defeats death by dying for his people and bearing their curse. As the author of Hebrews will mention in just a few verses, this death was to "make propitiation," that is, to remove the wrath of God that was justly against us due to our sin. Yet, even more than that, Christ defeats death by rising again from the dead, thus giving resurrection hope to all of God's people. He is the firstfruits of the resurrection (1 Cor 15:20), and we are the harvest he will reap in the eschaton (1 Cor 15:22-23). Christians can truly rejoice: "Death has been swallowed up in victory. Where, death, is your victory? Where, death, is your sting?" (1 Cor 15:54-55).

Hebrews 2:16 reengages the author's exposition of the incarnation and the atoning work of Christ with the overall argument in chapters 1 and 2 of Christ's superiority over the angels. The author reminds us that the last Adam is restoring humanity to God's good purpose of having dominion over the world and displaying God to all of creation. Christ is superior to the angels because he himself is the image of the invisible God and the redeemer of the pinnacle of God's creative activity—mankind. Indeed, as the One who helps "Abraham's offspring," his work is intimately interwoven within the entire fabric of redemptive history. Christ is the white-hot center of God's purposes and plan for humanity.

Priesthood and Propitiation
HEBREWS 2:17-18

These verses are heavily loaded with important theological assertions. First, notice that the author says that Christ "had to be" incarnated and sacrificed in order to forgive the sins of God's people. I am often asked if God could have secured our salvation in any other way. This text indicates that the answer to that question is no. God only acts in the way that corresponds with his character and most displays his glory. Thus, in order to both satisfy his justice and display his mercy, God put Christ forward as a propitiatory sacrifice. No external necessity is forced on God, but God is always consistent with his own character.

The author also reasserts the absolute indispensability of the incarnation. Christ "had to be" made "like his brothers and sisters." In order to conquer death through death, the Son of God became a human being. Yet the author also explains that Jesus became a man in order to become a "high priest" on our behalf. It is critical that we rightly understand the Old Testament's teachings on the priesthood. The original readers of Hebrews were likely Hellenistic Jews who recognized the need for a priest specifically in matters of sacrifice. In the Old Testament, the people of Israel looked to the priests for mediation before God. On the Day of Atonement the high priest represented all the people before God and offered a substitutionary sacrifice on their behalf. Hebrews fully explains the relationship between Jesus and the priesthood in the chapters to come, but in this verse the author simply introduces us to the relationship. He presents the notion that in order to make a propitiatory sacrifice for the people, Jesus had to function as a priest; and in order to be a priest, the Son of God had to become a man.

Atonement is a massively important word that encapsulates the meaning of Jesus's work on the cross. The meaning of propitiation—an atoning sacrifice—has been hotly contested. For example, in the early twentieth century one of the chief aims of liberal theologians was to redefine the meaning of the atonement. The primary word they sought to expunge from the Christian theological vocabulary was *propitiation*. In fact, one of the most famous New Testament scholars in the liberal academy, C. H. Dodd, staked his academic reputation on asserting that propitiation was synonymous with expiation. Since the terms still confuse many Christians, we will examine each of them in turn.

Expiation refers to the washing away of sin. It cancels the debt of sin and closely relates to the forgiveness of sins. Yet expiation requires no change in God himself. It fails to answer *how* a holy God can forgive sins. *Propitiation* answers this question. Propitiation refers to the satisfaction of God's justice. At the cross, God poured out his wrath against sinners on Jesus, thereby satisfying God's demand for the just punishment of sin. Thus, God's wrath was satisfied and his righteousness was vindicated. Paul describes the atoning sacrifice of Christ with the same language in another important passage on the meaning of the cross in Romans 3:21-26:

> But now, apart from the law, God's righteousness has been revealed, attested by the Law and the Prophets. The righteousness of God is through faith in Jesus Christ to all who believe, since there is no distinction. For all have sinned and fall short of the glory of God. They are justified freely by his grace through the redemption that is in Christ Jesus. God presented him as an atoning sacrifice through faith in his blood, to demonstrate his righteousness, because in his restraint God passed over the sins previously committed. God presented him to

demonstrate His righteousness at the present time, so that he would be
righteous and declare righteous the one who has faith in Jesus.

Propitiation enables God to be both just and justifier. Without the satisfaction of God's righteousness in the punishment of sin, he could not justly declare sinners righteous. Thus, propitiation stands at the very heart of the gospel. The logic of propitiation makes the good news good. Without propitiation, there is no gospel. In fact, the nature of Christ's atoning work is so central to the argument of Hebrews that the author revisits the entire discussion at length in Hebrews 9 and 10. He continues to clarify exactly how Jesus's priesthood and his propitiatory sacrifice work together to bring about our redemption.

Verse 18 reminds us to look backward to the temptations and sufferings of Christ to find encouragement in meeting our own temptations. This is a regular pattern throughout Hebrews: the Christian faith continuously alternates between looking backward and looking forward. We look forward to the hope of resurrection and the perfection of our salvation, but we also look backward at the life and ministry of Christ. In so doing, we look back to the source of our salvation. When we pray to Christ for rescue from sin, we pray to One who has himself walked through suffering and temptation. He is no stranger to our difficulties. He truly has been made like his brothers and sisters "in every way" (2:17).

These two introductory chapters of Hebrews are remarkable. In the midst of the author's argument that Christ is superior to the angelic host, we have already seen tremendous glimpses of the gospel of grace. This gospel is the solution to our biggest problems in life, from death to the devil. Yet because of the nature of the gospel, it is also the solution to our day-to-day trials and temptations. Christ sympathizes with our weaknesses at every level. As our incarnate brother, he suffered and was tempted just like us. Therefore, we can approach him with confidence and in faith.

Reflect and Discuss

1. The Trinity is distinctly Christian. In what ways do the Father, Son, and Holy Spirit act for our salvation?
2. What are some other verses or phrases in Scripture that beautifully capture a summary of the work and ministry of Jesus the way "bringing many sons and daughters to glory" does in Hebrews 2:10?

3. In what ways do you magnify the glory of God in your life? At work? At home? In what areas could you improve your magnification of the Lord?

4. Do you find yourself underestimating the devil? What about overestimating him? How does Christ's victory over the devil affect your view of the enemy?

5. Do you fear death? How does this passage prepare Christians to handle the inevitability of death? How can Christ's accomplishments over death calm fears about death?

6. How does the fact that Jesus "had to be like his brothers and sisters" comfort you? How does the indispensability of his incarnation encourage you in your day-to-day life?

7. Explain the concepts of *expiation* and *atoning sacrifice* in your own words. Why does atoning sacrifice stand at the heart of the gospel? What does it say about the seriousness of our sin?

8. Why do you think *atoning sacrifice* is such a hotly contested theological term? Why do so many still try to expunge or redefine it today?

9. How does Jesus's priesthood relate to his propitiatory death?

10. Do you regularly look back to the temptations and sufferings of Jesus to help you in the fight against your temptations? What are some of the ways that the temptations and sufferings of Jesus could help you in the particular sufferings and temptations you face?

Jesus Is Greater Than Moses

HEBREWS 3:1-6

Main Idea: Consider Jesus, the high priest who has performed a superior sacrifice on your behalf, and hold on to your hope in Jesus, the One who is greater than Moses as the Son and architect of God's house.

I. **An Apostle and High Priest Better Than Moses (3:1-4)**
   A. A holy brotherhood
   B. Consider Jesus as the Scriptures portray him.
   C. Consider Moses . . . in light of Christ.
II. **The Hope of God's House (3:5-6)**
   A. The servant of the house
   B. The heir of the house
   C. The perseverance of our faith

Hebrews 3 begins a new section in the overall argument of Hebrews. Chapters 1 and 2 introduced some of the epistle's major themes and argued for the superiority of Christ over the angels. In this chapter the argument shifts to the superiority of Christ over Moses. This transition takes readers one step closer to the center of the theology of Hebrews: Jesus Christ is the climax of redemptive history and the fulfillment of all of God's Old Testament promises, prophecies, and patterns.

An Apostle and High Priest Better Than Moses
HEBREWS 3:1-4

Similar to what we saw with "for this reason" at the beginning of Hebrews 2, "therefore" in 3:1 connects the preceding argument with the author's moral exhortation to the church. The logic is simple: in light of the great salvation provided, consider Jesus! Thus, because Jesus is the merciful and faithful high priest who has tasted death for everyone and is the source of our salvation, Jesus merits our full consideration.

A Holy Brotherhood and Heavenly Calling

Before coming to the exhortation, the author identifies his readers as "holy brothers and sisters" and those "who share in a heavenly calling." It is easy to skip over little descriptors like these, but we must remember that the biblical authors often embed an entire theology in the words they use to describe the church. The use of "brothers and sisters" recapitulates the preceding argument that Christ is not ashamed to call us "brothers and sisters." By virtue of becoming Christ's siblings, we become brothers and sisters to one another in the church—the family of God. Our common brotherhood in Christ produces our new familial relationship and ultimate unity.

The word *holy* is important as well. Other biblical authors designate the people of God as a "holy" people (1 Cor 3:17; Eph 2:21; 1 Pet 2:5,9). This word emphasizes that the blood of Christ has sanctified and cleansed the church. The context of Hebrews gives the word an even richer significance. Holiness was an important feature of the Levitical system. Worshiping God rightly under the old covenant required holiness in every aspect of life among the old covenant people. This is why Leviticus contains such detailed instructions about sacrifices and purifications. Holiness could only come through sacrifice, which is to say, holiness was not a human achievement. Thus, when the author designates these people as a holy brotherhood, he makes a Christological claim. He is not congratulating them for achieving the status of holiness; he is rendering them holy on the basis of the priestly sacrifice Christ offered on their behalf.

The "heavenly calling" shared by believers refers to God's purposes in our salvation and our glorification. Again, the description accents the fact that God has acted to rescue the church. He makes us what we are. We do not transform ourselves into something and then become God's people; God transforms us into his people. These designations also remind us that believers compose the church. "Holy" unbelievers do not exist. It is impossible to share in God's heavenly calling while remaining unrepentant. To be a part of Christ's church requires repentance and faith. It means that the blood of Christ has cleansed you and that you are now destined for a heavenly glory according to God's infallible purpose.

Consider Jesus as the Scriptures Portray Him

As already mentioned, the author exhorts the church to "consider Jesus." The word *consider* communicates the idea of meditation. Jesus is the heart of Christianity, which means his person and work are the best objects for Christian meditation. We should remember that all people have a worldview. That means we interpret all the data we encounter through a particular grid, through our preconceptions about the world. The author of Hebrews reminds us that the ultimate axiom for the intellectual thought life of the believer is Jesus Christ. He is not simply the author and finisher of our faith; he is the author and finisher of our thoughts as well. Considering Jesus should animate the intellectual patterns of all believers and recalibrate their biblical worldview.

However, we must never "consider Jesus" outside of the biblical and theological context in which he is presented. If we think on Christ, we must think on him rightly. That is why the author of Hebrews clarifies that we must think on Christ according to how Scripture reveals his character. The author specifically highlights two aspects of Christ's ministry: he is our "apostle," and he is our "high priest." We rarely use the term *apostle* to refer to Christ. This is because we never think about the meaning of the term. *Apostle* simply means "sent one." Thus, the twelve apostles are those specifically commissioned by Jesus Christ and "sent" out on his behalf. In the same way, Christ is the apostle of the Father, the One sent from heaven with a specific message and mission to accomplish. Jesus is also the "high priest," a designation the author will continue to unfold throughout the rest of Hebrews.

Consider Moses . . . in Light of Christ

The author of Hebrews primarily wants us to consider the faithfulness of Christ. He demonstrates the faithfulness of Christ by comparing him with Moses. Jesus "was faithful to the one who appointed him, *just as* Moses was in all God's household" (emphasis added). The introduction of Moses into the argument at this point may initially seem strange, but when we remember the overall argument of Hebrews, then we can see that this is absolutely necessary.

Hebrews is written to believing Hellenistic Jews. Thus, the primary theological background for Hebrews is the Old Testament. The Jews steeped themselves in the Old Testament Scriptures and exercised the utmost reverence for their major historical figures like Moses. In order to assure his audience that Christ superseded Judaism, the author of Hebrews constructs several arguments to show Christ's superiority to the old covenant. Hebrews 1 and 2 already demonstrated Christ's supremacy to the angels. Now the author contrasts him with Moses.

It is impossible to think about the old covenant and Judaism without considering Moses. God used Moses to liberate his people in the exodus, which the Old Testament treats as the paradigmatic example of how God acts on behalf of his people. Moreover, God used Moses to deliver the law to Israel. The old covenant is essentially the legacy of Moses's ministry to the people of Israel.

Even without Hebrews, a careful reading of the Pentateuch and the Gospels would be enough to demonstrate that Christ is greater than Moses. Moses was a man; Christ is the God-man. Moses was a sinner judged for his sin; sinless Christ is judged for the sins of his people. Moses turned the water of the Nile into blood; Christ changes water into wine. Moses led the children of Israel out of bondage to Egypt but failed to lead them into the land of promise; Christ, the second Moses, leads his people out of bondage to sin and takes them all the way into the eschatological land of promise.

Yet, as true as these observations are, we must not allow them to detract from the specific argument made by the author of Hebrews in the following verses. The argument does not contrast the faults and failures of Moses with the successes and achievements of the Lord. Instead, it highlights the faithfulness of Moses (3:2) and his achievement of faithfully discharging his office as a servant in the house of God. If Moses is worthy of glory as a servant, how much more worthy is Christ—the One who built the house?

At a glance, the logic of verse 4 can be difficult to understand. Fundamentally, however, the author makes a simple point. The "house," later identified as the people of God, had to be built by someone. Every house needs an architect. Christ functioned as the architect of God's house—that is, God's people. Thus, Christ is greater than Moses simply because he created Moses.

The Hope of God's House
HEBREWS 3:5-6

The author continues to demonstrate Christ's superiority over Moses in verses 5 and 6. Whereas Moses was faithful over God's house as a servant, Jesus Christ is faithful over God's house as a Son. Sonship is greater than servanthood.

The Servant of the House

The typical word translated "servant" in the New Testament comes from the Greek word *doulos*. While "servant" is certainly an acceptable translation, it may not capture everything that the word *doulos* conveys. Some scholars, for example, translate the word as "slave." Many modern translations avoid this rendering due to the negative connotations it produces for American readers. The language of slavery often conjures up images of the brutal, ethnically based slavery of the antebellum American South. Nevertheless, "slave" does capture the lowly stature of a *doulos*.

However, the word translated "servant" in this passage does not come from *doulos*. It comes from the Greek word *therapōn*. A *therapōn* held a position of nobility under the authority of the one who appointed him. Thus, verse 5 highlights Moses's place of rank and honor. In fact, Hebrews 3:5 echoes God's own words concerning Moses in Numbers 12:7. He was a faithful servant and an able man in God's household.

But what did it mean for Moses to be a faithful servant? The author clarifies that by faithfully discharging his ministry, Moses testified "to what would be said in the future." In other words, Moses's life and ministry displayed the superiority of Christ. They meant to point away from Moses and toward the Messiah. Moses's ministry existed to testify about things to come. Passages such as Deuteronomy 18:15 demonstrate this. As the author of Hebrews will later show, the priesthood, sacrifices, and entire old covenant system serve the same purpose.

Paul makes a similar claim in Romans 3:21. The Law and the Prophets bore witness to the righteousness of God available to sinners in and through Jesus Christ. The entire Old Testament is one large arrow pointing to the coming Messiah. Whether through typological patterns, promises, or prophecies, Moses faithfully discharged his service in the household of God by pointing to one greater than himself, Jesus Christ. Christ fulfilled all that Moses said in ways beyond Moses's own understanding. Christ then is superior to Moses, just as Moses himself would affirm.

The Heir of the House

Hebrews 3:6 draws an explicit contrast between Jesus and Moses. Moses was a servant. He was a faithful servant, but still just a servant. Jesus, however, is the Son. Jesus is not just a servant in the household; he is the One who inherits the house and functions as its Lord. As the writer of Hebrews explains, the household is nothing less than the people of God, those who "hold on to" their confidence and "boast" in their hope. This means that the household over which Jesus is faithful is the household he built by shedding his blood for sinners.

Other passages in the New Testament also use house language (the Greek word *oikos* means "house" or "household") to describe the church and to show that Christ serves as its foundation (Acts 4:11; Eph 2:19-20; 1 Pet 2:5). To say, then, that Moses was a faithful servant in God's household is to say that he was a servant among God's people. Christ, however, is the Savior of God's people. When the author says, "we are that household," he also subtly affirms the deity of Christ. Verse 5 calls it "God's household." "His" in verse 6, however, refers to Christ. Thus, the writer of Hebrews affirms the divine sonship of Christ. He is both the eternal Creator (3:4) and Redeemer (3:5-6) of God's people.

The Perseverance of Our Faith

The final phrase of 3:6 troubles Christians because it seems to suggest that our salvation is conditional. Obviously the people of God are those who "hold on to" their confidence and "boast" in their hope, but why would the author include the conditional "if"? Is the author casting doubt on the certainty of eternal salvation available in Christ?

Hebrews, perhaps more than any other New Testament book, affirms the sufficiency of Christ and his work for our salvation. Nevertheless, warnings against failing to persevere in the faith appear throughout the book. This verse introduces that major theme in Hebrews. The author of Hebrews and the rest of Scripture teach that only those who persevere in faith will be saved, and that all who have genuine faith will persevere. Believers constitute the household of God, which is to say that the church is made up of persevering believers who have authentic faith.

Our works neither save us nor keep us saved. Only Christ can save us. We must hold on to our "confidence" and retain our "boast" in the gospel and in the Lord. We do not boast in ourselves and our own spiritual achievements. We boast in the cross and in the hope of resurrection. The doctrine of the perseverance of the saints does not mean we enter God's kingdom by faith and stay in God's kingdom by works. Instead, it means we enter God's kingdom by a faith that will persevere and never fail. By faith, we confidently trust that Christ's righteousness belongs to us. He is our only boast. He is our unfailing hope.

Reflect and Discuss

1. How does the description of "holy brothers and sisters" inform how we should live both in the context of the church and in the world? Do you think about your church in familial terms? What are some ways you can become a better "brother" or "sister" within your church?
2. What does it mean for Jesus to be the high priest of our confession? What are some ways this applies to our lives?
3. What does holiness look like in the life of the New Testament believer?
4. The author of Hebrews urges us to consider Jesus. The world urges us to consider anything else. What are some of the most prominent things the world urges you to consider instead of Christ? What are some helpful ways you can learn to consider Jesus more frequently and rightly in your current context?
5. What evidence does the text give that suggests Christ is superior to Moses? What other places in the New Testament point to Christ's superiority over Moses?
6. The author of Hebrews highlights faithfulness in the lives of Jesus and Moses. What should Christian faithfulness look like in our current cultural context?
7. How does considering Jesus and meditating on his work aid and fuel faithfulness?
8. What does it mean for Christ to be the builder of the house? How does Christ's role in God's household differ from Moses's role in God's household? What is our role therein?
9. In light of the way Moses is described as a faithful servant, in what specific ways are we to serve Christ?
10. What does holding on to our confidence and boasting in our hope look like from day to day? How does the author use the conditional "if" to encourage us and solidify our hope in Christ and in his work for our salvation?

Exhort and Encourage for the Sake of Faith

HEBREWS 3:7-19

Main Idea: Israel failed to enter God's rest because they presumed on God's kindness and had their hearts hardened by sin. Therefore, exhort and encourage one another to hold firmly to your confession until the end so that an evil, unbelieving heart will not lead you away from faith in the living God.

I. **Learning from a Bad Example (3:7-11)**
    A. The Holy Spirit says: Hebrews and inspiration
    B. The urgency of believing today
    C. Rebellion and rest: why Israel failed
II. **Exhorted to Endure (3:12-19)**
    A. An evil, unbelieving heart
    B. Holding firmly to faith

Years ago I attended a lecture that profoundly impacted me. The lecturer was Heiko Oberman, a prestigious history professor from the University of Arizona and one of the world's greatest scholars on the Reformation. Oberman was about seventy years old at the time; I was in my early twenties.

Halfway through the lecture, Oberman became unusually frustrated with the class. The group did not frustrate him because of misbehavior or lack of attention. The class frustrated him simply because we were young! "Young men will never understand Luther," he said, "because you go to bed every night confident you will wake up healthy in the morning. In Luther's day, people thought that every day could be their last. They had no antibiotics. They didn't have modern medicine. Sickness and death came swiftly." Oberman was right. To fully understand Luther, we needed to know he faced the reality of eternity each day—and so do we!

Closing his eyes at night terrified Luther because he was afraid he would wake up in hell. His angst grew out of his recognition of God's holiness and man's sinfulness. Only the imputation of Christ's righteousness found in the gospel delivered him from that fear.

The prospect of God's judgment is indeed terrifying. Only the gospel provides us the assurance we need that we can have a right standing before a holy God. Yet as the author of Hebrews reminds us, the gospel not only delivers us from the penalty of sin but from the power of sin as well. Christians must persevere in the faith in order to reach the promised land. We must continue to hold firmly to the gospel, lest the holiness of God shut us out of his rest and Luther's nightmare become an endless reality for us. This is the message of the remainder of Hebrews 3. The author exhorts God's people to endure.

Learning from a Bad Example
HEBREWS 3:7-11

In verses 7 through 11, the author draws attention to the first generation Israelites and their rebellion against God in the wilderness. God warned those Israelites to endure in their faith, but many of them failed. Instead of trusting in the One who rescued them from slavery, they provoked God and were shut out of the promised land. Hebrews 3:7-11 admonishes us not to be like faithless Israel.

The Holy Spirit Says: Hebrews and Inspiration

The writer of Hebrews does something spectacular with the introductory clause in verse 7. He prefaces a quotation of the Psalms with the words, "as the Holy Spirit says." In doing so, the author dramatically affirms the divine inspiration of Scripture. The author highlights the Holy Spirit's role in the formation of Scripture a little later in the book as well (Heb 10:15).

"As the Holy Spirit says" accomplishes two tasks. First, it teaches us that God is the author of Scripture. It teaches us, "men spoke from God as they were carried along by the Holy Spirit" (2 Pet 1:21). When Scripture speaks, God speaks (Warfield, *Inspiration and Authority of the Bible*, 119). When we hear Scripture, read Scripture, study Scripture, or encounter Scripture in any way, we can be confident God is speaking to us.

Second, it affirms the living character of Scripture. The author does not use the past tense. He does not say, "The Holy Spirit said." He uses the present tense. Every time we open the Bible, the Holy Spirit speaks. Even though the biblical authors recorded these words long ago, they are still living words. The author of Hebrews explicitly argues this in the next chapter: "For the word of God is living and effective and sharper than any double-edged sword" (Heb 4:12).

The Urgency of Believing Today

In the main argument of this text, the writer of Hebrews returns to the Psalms for support and to model how to read the Old Testament in light of Christ. The verses quoted here are from Psalm 95:7-11. In stark contrast to Moses, the people of Israel in Moses's time were faithless to God. Thus, the author uses these verses from the Psalms to exhort us not to repeat the faithlessness of the Israelites. Psalm 95 warns God's people not to harden their hearts and turn away from the God who saved them. This is precisely what happened to Israel. They murmured against the Lord, grew discontent with his redemption, and pined for the pleasures of Egypt (Ps 106:6-43).

The author presses the word *today* on his hearers with a sense of urgency. The urgency remains for us in our current context just as much as it did for the original audience. Today is the day of decision. Today we will either walk with God or walk away from him. As Luther recognized, today is the day of salvation because today may be our last. The original audience could not presume upon another day. Neither can we.

The phrase "if you hear his voice" is very important. Entering God's final rest depends on hearing and heeding the voice of God. For anyone to hear God's voice is a result of an act of mercy and salvation. God speaks in order to save his people. The original author teaches his audience that God has graciously spoken so that they might be saved. Now they must obey God's voice and faithfully follow it into eternity.

Rebellion and Rest: Why Israel Failed

The author also shows his audience why Israel failed to enter the promised land: they hardened their hearts. The Lord tested them in the wilderness (v. 8) and they failed. The forefathers of the nation failed to keep their hearts God-oriented. Though they saw the "works" of God "for forty years" (v. 9), they put God to the test and rebelled against him.

Israel presumed on God's kindness. God graciously preserved them for forty years. He delivered them. He kept them alive. He provided manna for them. He guided them through the desert with a pillar of fire by night and a pillar of cloud by day. And yet they presumed on that grace and grumbled against the Lord.

What is the "rest" Israel failed to enter? The word *rest* in verse 11 refers to the land beyond the Jordan River. God swore in his wrath that the people of Israel would not enter Canaan, the land he had first promised to Abraham and his descendants (Gen 15:18-21). However, the context of the author's argument indicates that Canaan looked back to the rest of Eden and also typologically foreshadowed the future eschatological rest of the new creation. This is why the writer of Hebrews uses this Psalm and the story of Israel in the wilderness to exhort his readers to remain faithful. He wants them to make it to the true land of rest.

Rest in Scripture metaphorically refers to God's blessings of safety, security, and salvation. Hebrews develops this picture by bringing a uniquely Christological component to a theology of rest. Hebrews 4 teaches that Jesus Christ is our Sabbath rest. Not a place but a person— Jesus Christ—most fundamentally gives us rest.

The warning in these verses is sobering and serious. Just as he did with Israel, God will shut out from his rest those who rebel, walk in unfaithfulness, and presume on the grace of God. Like faithless Israel, those who presume on the grace of God will die on the wrong side of the Jordan. We must hold firmly today lest we wake up outside God's eternal rest.

Exhorted to Endure
HEBREWS 3:12-19

In verses 12-19 the author shifts away from showing his audience Israel's unbelief to exhorting his audience not to fall into unbelief. He exhorts his people not to follow in first generation Israel's faithless footsteps. Instead, he encourages them to endure in the faith so that they can enter into God's eschatological rest.

An Evil, Unbelieving Heart

Verse 12 begins the author's application of Psalm 95 to his audience. Israel sinned because they did not believe God. They had an "evil, unbelieving heart." This type of heart ultimately sets us on the path that leads away from the living God. Thus, the author exhorts his brothers and sisters to check their hearts so that they will not end up hard-hearted like Israel.

How do we combat evil, unbelieving hearts? Verse 13 provides the remedy. Christians "encourage each other daily, while it is still called today." Paul gives the same command to the Colossians when he encourages them to teach and admonish one another "in all wisdom . . . through psalms, hymns, and spiritual songs, singing to God with gratitude in your hearts" (Col 3:16). Immersing oneself in the community of saints, in the care and watchfulness of the local church, in the preaching of God's Word, and in the exhortation of fellow believers remedies an evil, unbelieving heart. These things protect us from falling away. The author again highlights the urgency of this task. We must immerse ourselves in these things "today." Tomorrow is no guarantee.

The author also describes an "evil, unbelieving heart" as one that has been hardened by the deceitfulness of sin. The Old Testament diagnoses the hardening of the heart as a terminal disease. A hardened heart leads to eternal death. Each of us at some point had a hard heart, but God, because of his love for us, replaced our hearts of stone with hearts of flesh (Ezek 36:26). While we were dead in our sins and opposed to God, God brought us to life by his grace (Eph 2:1-7). God's miraculous work on hearts of stone grounds our endurance and helps us fight evil, unbelieving hearts.

The danger of having a hard heart is not just that you might stumble. The danger of a hard heart is that it will lead to a final denial of God and rejection of his grace in Jesus Christ. The danger of a hard heart is unbelief. Hard hearts do not recognize or accept their need for a savior. Therefore, the ministry to which the author exhorts his brothers and sisters is no small ministry. Exhorting brothers and sisters in Christ to watch out for an evil and unbelieving heart is an urgent task for gospel faithfulness with eternal significance.

Holding Firmly to Faith

The "reality that we had at the start," mentioned in verse 14, is a conversion—one's first confession of Christ when God regenerated the heart by the power of the gospel. While the author reminds us that God sovereignly ignites our conversion, perseverance in our faith (fueled and motivated by God's grace) is our responsibility. Ultimately, we cannot keep ourselves. God is the One who began a good work in us and will bring that work to completion in the end (Phil 1:6). God is the One who will uphold and guard us by his power through faith (1 Pet 1:5).

Verses 15 through 18 push forward the author's argument for perseverance in the faith. In verse 15 the author quotes Psalm 95:7-8 to once again reiterate the importance and urgency of hearing and obeying God's voice. The questions the author asks in verses 16-18 underline a central theological issue—the fatal error of unbelief. The Israelites committed many sins in the wilderness but only one prevented their entry into the land of promise, the sin of unbelief. Verse 19 powerfully demonstrates the need to persevere *in faith*. Without faith we will not enter the promised land. The faithless will not enter God's eschatological rest. The faithful hold firmly until the end.

Reflect and Discuss

1. The author of Hebrews argues that one of the reasons Israel fell away was because their hearts were hardened by the deceitfulness of sin. Is there any sin in your life that you entertain and refuse to put to death? Are you at total war with your sin, or do you pick and choose your battles? Explain.

2. Do you regularly confess your sin to other brothers or sisters in your church as a means to prevent the hardening of your heart? Which relationships exhort you to endure in the faith? How do you encourage others to endure?

3. In what ways do you, like Israel, presume on God's kindness? Do you expect God to grant you tomorrow? Would today look any different in your relationship with the Lord if you knew it was your last?

4. How does the author of this passage use the reality of God's wrath to motivate his audience to hold firmly until the end? Do you typically think about God's wrath as a motivation for persevering in your faith? Why or why not?

5. In what practical ways can you encourage brothers and sisters in your church to persevere in the faith? Identify other places in Scripture that show us how Christians can exhort one another.

6. How does the miracle of rebirth help us endure in the faith? Does the miracle still flame your affection for Christ, or have you simply grown accustomed to it?

7. In what activities or things do you pursue rest? If Jesus Christ is our ultimate rest, what does that say about the "rest" we experience this side of heaven?

8. The perseverance of the saints is one of the most comforting doctrines in all of Christian theology. How might it help you and others to endure in the faith?

9. In what ways is the divine inspiration and living character of Scripture tied to perseverance in the faith? How does the author of Hebrews use Scripture to spur his audience forward toward God's eschatological rest?

10. Spend time reflecting on "the reality that [you] had at the start," to which the author of Hebrews refers in verse 14. What is the significance of the word "if" in this verse?

Let Us Enter His Rest!

HEBREWS 4:1-13

Main Idea: God invites us to enter his rest today. Therefore, let us hold on to our faith in Christ, maintaining the urgency of our belief, and let us encourage one another with God's sustaining Word.

I. **Entering by Faith (4:1-2)**
II. **Entering with Urgency (4:3-10)**
III. **Entering with the Word (4:11-13)**

Every generation of Christians faces theological crises, so every generation of Christians must fight to maintain the theological purity of its gospel proclamation. Getting the gospel wrong results in spiritual death. Because the good news of the gospel is the only means by which sinners can be saved, it must be preserved and protected at all costs by all Christians in every generation.

The author of Hebrews recognized the gravity of this reality. His letter strongly defends and defines the gospel for a people who found themselves in the middle of theological crisis. As we have seen elsewhere in the letter, one of the ways the author combats misconceptions about the work of Christ is by modeling how Christians should read the Old Testament. After demonstrating the superiority of Christ over the angels and over Moses, the author turns his attention to the theme of rest and demonstrates how Christ is the only foundation for true spiritual rest.

A brief survey of the word *rest* in Scripture reveals that the biblical concept of rest communicates a great deal more than taking a nap or going on vacation. As we have already seen in Hebrews 3, "rest" in the Bible is a deeply theological concept and one the author does not use apart from the metanarrative of Scripture. The same is true in Hebrews 4.

Entering by Faith
HEBREWS 4:1-2

In Hebrews 3 we see how entering into "rest" in the Old Testament pointed to the people of Israel entering the land of promise. That land of promise was more than just a piece of territory. The land was indicative of God's promise to Abraham and signified God's plan to restore creation after the fall corrupted it. Thus, entering the promised land meant more than just entering a piece of real estate. It meant enjoying and entering God's plan of salvation and inhabiting the very place where God set his dwelling.

Throughout most of the Old Testament, Israel disobeyed God and did not enter God's rest. They were "found to have fallen short." The old covenant people, by and large, did not have circumcised hearts and therefore did not respond to the grace of God with faith. While they may have physically entered the territory of Canaan, they never truly entered into the spiritual rest that the territory typified.

The author not only reminds his readers that those under the old covenant failed to enter into God's rest, but he also uses this information to warn them. This is why he begins this verse with the word *therefore*. He reminds his readers of the failure of the Israelites to enter into God's rest in order to exhort them to continue in the faith lest they too end up outside God's rest. The author's exhortation comes out even more forcefully in verse 2. The "good news" was preached to the ancient Israelites, just as it has also been preached to the author's audience. But the Israelites failed to respond to that good news with faith.

A number of important points emerge from these two verses. First, this passage reminds us that simply hearing the message of the gospel is insufficient for salvation. Jesus himself (quoting from Isaiah 6) spoke of this when he reminded his disciples that there are those who hear the message of the gospel but do not believe it (Matt 13:10-15). Second, it reminds us that the only appropriate response to the gospel is faith. Israel heard the promises and warnings of God but did not respond with faith. As a result, they perished in the wilderness.

Third, this passage reminds us that faith is something much more than just intellectually apprehending the gospel message. The Israelites surely understood the promises and warnings God gave them, yet they did not rest on those promises. They disregarded the word of God and acted disobediently because they did not *believe* the word of God.

Finally, these verses remind us that the message of salvation was not different for those in the Old Testament. Regrettably, many false teachers have pointed to the numerous commands in the Old Testament and argued that works saved old covenant saints, but now, by the work of Christ, grace saves new covenant saints. This text, however, demonstrates that the same "good news" preached in the new covenant was also preached in the old covenant. Of course, now that Christ has come and fully revealed the Father (John 14:8-9), new covenant believers have a fuller picture and a greater understanding of how God has acted to save. Nevertheless, old covenant saints were saved *by faith* in the promises of God just as we are today. Paul makes this clear in Romans 4:1-25 when he argues that Abraham was justified by faith.

Entering with Urgency
HEBREWS 4:3-10

In verse 3 the author once again quotes from Psalm 95:11, on which he has been basing his argument since Hebrews 3:7. "They will not enter my rest" resoundingly condemns the wilderness generation for its failure to trust the promises of God and enter his Sabbath rest. While Psalm 95:11 convicts the wilderness generation for its unfaithfulness, the author of Hebrews uses it to reiterate a great theme of this passage: those who *believe* enter God's rest. In fact, the end of verse 3 affirms the availability of that rest to all generations—even the wilderness generation—since God's rest started at the foundation of the world, a notion the author grounds in verse 4 by drawing from the creation narrative. Since the seventh day of creation, the opportunity to join God in his rest remains.

The repetition of Psalm 95:11 in verse 5 emphasizes the urgency of entering God's rest. When a biblical author repeatedly returns to the same issue, it is most likely because the hard-heartedness of sin-prone people requires the repetition. Only one thing can satisfy the restlessness of the human soul—the "rest" of God. And the only way we can access God's rest is by faith in Jesus Christ, the One who secures God's rest for believers through his death and resurrection. If we reject the promises of the gospel, then we will die in the wilderness. But if we trust in its promises and in the God who makes them, we will enter God's rest. This is a message stubborn sinners need to hear over and over again.

In verses 6 and 7 the author brilliantly applies what he said previously, as the words "therefore, since" indicate. These verses are also rich with theological and hermeneutical treasures. The author affirms both David's authorship of Psalm 95 and the historicity of the events surrounding the wilderness generation. Moreover, just as David did for his original audience, the author of Hebrews applies the significance of the wilderness events to the current situation of his congregation. In other words, Psalm 95 simultaneously condemns the wilderness generation for its disobedience and invites its original hearers to respond to God's promises in faith, which the author of Hebrews picks up and applies to his own audience.

Furthermore, just as David urged his original hearers to respond to God in faithfulness "today," so too does the author of Hebrews urge his readers to respond to God in faithfulness "today." David's words to the Israelites in his own time are just as valid and urgent now. God has appointed today for us so that we might respond to his call in faith and not harden our hearts. We cannot presume upon tomorrow. Today may be the only day we have left. But as long as you have today, you have an invitation to faith.

Joshua's name in verse 8 can seem somewhat unexpected. However, once we understand the context of Psalm 95 and the theological rationale of the author, the introduction of Joshua at this point in the argument no longer seems strange at all.

Until this verse, the author has essentially given his readers a biblical theology of Israel's disobedience. Psalm 95 anchors his biblical theology because it both rehearses the story of Israel's disobedience and provides God's interpretation of those events. As we have seen, Psalm 95 specifically focuses on Israel's rebellion against God and against Moses in the wilderness—a rebellion that kept them from entering the promised land.

Moses, however, did not lead the people into the promised land. His successor Joshua did that, which is why the author introduces him in verse 8. The author has already demonstrated that Christ is superior to the angels and Moses. Now he must demonstrate that Christ is superior to Joshua.

As the writer notes, even though Joshua led the people of Israel into Canaan, he did not lead them into God's "rest." Even in Canaan the people of Israel continued to rebel against God. When the people of Israel journeyed across the Jordan River into the land of Canaan, they did not journey into rest; they simply moved from one place to another. Thus Psalm 95, written by David long after the events of the conquest, still speaks of a Sabbath rest that remains for the people of God.

How do we enter this Sabbath rest? The whole letter of Hebrews tells us: by believing in Jesus Christ, the Lord of the Sabbath. Joshua led Israel into the land, but Jesus leads his people into God's true eschatological rest. Verse 10 elaborates on this. We rest from our works and enter God's rest when we trust in Christ. We no longer have to live our lives trying to "prove" our righteousness before God. Instead, we "rest" from that labor because Christ has already proved that righteousness on our behalf.

Like John 3:16, Hebrews 4:10 powerfully captures the message of the gospel in a single verse. The gospel is not morality. The gospel is not external religion. Nor is it a seven-step program for obtaining a better life. The gospel is the message of Christ's accomplishments on our behalf so that we might "rest" from our works by trusting in his work. When we trust in Christ's work, we rest from trusting our own.

Excursus: Hebrews and the Inspiration of Scripture

I have noted several times throughout this commentary how unashamedly clear the author of Hebrews is regarding his high view of Scripture. As we saw in Hebrews 3:7, the author often introduces Scripture with the words "the Holy Spirit says," even when the Scripture he's quoting comes from a historical person (David in this case). Such instances demonstrate that the author of Hebrews wholeheartedly believes Scripture's ultimate origin is God himself.

Hebrews 4:7 gives us another important example of the author's theology of Scripture. The author believes the words of Psalm 95:11 ultimately come from God, but he does not ignore the fact that they also come "through David." Thus, the writer of Hebrews simultaneously affirms the divine and human authorship of the Bible. God speaks in Scripture, but he speaks through certain individuals. B. B. Warfield called this the "concursive" theory of inspiration (*Inspiration and Authority of the Bible*, 95).

The apostle Peter speaks about the divine and human authorship of Scripture in 2 Peter 1:21: "No prophecy ever came by the will of man; instead, men spoke from God as they were carried along by the Holy Spirit." God used real, historic people with peculiar vocabularies and personalities to write the Bible, but he also providentially "carried them along" so that they would write exactly what he intended. Article VIII of the "Chicago Statement on Biblical Inerrancy" (which makes a series of affirmations and denials about the doctrine of Scripture) states the doctrine this way: "We affirm that God in His work of inspiration utilized the distinctive personalities and literary styles of the writers whom He had chosen and prepared. We deny that God, in causing these writers to use the very words that He chose, overrode their personalities."

Amazingly, God used the personalities, writing styles, experiences, and life situations of the human authors in order to accomplish the production of an "inscripturated" text; men, inspired by the Holy Spirit, wrote God's Word. This does not mean the authors passively entered trances as they composed Scripture. Nor does it mean God merely dictated the words to them. The authors actively engaged in the composition process, yet God carried them along in such a way that everything they wrote was exactly what he intended; Scripture is the actual word of God.

Entering with the Word
HEBREWS 4:11-13

Verse 11 introduces the "so what" of the preceding section. In light of what has preceded, "Let us *then* make every effort to enter that rest" (emphasis added). The accent in this verse is on the exhortation to strive for God's rest so that the threat of falling by disobedience will not come true for these believers as it did for the wilderness generation. We must not be like the Israelites in the wilderness. We must strive to enter God's rest. In other words, we must work at resting. This means we must work *against* all of our efforts to prove our righteousness. We must strive *against* all our efforts to justify ourselves.

One of our chief responsibilities in the Christian life is to exhort one another to faithfulness. This is one of the things we do every Sunday in corporate worship when we sit under the preaching of the Word of God. This is what we do when we sing together. This is what we do when we pray together. This is what we do when we fellowship together. We gather in corporate worship to encourage one another to be fully satisfied in Christ and in him alone, lest we fail to enter his rest.

The author also underlines the role of God's Word in our perseverance in verses 12 and 13. The designation "word of God" requires some definition. The author uses the phrase to point to the entirety of divine revelation—both written and incarnate. Regrettably, many Christians divorce the Bible from Jesus. "I don't need theology or the Bible, I just want Jesus," some may say. This is a misguided assessment. Christ cannot be divorced from Scripture. Our knowledge of Jesus as the divine Son of God and his accomplishments for us only come *through* Scripture. We cannot have Jesus Christ apart from the witness of the Bible. The two are inseparably wedded.

The author establishes two characteristics about the Word of God in verse 12. First, the Word of God is "living and effective." This highlights the enduring vitality of Scripture. Since God is the author of Scripture, it is not a dead book. As God lives, Scripture lives. Furthermore, as we see throughout Scripture, when God speaks, God acts. This is what is meant by the adjective *effective*. For example, God created the heavens and the earth with his word. Thus, Scripture, because it is God's Word, is alive and life giving. The Bible is not a bunch of dead, lifeless words. It is the living Word of God. It accomplishes everything God wills. As the Lord says through the prophet Isaiah, "so my word that comes from my mouth will not return to me empty, but it will accomplish what I please and will prosper in what I send it to do" (Isa 55:11).

Second, the author describes Scripture as "sharper than any double-edged sword." As a sword, Scripture is "penetrating as far as the separation of soul and spirit, joints and marrow. It is able to judge the thoughts and intentions of the heart." The description of the Bible as a sword that can pierce and divide the soul demonstrates the invasive quality of the Word. When we approach Scripture with a humble hermeneutic of submission rather than a haughty hermeneutic of suspicion, then it is not we who read Scripture, it is Scripture that reads us. Scripture untangles the human heart and unearths sin like no other book can. No other book can discern the thoughts and intentions of our hearts. Only God's Word can do that.

Scripture is like a scalpel wielded by God to perform spiritual surgery. In conjunction with the Holy Spirit, the Word of God cuts through the sin and darkness of the human heart to restore spiritual health and vitality for Christ. Without the Word, we are as good as dead. God's Word, however, eradicates the disease of the human heart and breathes life where there is death.

Verse 13 shifts from the Word of God to God himself, which shows the intrinsic link between God and Scripture. Just as God's Word graciously reveals God to man, it also makes man accountable before God as Judge. When God reveals himself to us, we in turn realize that we all "are naked and exposed to the eyes of him to whom we must give an account." Scripture strips us bare before our own eyes and before the eyes of God because it exposes God's ineffable character. As Calvin famously stated, "It is certain that man never achieves a clear knowledge of himself unless he has first looked on God's face, and then descends from contemplating him to scrutinize himself" (*Institutes*, I.I.2).

God gives us the gift of Scripture so that we will not follow the example of Israel's disobedience. The Bible is our guide to trusting God and finding full satisfaction in him. Furthermore, God has revealed the truth about Christ to us in his Word. This is why we must be students of God's Word and maintain the centrality of its teaching. Scripture leads us to Christlikeness. If we are to become like the incarnate Word, we must study the inscripturated Word.

Reflect and Discuss

1. What are some theological crises the evangelical church faces today? How are these crises threatening the purity of gospel proclamation? In what ways can we better defend and define the gospel in light of these issues?

2. Many unbelieving Israelites entered the physical land of Canaan but still failed to enter into God's rest. What does that tell us about the heart of these Israelites? What does it suggest about the importance of the heart in regards to salvation?

3. How does the creation narrative and God's Sabbath rest on the seventh day of creation serve the argument of this passage?

4. In what ways does the author's treatment of Scripture in this passage, particularly the Old Testament, bolster your confidence in the inerrancy and divine inspiration of Scripture? Explain in your own words the concursive theory of inspiration and the role of the human author in the composition of Scripture.

5. Why is it so difficult for us to rest from our attempt to merit our own righteousness? Why is resting such a constant struggle for Christians? How does our union with Christ and his righteousness help us in this matter?

6. How does Scripture help us strive to enter God's rest? How do the attributes of Scripture described in this passage strengthen your perseverance?

7. How would you respond to someone who says, "I don't need theology or the Bible; I just need Jesus"? How could you use this passage to support your argument?

8. How is the author using Joshua to illustrate his point? Why is Jesus
    superior to Joshua in the context of this passage?
9. What was the "good news" preached under the old covenant? Why
    was it the same message we have heard preached under the new
    covenant? What does it mean to have faith?
10. Explain the many ways Psalm 95 is functioning in the author's
    argument.

Jesus: Our Tempted Yet Sinless High Priest

HEBREWS 4:14-16

Main Idea: Jesus, our elder brother and great high priest, was tempted like us but did not sin. As a result, we now have access to God, to whom we can confidently draw near in our times of need.

I. **Holding Fast to Our Confession (4:14)**
    A. Our confession of the historical Jesus
    B. Our confession of the Christian faith
II. **Remembering Our Sinless High Priest (4:15)**
III. **Boldly Approaching the Throne of Grace (4:16)**

The truths and doctrines the author presents in Hebrews 2 undergird the claims and conclusions he makes here in the final verses of chapter 4. Thus, the author uses both chapters to develop the same argument about the function of Jesus's humanity. They both explain that Jesus had to be made like his brothers and sisters in every respect so that he could become a merciful and faithful high priest in the service of God, and so that he might make propitiation for the sins of the people.

Holding Fast to Our Confession

HEBREWS 4:14

The words "therefore, since" in Hebrews 4:14 link this section back to the arguments in Hebrews 2. The author now begins to develop the priestly ministry of Jesus in more detail. In Hebrews 4:14 the author identifies Jesus not only as a high priest but as "a *great* high priest" (emphasis added). High priests are prominent throughout Scripture, but only one *great* high priest exists—Jesus, the Son of God. As the great high priest, Jesus redefined the office because, even though he was tempted in every way as we are, he never sinned and he has passed through the heavens into the very throne room of God to be our mediator. Later verses also show that this spatial language refers to the fact that Jesus's priestly work for us did not take place in the earthly tabernacle but in the heavenly tabernacle (Heb 9). Jesus—because he is the great high priest and on account of the superiority of his sacrifice—has entered the actual presence of God on our behalf and has now brought us near to God. The author of Hebrews uses this priestly work of Christ as the grounds for exhorting his audience to "hold fast to our confession." This confession is a two-fold confession: our confession of the historical Jesus and our confession of the Christian faith.

Our Confession of the Historical Jesus

For the first time in the letter, the author refers to Jesus by name in verse 14. In doing so, the writer makes clear that the historical Jesus is the ground of the believer's faith. The author declares that the one with the titles "great high priest" and "Son of God" is none other than Jesus of Nazareth—the One who equips us to hold fast to our confession. He reminds us that our faith is grounded in the incarnation that took place in space, time, and history. This verse emphasizes that Christ's work is not distant from our own experiences. Even though he has passed through the heavens as our great high priest, Jesus identifies with human beings in his own humanity.

Our Confession of the Christian Faith

In addition to our confession of the historical Jesus, the confession also refers to every Christian's confession of the gospel. In Romans 10:9 Paul says, "If you confess with your mouth, 'Jesus is Lord,' and believe in your heart that God raised him from the dead, you will be saved." This is the message that makes up the heart of the Christian faith and is what Christians throughout the centuries have been claiming as their confession. The second clause of Paul's confession—"and believe in your heart that God raised him from the dead"—is not a sacred mantra or a kind of secret linguistic key. It is the very identity of the Christ we follow and the very heart of the confession we make. Christians believe and confess Jesus Christ as the resurrected Lord.

Hebrews 4:14 urges Christians not to abandon this confession, particularly in the face of temptation and trial. As we have already seen, Israel's way of responding to temptation is not one that the author encourages his readers to emulate. Israel let temptation and trial erode their confession in Yahweh. They had heard God speak words from the fire, witnessed the plagues and the parting of the Red Sea, received the covenant passed on by their forefathers, and heard the message of the prophets, yet they failed. They did not hold fast. In contrast, the author exhorts his people to keep clinging to their confession of faith, not by their own strength or through the mediation of a prophet or a priest, but by faith in their great high priest, Jesus, the Son of God.

Remembering Our Sinless High Priest
HEBREWS 4:15

Hebrews 4:15 demonstrates the sinless nature of Christ's high priesthood and continues the exposition of Christ's humanity started in Hebrews 2:17-18. The author of Hebrews does not engage here in theological theory but instead formulates a real and tangible theology on which readers can anchor their lives. Why do we need a high priest who is able to sympathize with our weaknesses? Hebrews 4:15 answers that question by explaining that Jesus could not have fully identified with us and fulfilled his ministry of propitiation if he had not also identified with us in our temptations and remained without sin.

This naturally leads to an important theological investigation: What distinguishes temptation from sin? If Jesus was tempted in every way as we are and yet did not sin, doesn't this logically assume that it is possible to be tempted and not sin? After all, if temptation itself were sin, we would not have a sinless Savior.

The typical understanding of *temptation* is the enticement to wrongdoing that confronts us every day. We typically think about it in its most graphic forms: the temptation to sin sexually, the temptation to elevate ourselves over others, the temptation to steal and cheat, or the temptation to lash out in anger. Yet when we examine Jesus's temptations in Matthew 4, we see just how basic temptation can be. That narrative demonstrates that even eating can be a temptation if satisfying physical hunger results in disobedience to God. Thus, Scripture shows us that temptation can take the most graphic of forms and the most basic of forms. Nevertheless, Scripture instructs us to go to Christ when we are tempted because he is the only one who was tempted in every way common to humanity and yet did not sin.

Consider Jesus's words in the Sermon on the Mount. Jesus says that to lust after a woman is to commit adultery in the heart (Matt 5:28). Does this imply that a man commits adultery in his heart every time he sees a woman he considers attractive? The answer cannot be yes because

Jesus is not calling men to stop looking at women; he is calling them to fight looking at women *with lustful intent*. He is calling them to fight the temptation to turn attraction into sin. Every man knows a line is crossed when he moves from an initial attraction to allowing that attraction to captivate his mind with lustful thoughts. When a man crosses that line, he is giving permission to his temptation to manifest itself into full-blown sin. Even without giving himself to that sin in a physical sense, that man is still committing adultery.

Jesus never crossed that line. He was tempted in every respect that we have been tempted, but never once did he permit that temptation to become sin in his heart, in his thoughts, or in his actions. Thus, temptation that resists or rejects sin falls short of sin, while temptation that gives over to sin is sin. In other words, millions upon millions of people who have never committed adultery in the flesh have committed adultery in their hearts. Moreover, every person has in some respect given permission to some temptation to become sin. Thus, the author of Hebrews is exhorting his readers to find rescue from their temptations in Christ, the only high priest who can deliver us from temptation. While temptation may always hinder us this side of heaven, Jesus's priestly ministry promises that it will never ultimately triumph over those who claim Christ as their high priest.

Amazingly, the author tells his readers that Jesus was tempted in every way that they are tempted, but Jesus never let his temptations cross over into sin. He *always* resisted. This perfect sinlessness is indispensable to Christ's ministry as our high priest. If Jesus had sinned, his atonement would not have been sufficient because he could not have propitiated God's wrath against sin. In Romans 3 Paul explains that God overlooked the sins of the past in his forbearance in order that full atonement would be made in the cross of Jesus Christ. In other words, Israel lived under the threat of the wrath of God day by day. Old Testament priests could only offer sacrifices that would delay God's judgment against sin. Their sacrifices could only buy time. Jesus's sacrifice, however, accomplished complete atonement for sin once and for all. This was only possible because he was without sin, totally unlike every other high priest and totally unlike every other human being.

Boldly Approaching the Throne of Grace
HEBREWS 4:16

On account of their great high priest who intercedes on their behalf and sympathizes with their weaknesses, the author of Hebrews exhorts Christians to approach the throne of grace with confidence. This throne is the throne of God. For those who are in Christ, God's throne is a throne of immeasurable grace. At his throne, Christians are able to find grace to help them in their times of need. Even in our weaknesses, we can approach the throne of God with confidence because we know that God has fully and finally put away all of our sin in Jesus Christ, our great high priest. However, for those who are not in Christ, God's throne is a throne of terrible judgment. At his throne, those who reject Christ bear the full penalty of their sins. For those who reject Christ, the "throne of grace" is a throne of wrath.

Furthermore, the author says that this throne of grace is a place Christians can confidently "approach" in order to find the grace they need to face every situation in life and to receive the mercy they need to cover the sins they commit. If we could not draw near to God with confidence on account of Christ's work, then the Christian life would be futile and hopeless. We would not dare enter God's presence if we did not know Jesus as the One who is faithful and righteous to forgive us our sins and to cleanse us from all unrighteousness (1 John 1:9).

Christians have a great high priest, one who has passed through the heavens, atones for sin, and intercedes for us before the Father. Jesus, our intercessor, identifies with us because he experienced in every respect the same temptations that we experience. Therefore, we can come before the throne of God every day as well as on the last day with confidence because we know Christ mediates for us before the Father.

If Christ were not our great high priest, we could not stand before God. We would be cast from his presence for all eternity. And yet, no Christian lives under this threat. Righteous judgment has been replaced by radical mercy. Therefore, let us not shrink from God's presence. Instead, let us draw near to him with all boldness and confidence, knowing that he is willing to equip us with mercy and grace in our times of need.

Reflect and Discuss

1. Look back to the truths and claims the author makes about Jesus in Hebrews 2. Explain how they complement and fortify the truths

and claims he makes in Hebrews 4:14-16. How are the two passages related?

2. What three characteristics does Hebrews 4:14 ascribe to Jesus? How do these attributes and identifications help us hold fast to our confession? How do they help us inform and articulate our confession?

3. Why is it essential that we not compromise on our confession of the historical Jesus and our confession of the Christian faith? How does holding fast to our confession in times of trial and temptation work to reveal the genuineness of one's faith? Describe a situation in which you've seen someone claim the name of Christ and yet compromise on our two-fold confession.

4. Why is it so important that we understand that Jesus can sympathize with sinners? How does that fact affect your outlook on the Christian life? How does it equip you in your fight against sin?

5. Why is Jesus's sinlessness in the face of temptation indispensable to his identity as the Son of God and as our great high priest? Why do we need Jesus to be tempted in every respect as we are and yet remain without sin?

6. Explain the difference between temptation and sin. How could Jesus be tempted and yet remain without sin?

7. How do the author's assertions about Jesus in Hebrews 4:15 relate to the author's exhortation in 4:14? How do the contents of verse 15 help us hold fast our confession?

8. Why are only Christians able to draw near to the throne of grace with confidence? What causes you to be apprehensive in approaching the throne? What things in your life prevent you from approaching the Lord with confidence?

9. Are receiving mercy and finding grace synonymous terms, or do they convey two different realities?

10. How do Christ's sympathy and sinlessness as identified in Hebrews 4:15 ground the command to boldly approach God's throne in 4:16?

The Chosen High Priest

HEBREWS 5:1-10

Main Idea: Christ's appointment as high priest was greater than any other high priest's appointment; therefore, he can grant eternal salvation to all who obey him.

I.   **The Typical High Priest (5:1-4)**
    A.   The gentle and solidary high priest
    B.   The obligated and called high priest
II. **Our Appointed High Priest (5:5-6)**
III. **Our Perfect High Priest (5:7-10)**

Chapter 5 continues the line of thought the author began in 4:14. Whereas Hebrews 4 showed us Christ's superiority in his sinlessness as high priest and in his ability to sympathize with us in our weaknesses, Hebrews 5 focuses on the superiority of Christ in his appointment as high priest—an appointment that comes from God alone. Hebrews 5, like the final verses of chapter 4, continues explaining why Christians can hold fast their confession: they have a better high priest.

The Typical High Priest

HEBREWS 5:1-4

Hebrews 5:1 identifies one of the defining marks of Judaism. Israel could trace a succession of high priests back to Aaron. Aaron, brother of Moses, was the first high priest and representative of the people, chosen "from among men." But who chose him? Did the people through some kind of democratic process choose him? No. Only God appointed high priests. This process was no different with Jesus. God, just as he had with every other prior high priest, appointed Jesus singularly. The Father chose and assigned him to his priestly task.

Israel saw the appointment of the high priest as a demonstration of God's sovereignty. Although God used angels and other agents to declare Christ's divine appointment, God alone ultimately appointed him. The purpose of God appointing high priests was so that the high

70

priest could act "for the people"; it was thus necessary for the high priest to be chosen from among the people. He represented the people as he ministered in the most holy place before God. When the high priest performed sacrifices, burned incense, offered gifts, and did other priestly duties, he did them on behalf of Israel. He did them in the people's place.

The Gentle and Solidary High Priest

"Those who are ignorant and are going astray" paints the picture of unfaithful people and highlights the high priest's solidarity with sinful human beings. The "ignorant" identified in this verse probably refers to those who were ignorant due to their lack of knowledge of God. No Israelite should have been unfamiliar with the covenant, the law, and God's requirements. The Lord commanded Israel to know the law, to train their children in it, to meditate on it night and day, and to write it on their hearts (Josh 1:7-8; Deut 6:4-9; Prov 7:1-3). Moreover, God instituted festivals for Israel that included the public reading of the Law and public recitation of his deeds precisely so that the Israelites would better know and fear him (Deut 31:9-13). Thus, to be an Israelite and to be ignorant of God meant deliberately disregarding and forsaking God's law.

Knowledge of God alone, however, does not demonstrate faithfulness. The faithful follower of God must also apply that knowledge to the situations of everyday life. Not to apply knowledge was to go astray. The word *astray* does not necessarily mean acting in outright rebellion against God. It can refer simply to being wayward in our thoughts or habits and allowing ourselves to wander from the things of God. The high priest identifies with the ignorance and waywardness of his people because he too is a finite human beset with weaknesses. He can deal gently and compassionately with their ignorant and wayward sinfulness because he himself understands it.

The Obligated and Called High Priest

If the comprehensive solidarity of the high priest with the people was not clear enough from the previous verses, the author makes it perfectly clear in verse 3—the high priest even shares with his people in his own sin. Just as the people were beset with sin, so also was the high priest beset with sin. Therefore, he was obligated to offer up sacrifices for his own sin before he could offer up sacrifices for the sins of the people. His own sin required atonement before he could enter the most holy place. It tarnished him to the point that he could not enter God's presence and intercede on behalf of the people without first purifying himself through sacrifice.

Verse 4 reiterates that the priesthood was not a volunteer position. The priest did not just take the position for his own honor. He only assumed the position after God "called" him, just as God called Aaron. Aaron did not apply to become high priest. He was not elected for the people by the people. God called him to become high priest (Exod 28:1). God's calling emphasizes the servant nature of the high priest's role. Even though the high priest held an exalted office, his office was motivated by service and marked by humility.

Our Appointed High Priest
HEBREWS 5:5-6

Here the author shifts focus from the human high priest to the God-man high priest, Jesus Christ. Jesus is like all other high priests in his appointment. This is what the quotation from Psalm 2:7 highlights. Jesus did not exalt himself to be high priest or seek his own glory in any way. The Father sovereignly appointed the Son, and the Son obediently accepted the role.

But then, you may ask, What does Melchizedek have to do with the high priesthood of Jesus? Who is Melchizedek anyway? Melchizedek is a rare figure in the Old Testament. He appears in only two specific Old Testament texts. We first meet him in Genesis 14:17-24:

> *After Abram returned from defeating Chedorlaomer and the kings who were with him, the king of Sodom went out to meet him in the Shaveh Valley (that is, the King's Valley). Melchizedek, king of Salem, brought out bread and wine; he was a priest to God Most High. He blessed him and said:*
>
>> *Abram is blessed by God Most High,*
>> *Creator of heaven and earth,*
>> *and blessed be God Most High*
>> *who has handed over your enemies to you.*

And Abram gave him a tenth of everything.
Then the king of Sodom said to Abram, "Give me the people, but
take the possessions for yourself."
But Abram said to the king of Sodom, "I have raised my hand in
an oath to the LORD, God Most High, Creator of heaven and earth, that
I will not take a thread or sandal strap or anything that belongs to you,
so you can never say, 'I made Abram rich.' I will take nothing except
what the servants have eaten. But as for the share of the men who came
with me—Aner, Eshcol, and Mamre—they can take their share."

Melchizedek appears and then disappears quickly. Genesis first identifies him as a king of Salem, a Gentile and pagan territory. Melchizedek is a king and yet performs a task not common to kings: offering bread and wine. Genesis then identifies Melchizedek as a priest of God Most High. Thus, in some mysterious way, God appointed a priest from a foreign people unto himself. He then brought this foreign king who was a priest to Abraham, the one with whom God had established his covenant. Melchizedek first blesses Abraham, and Abraham responds by giving him a tenth of everything. Then Melchizedek abruptly disappears.

He appears again in Psalm 110:

This is the declaration of the LORD to my Lord:
"Sit at my right hand until I make your enemies your footstool."
The LORD will extend your mighty scepter from Zion.
Rule over your surrounding enemies.
Your people will volunteer on your day of battle.
In holy splendor, from the womb of the dawn,
the dew of your youth belongs to you.
The LORD has sworn an oath and will not take it back:
"You are a priest forever
according to the pattern of Melchizedek."
The Lord is at your right hand;
he will crush kings on the day of his anger.
He will judge the nations, heaping up corpses;
he will crush leaders over the entire world.
He will drink from the brook by the road;
therefore, he will lift up his head.

This psalm's immediate fulfillment happened in David's own kingship, but its ultimate fulfillment came later in David's line—in the one who sits at the Father's right hand, Jesus Christ. Given that Melchizedek seemingly has little to do with the messianic nature of this psalm, the inclusion of his name likely would have surprised the original audience.

"A priest forever" points to the messianic figure who fulfills this prophecy and distinguishes the order of Melchizedek's priesthood from other priesthoods. Other priesthoods had a termination date because all other priests died. Death prevented them from serving as priests forever. Jesus Christ, however, on account of his resurrection from the dead, serves as a priest forever. His priesthood knows no end.

What does it mean for Jesus's priesthood to be "according to the order of Melchizedek"? While it is tempting to think that "according to the order" refers to a Melchizedekian line of priestly succession or that Jesus came from outside the tribe of Israel as Melchizedek did, this is not the case. There was no Melchizedekian line of priestly succession, and only someone from within Israel could fulfill the Davidic monarchy. Therefore, "according to the order" must mean that Jesus's priesthood, like Melchizedek's, is born out of the sovereign purposes of God. The order—that is, the nature—of Jesus's priesthood is of a sovereign order, a sovereign nature. Like Melchizedek, Jesus did not take the honor of priest upon himself; he was sovereignly appointed. And in his appointment and service as high priest, he was exalted above all others.

Our Perfect High Priest
HEBREWS 5:7-10

Here the author steps away from the theological groundwork he has been laying to turn his attention to the incarnated life of Jesus. "During his earthly life" points the reader to the ministry of Jesus. Even though Jesus was totally without sin, this did not make him exempt from the frailty of human experience. Even Jesus was beset with the heartache and grief associated with human existence. This is what Jesus's prayers and supplications signaled. They signaled that he depended on God to meet his needs and to sustain him at all times. Jesus was just like any other human being in this regard.

"With loud cries and tears" recalls Jesus's experience in the garden of Gethsemane. "To the one who was able to save him from death" certainly corresponds with this thinking. But this reference does not limit Jesus's loud cries and tears to his experience in Gethsemane, for Jesus faced the anguish of becoming sin for those who believed in him and bore the burdens of human existence all the days of his flesh. Scripture shows us Jesus offering up prayers and supplications even before the cross. One example of this is in the high priestly prayer of John 17. Loud cries and tears were regular features in Jesus's prayer life.

Christ's prayers to "the one who was able to save him from death" were not prayers expressing a desire to escape the cross and the grave. He predicted his own death many times throughout the Gospels and said that death was the purpose for which he was sent into the world (John 12:27). Jesus did not pray in order to be saved from dying; he prayed in order to be saved out of death through the resurrection. Jesus's prayer to be saved from death was a prayer to be raised from the grave. The One who was able to save Jesus from death answered his prayer when he delivered him from death in the resurrection.

The Father was not deaf to the loud cries and tears of his Son. He heard and answered the Son's prayers "because of his reverence." A good way to think of this reverence is in terms of awe, devotion, or submission. The Father heard the Son because Jesus feared God and because he totally submitted his will to his Father's.

In verse 8 the author explains that Jesus learned obedience to God through what he suffered, even though he was God's Son. That Jesus learned obedience should not cause us to think that Jesus needed to be taught obedience because he was disobedient at one point. Hebrews is clear that Jesus never disobeyed. Rather, this verse highlights his humanity. As Jesus experienced the trials associated with human existence, he learned how to obey his Father in them. Suffering taught Jesus how to submit his will to his Father's will. We see this lesson at its sharpest point in Gethsemane and on Calvary. The cross meant terrible agony of heart and body for Christ, but he remained resolute in his willingness to be obedient, even obedient to the point of death (Phil 2:8). By faithfully enduring the suffering ordained by the Father's plan to redeem sinners through his own blood, Jesus learned obedience.

Verse 9 tells us that Jesus "was perfected" through suffering—so much so that "he became the source of eternal salvation for all who obey him." What does it mean that Jesus was made perfect? Wasn't he already perfect? Furthermore, what does it mean that Jesus became the source of eternal salvation? We have already seen how suffering played a part in Jesus's perfection in Hebrews 2:10. The author is echoing the same reality in this verse. Jesus was not made perfect in the sense that his nature was once impoverished and needed to be improved. Rather, he was made perfect in the sense that learning obedience through suffering was a prerequisite for becoming a qualified and sufficient high priest. In being made perfect through suffering and death, Jesus became "the source of eternal salvation." This simply means that Jesus's suffering stands as the basis for our salvation. Christ as the source of our salvation is synonymous with Christ as the founder of our salvation (cf. 2:10).

The eternal salvation that Jesus pioneers is only granted "for all who obey him." It is fitting that the One who learns obedience through what he suffered would stand as the source of eternal salvation for all who obey him. In keeping with one of the major themes of the book, the author of Hebrews is once again encouraging his people to obey Jesus and not abandon the faith.

The writer concludes his discussion about the priesthood of Jesus by returning to the reality that God designated Jesus to be a priest according to the order of Melchizedek. The assurance of our faith is in the fact that Christ himself is a priest forever after this order. Thus, the assurance of our salvation and our standing before the Father are rooted in Jesus's priesthood—a priesthood that sovereignly comes from the Father's appointment. It is a priesthood that was made perfect through suffering and death on a cross.

Reflect and Discuss

1. What was the purpose of Old Testament priests? In what ways did Jesus fulfill these duties in his service as high priest of the people? What similarities does this passage show between Jesus's priesthood and typical priesthoods?
2. Why was the divine appointment of the high priest significant? How does Jesus's priesthood relate to Melchizedek's in this regard, and what does it tell us about God's purposes?
3. Why does the author compare Jesus to Melchizedek? What does it mean for Jesus to be according to the order of Melchizedek?
4. What part does Jesus's humanity play in his priesthood? How does it help him be the best possible high priest for us?
5. Explain how Jesus can be weak and dependent in his human existence yet remain sinless.
6. How are the ignorance and waywardness of the people related to the high priest? How might you guard against ignorance and waywardness in your own life? How does the priesthood of Jesus help us in our ignorance and waywardness?

7. How do Jesus's prayers and supplications during his earthly life show his solidarity with human beings?

8. What does it mean for Jesus to be a priest forever? How does Jesus's remaining a priest forever assure our faith and help us endure?

9. In your own words, explain what it means for Jesus to be made perfect through suffering.

10. Why was it necessary for Jesus to learn obedience through suffering? What part do suffering and death play in Jesus's perfection? His sonship? What part do they play in his becoming the source of eternal salvation?

Warning against Stagnation

HEBREWS 5:11-14

Main Idea: We must steadily pursue maturity in the faith by digesting the deep truths of God's Word.

I. **The Diagnosis: Dull Hearing (5:11)**
II. **The Symptom: Childish Understanding (5:12-13)**
    A. A failure to know and grow
    B. Getting back to the basics
    C. Milk and moral immaturity
    D. The word of righteousness
III. **The Remedy: Discerning Power (5:14)**
IV. **Our Responsibility**

Certain moments are crystallized in our memories. I vividly recall an event that occurred when I was just ten years old. I was complaining to my father about an ailment I was experiencing. When he asked me what was wrong, I replied, "I have a tummy ache."

My father responded in a way I'll never forget. "You're ten years old," he said. "You don't have a tummy anymore, you have a stomach." There was a little bite to my father's words, but it was necessary. In my father's eyes, the word *tummy* did not demonstrate my maturation into adolescence. I do not think he expected me to remember this story forty years later, but he certainly expected me to grow up a little by developing my vocabulary and learning to act my age.

Similarly, the author of Hebrews rebukes and exhorts his readers in a way that only a loving, spiritual father could. He admonishes them for their willful ignorance and immaturity in the faith. They still need milk when they should be eating solid food. The author urges them to leave behind their spiritual childishness and to move into spiritual adulthood by developing an appetite for the solid food of God's Word. Like my father did with me over forty years ago, the author is telling his people, "It's time to grow up."

The Diagnosis: Dull Hearing
HEBREWS 5:11

The phrase "about this" refers to the author's previous discussion about the differences between Christ's priesthood and Aaron's priesthood (4:14–5:10). In that discussion, the author teaches us that the great high priesthood of Christ is infinitely superior to that of the priests of the old covenant since Christ is a priest according to the order of Melchizedek. The writer returns to the topic of Jesus's priesthood later in the letter, but he interrupts the discussion here in order to exhort and chastise his people for their spiritual dullness and immaturity in the faith.

The author wants to continue talking about Christ's priesthood, but he stops. Why? Is it because Christ's priesthood is inherently difficult to understand? The author says the priesthood of Christ is "difficult to explain," but is it because Christ's priesthood itself is too perplexing? No. It is difficult to explain because the people have become "too lazy to understand." They don't have the mature ears, minds, or hearts for grasping the concept. Those who are trained in Scripture and are progressing in the faith are better equipped to understand Christ's priesthood, but those who shut their ears to God's Word regress in their faith and fumble in their comprehension. Spiritual concepts like Christ's priesthood are difficult only for the spiritually immature, those who have become "too lazy." The spiritually mature, on the other hand, have the energy to investigate and understand spiritual concepts that are hard to explain.

Believers have a moral responsibility to know and understand Scripture. We often act as if our biblical ignorance is merely a matter of God hiding or withholding knowledge from us. Yet Scripture teaches us that our ignorance of God's Word is a moral problem, not an intellectual one. When we deliberately ignore God's Word for whatever reason, we sin against the Lord. In the case of the Hebrews, the congregation became intellectually sluggish by their own negligence. Their spiritual immaturity was their fault. They grew intellectually dull because they became sluggish of heart. Christ's priesthood became difficult to understand because their hearts became indifferent to Scripture. Thus, the author must stop explaining Christ's priesthood in order to admonish his people and prod them out of their lethargy.

The Symptom: Childish Understanding
HEBREWS 5:12-13

In verse 12 the author more acutely pinpoints the root cause of this congregation's spiritual immaturity. Not only can they not understand spiritual concepts like Christ's priesthood, but they have also forgotten the fundamental things of the faith! Even though they have had plenty of time to become teachers themselves, they actually need teachers to reteach them the elementary doctrines of the Christian faith.

A Failure to Know and Grow

This reference to "teachers" is not a reference to those who hold a particular teaching office such as a pastor or elder. Rather, by using the term *teacher*, the author is addressing their responsibility to disciple other believers. Not all Christians are expected to be pastors or elders. All Christians, however, are expected to be teachers in the sense that they should be prepared to train new believers in the fundamentals of the faith. The congregation should consist of willing and maturing disciples who are training up newer and less developed disciples. They ought to be teaching others. Instead, they are lapsing spiritually and need others to teach them the basics of the faith again.

The word *again* is critical here because it indicates that the congregation did not internalize the teaching they already received. They do not need to be taught for the first time. They have already been taught "the basic principles of God's revelation." The word *again* implies that the congregation has forgotten what they should know by heart by now. This is not a simple case of their needing review. Christians, no matter their maturity in the faith, should always review the elementary things of the faith. This congregation, however, needs more than recap: they need to relearn. Thus, we must be careful to internalize the teaching we receive and to take the fundamentals of the faith to heart so that we are established in the faith and able to fulfill our responsibility as "teachers," that is, as disciples.

The issue the author addresses here is the Christian's intellectual responsibility. But we must not limit this particular warning only to the Christian's intellect. This warning is ultimately about the entirety of the Christian's spiritual life. Our spiritual life should be such that we are learning to take responsibility for our own growth. We must be developing an appetite for grace, knowledge, and understanding. The more we know, the more we should want to learn. We are called to do this not only for ourselves but so that we can teach those who are less spiritually mature. Our spiritual growth has both inward and outward dimensions. We grow in the faith for our own sake and for the sake of others.

Getting Back to the Basics

This text also teaches another important truth about the Christian life. Certain fundamental principles and doctrinal foundations are prerequisites for understanding more mature and complex truths. Before we can handle the upper-level courses, we must master the entry-level classes. We must grasp basic truths at basic levels before we can move forward. What are these basic principles? The author lays them out at the beginning of chapter 6, so we will look at them more in depth in the next chapter. For now, it is sufficient to say that the basic principles are the truths that make up the basic storyline of Scripture.

Labeling these principles as "God's revelation" communicates that Scripture is God's spoken word. This also points to God's self-disclosing and decisive acts in redemptive history. These acts, which the author lays out in fuller detail later on in the letter, are seminal moments in the history of Israel and the church. In these acts God reveals truths about himself that inform our understanding of who he is and establish the fundamental doctrines of our faith. The author's readers are indicted for their failure to put this revelation into practice. As a result of their spiritual lethargy, they remain infants in the faith. Their digestive systems can only handle spiritual milk, not solid food.

Milk and Moral Immaturity

The writer of Hebrews speaks pastorally in these verses. We might even say he speaks paternally. What ought to be taking place in the spiritual lives of the congregation is not taking place. They ought to be feasting on the solid foods of the faith, not continuing to nurse on the milk of spiritual infancy. This is why the author rebukes them as he does. He rebukes them the way my father rebuked me when I told him my tummy hurt.

There is *nothing* wrong with giving milk to an infant. It is natural for an infant to live on a diet of milk. In fact, despite all of our scientific and technological advancement, we have never been able to develop something that can nourish an infant quite like a mother's milk. It would be pointless to put a steak dinner in front of a baby. The child is simply not ready for it. But *everything* is wrong with offering mother's milk when the child is ready for steak. That is why the word picture in this text is so powerful. This congregation ought to be eating spiritual steak by now. Instead, they're still living on milk.

Paul uses the metaphor of milk in a similar way in 1 Corinthians 3:1-2. He writes,

> For my part, brothers and sisters, I was not able to speak to you as spiritual people but as people of the flesh, as babies in Christ. I gave you milk to drink, not solid food, since you were not yet ready for it. In fact, you are still not ready.

A remarkable symmetry between Paul's statement and Hebrews 5:13 exists. Just as Paul contrasts the spirit and the flesh, the author of Hebrews contrasts those who are skilled and unskilled in the message about righteousness. When we place these two texts beside each other, we learn that spiritual immaturity leads to moral immaturity. Spiritual immaturity leads to believers who live according to the flesh rather than the spirit. To willingly remain an infant in Christ makes one a person of the flesh and unfit for righteousness.

The Word of Righteousness

"The message about righteousness" essentially means "the message that leads to salvation." While there is a moral element to this message about righteousness, the context points us toward the gospel and God's saving purpose. Believers who are childish are unskilled in the gospel because they lack the ability to turn to Scripture and see how God's plan to save culminates in the priestly work of Christ. They lack the maturity to live in a manner worthy of the gospel. Christians are not to be ignorant about the gospel. Nor are we to be untutored in the Scriptures. We are called to be skilled in the message about righteousness and to walk in the ways we have been taught.

If the writer to the Hebrews were merely making a diagnosis, then those who are spiritually immature would have little hope of remedying their situation. But the writer states that it is the believer's responsibility to become spiritually mature. He urges his readers to leave behind the milk of spiritual infancy and to draw near to God by feasting on the solid food of spiritual maturity. This moral imperative serves as good news because it implies that spiritual maturity is quite possible in the life of a believer. We cannot persist on a diet of milk when God offers us solid food.

The Remedy: Discerning Power
HEBREWS 5:14

We now arrive at the contrast between mature and immature believers. As we saw in 1 Corinthians 3, Paul refers to the meat of the faith as solid food—food that requires the hard work of chewing and digesting. Only by faithfully and diligently studying the Scriptures can we rightly train and exercise our spiritual power of discernment. Thus, only the mature can distinguish good from evil. The immature are too weak and have not had enough practice.

Discernment is critical to our lives. It often takes shape in ways that are not overtly intellectual. Think about it. We negotiate many of our day-to-day decisions on the basis of an intuitive discernment. To put it another way, discernment is like a theological grid or a worldview that helps us make instant moral and theological judgments about our circumstances. We would never get anything done if we made every decision on the basis of sheer intellectual reconstruction. Imagine a heart surgeon who has to stop and rethink cardiology in the middle of a surgery. Imagine how disastrous it would be if he needed to consult a textbook every time he entered the operating room. No one wants that kind of surgeon. We want surgeons who can use the intuition they have developed over years of dedicated practice. This need for discernment applies not only to surgeons but also to Christians.

Discernment is a higher order of thinking and can only be acquired through diligent training and experience. We want surgeons whose powers of discernment have been trained by constant practice. Similarly, if we want to mature as Christians, we must train our powers of discernment by constant practice. We should so thoroughly consider and internalize the fundamentals of the faith that we are able to teach them to others and discern good from evil. The author of Hebrews says that when we learn to practice discernment, we are ready for "solid food"— the weightier matters of God's Word.

This does not mean Christians eventually reach the point where they no longer need to study Scripture. All Christians, even maturing ones, always need the Bible. Discernment simply means that we find ourselves in familiar territory when we open the Word of God. Discernment means the Bible doesn't disorient us. We know how to read, study, understand, and reason from the Scriptures. When Christians possess discernment and can distinguish between good and evil, they have the capacity for spiritual reasoning. They can see how one doctrine relates to another and can logically apply those doctrines to aid decision making in all areas of the Christian life.

Our Responsibility

As we have seen, this passage indicts any Christians who are spiritually regressing when they should be growing. There is great and eternal peril in spiritual infancy, for it puts one in danger of falling away from God. Therefore, the author teaches Christians two important lessons about our responsibility to mature in the faith: (1) It is an individual believer's responsibility to grow in spiritual understanding so that the congregation as a whole is better equipped to faithfully minister the gospel to those in need. (2) It is the church's responsibility to teach the individual believer. Sadly, many congregations drink nothing but milk because that is all their pastors are feeding them. In other cases, congregations stubbornly refuse the solid food their pastors are offering them. Christians cannot accomplish what the author of Hebrews envisions if both of these barriers are not overcome. Healthy Christians serving in healthy congregations are essential to spiritual maturity.

The process of spiritual maturity is a long and challenging one. But the goal is to gradually move from a diet of milk to a diet of solid food. We may retain childish tendencies for a time, but we must be steadily growing out of them. We must learn to be mature in the faith as those who possess powers of discernment trained by constant practice to distinguish good from evil. If this is to happen, we can never stop feasting on the solid food of God's Word.

Reflect and Discuss

1. Evaluate your own life. Can you think of any areas in which you are spiritually immature and are thus still an infant in the faith? Name them. Are you currently growing in spiritual maturity? If so, in what ways?

2. What excuses do you often hear regarding one's ignorance of biblical knowledge or spiritual understanding? What excuses do you find yourself using? How does this passage address the excuses we usually give for our failure to grow in biblical literacy and spiritual maturity?

3. The author rebukes this congregation for needing teachers when they should be teaching others. Does this rebuke help you think differently about your responsibility to teach other Christians? If so, how? How is an individual Christian's responsibility to teach others different from an elder's or pastor's responsibility to teach the church?
4. What are the fundamentals of the Christian faith? Why do you think Christians are so prone to forget the spiritual truths they have been taught? What are some ways we can fight this forgetfulness?
5. What is the purpose of discipleship? What should the process of discipleship look like? Are you currently discipling a younger believer? Why or why not? Think of a less mature believer in your life you could disciple.
6. What is the difference between childishness and childlikeness? What does it look like to be both childlike and mature at the same time?
7. In your own words, explain what it means to be unskilled in the message about righteousness. How is this related to our spiritual maturity?
8. In what ways do you practice spiritual intuition on a daily basis? How can you sharpen this intuition? How does the local church help us develop a spiritual intuition?
9. When you open Scripture, do you feel like you are in familiar or unfamiliar territory? What does Scripture have to do with our discernment and spiritual maturity? How can knowledge of the Bible help us discern good from evil?
10. Who ultimately is responsible for the spiritual maturity of a Christian—the individual or the church?

Warning against Apostasy

HEBREWS 6:1-8

Main Idea: Ultimately, nonbelievers in the church will repudiate Christ and go back into the world. True believers, however, will be motivated to move forward in their faith and claim Christ as King until the end.

I. **Leaving the Elementary Foundation (6:1-3)**
   A. First couplet: A foundation of repentance from dead works and faith in God
   B. Second couplet: Instructions about washing and the laying on of hands
   C. Third couplet: Resurrection of the dead and eternal judgment
   D. "If God permits"
II. **The Danger of Irreversible Apostasy (6:4-8)**
   A. A warning against apostasy
   B. An illustration of apostasy

One of the most formative moments of my theological education occurred when I read a Jewish scholar defending the historicity of the resurrection of Christ. Sadly, the man was not a Christian. In that event, I learned that many people articulate right things about the gospel without truly being followers of Christ.

Fortunately, the Bible prepares us for these situations. Throughout the history of the church, Hebrews 6:1-8 has been one of the most difficult passages to interpret. To whom does this warning belong? To Christians? To non-Christians? To both? We must understand that this passage comes in the context of a larger argument: we should not neglect so great a salvation. Instead of maturing in their understanding of the greater truths of God, many in this church were neglecting the great salvation offered in Christ. As a result, they were stalling out in their spiritual growth and abandoning the faith.

Leaving the Elementary Foundation
HEBREWS 6:1-3

Leaving the elementary teaching of Christ does not mean leaving Christ behind. On the basis of knowing the elementary things, Christians should mature rather than settle for infancy. These Christians needed to move beyond the foundational things and the old covenant of their former Judaism. Foundations are good and necessary for building, but once they have been laid, they do not need to be laid again. The author exhorts his congregation to stop laying the same foundation repeatedly. Instead, they are encouraged to build on the foundation. The author uses three couplets to demonstrate these foundational truths about Christ:

- A foundation of repentance from dead works and of faith in God
- Instructions about washing and the laying on of hands
- Resurrection of the dead and eternal judgment

First Couplet: A Foundation of Repentance from Dead Works and Faith in God

The first couplet emphasizes repentance. Some forms of contemporary evangelical thought marginalize the necessity of repentance. However, Scripture teaches that there is no authentic faith without repentance from sin. In this text, repenting from dead works is in view. The author exhorts Christians to rest in Christ as their true Sabbath, which requires abandoning attempts at self-righteousness. Christians trust that Christ's righteousness, not their own, saves. The temptation to try to earn one's salvation is the author's central concern. He was afraid that many in the church were returning to Judaism and its emphasis on works.

This reinforces that justification by faith alone is essential to the gospel. Implied in this elementary truth is the necessity of leaving behind dead works and repenting of the fruitless attempt to establish our own righteousness before God. Jesus Christ, the great high priest, establishes our righteousness for us through his atonement. The author charges his people to leave behind their dead works by resting in that atonement and the righteousness God has provided for them in Jesus Christ.

Second Couplet: Washing and the Laying on of Hands

Ceremonial washing and the laying on of hands were both integral to Judaism. In order to move on to maturity, these Jewish believers needed to leave behind their confidence in ritualistic practices. Washing refers both to the washing of Israel in the past and to the once-for-all character of baptism. The washing of Israel under the law represented the purification of God's people, while Christian baptism symbolizes unity with Christ and identification with him in his life, death, and resurrection. Just as they were doing with dead works, some members of this church were placing their faith in ceremonial washings, not in the work of Christ.

The great diversity in matters associated with the laying on of hands makes it difficult to know what the author is addressing. In the Old Testament, hands were laid on people during blessing, on animals about to be sacrificed, on someone being devoted to a service, or on criminals in cases requiring the death penalty. In the New Testament, hands were laid on people for blessing, healing, commissioning, receiving the Holy Spirit, and receiving spiritual gifts. Whatever the case, these Christians were getting caught up in matters regarding the laying on of hands and not the righteousness secured for them in Christ.

Third Couplet: Resurrection of the Dead and Eternal Judgment

The third couplet concerns the final judgment and its eternal consequences. The two truly belong together: the resurrection of the dead is for the final judgment. Unless Jesus Christ stands as our advocate and our substitute, we cannot stand before God in the judgment that is coming. The resurrection of the dead should not be ignored; it should never be far from the horizon of our thinking. But there are other teachings that should also be addressed by the maturing Christian.

"If God Permits"

The final phrase, "We will do this if God permits," teaches us not to presume upon spiritual opportunities but to pray to God for our maturation in the faith. We cannot assume the future. Anything is done only if God permits. This awareness deepens dependence on God and drives prayerful expectation of perseverance. Nevertheless, this verse reveals that the author believes that his recipients will rise to the occasion. They *will* build on the elementary foundation if the Lord permits. The author is confident of this.

The Danger of Irreversible Apostasy
HEBREWS 6:4-8

A Warning Against Apostasy

These verses are some of the most difficult verses in the entire New Testament. The phrase "it is impossible" is used four crucial times in the book of Hebrews.

> *"It is impossible to renew to repentance those who were once enlightened, who tasted the heavenly gift, who shared in the Holy Spirit, who tasted God's good word and the powers of the coming age, and who have fallen away."* (6:4-6)

> *"It is impossible for God to lie."* (6:18)

> *"It is impossible for the blood of bulls and goats to take away sins."* (10:4)

> *"Without faith it is impossible to please God."* (11:6)

This particular passage focuses on the impossibility of restoring to repentance those who were once enlightened and partook of the goodness only God can offer. Who are these people who were "once enlightened" and "tasted the heavenly gift"?

The first option is that these people are genuine followers of Jesus Christ. They truly repented of their sin, were united with Christ, and were active in the body of believers. Then they fell away. If understood this way, the passage is a dire warning that many genuine Christians will fall away from the faith. Scripture, however, rules out this interpretation. The Bible repeatedly tells us that God keeps us (John 5:24; Rom 8:39; 11:29; 1 Cor 1:6-8; Phil 1:6; 2 Thess 3:3). In 1 John 2:19 and following, John describes apostates who had left the church. In leaving the faith, they showed they were not truly part of the faith in the first place.

When interpreting difficult texts, it is imperative that we look at other, clearer texts. Scripture is unified and does not contradict itself. Therefore this warning is not addressing Christians losing their faith because other passages say genuine faith cannot be lost. Rather, those who leave and apostatize never really had true faith.

The second option is to read the passage as a hypothetical warning (cf. Matt 24:24). This is a rhetorical technique used by the author to offer an ominous warning of something that cannot actually happen.

Nevertheless, because of its grim consequences, it incites believers to cling to Christ and to grow in grace. The problem with this interpretation is that this passage is not talking about something hypothetical.

The third option, which is the most faithful way to interpret this text, is to read this passage as a real warning. However, it is not a warning for the truly regenerate. Rather, it is a caution for individuals who have tasted the things of Christ but have not become genuine Christians. The author describes the people here as "those who were once enlightened." Many people hear and respond in a positive way to the gospel, but they do not truly believe it. They may know many things about the gospel, but they are not truly Christians. They have "tasted the heavenly gift." That phrase is a very strong expression. Blessings come to Christians, and these people have received some of those same blessings. They may even have demonstrated some of the gifts of the Spirit.

The third descriptive phrase is that they "shared in the Holy Spirit." This means they have demonstrated some of the new life attributed to the work of the Holy Spirit. They show signs of regeneration and even a commitment to identify with Christ and with his people. In other words, they look like believers. The last phrase, that they "tasted God's good word and the powers of the coming age," show that these people understand the gospel. Yet even in their understanding, they do not have true spiritual life; thus, they fall away.

How are we to understand this warning? First, we are told that they have fallen away. In falling away, they returned to their former state of Judaism. The question then becomes, Can a Jew who converts to Christianity and then repudiates Christ as they go back into Judaism come back to repentance again? The answer is no. At issue is more than just going back into Judaism. We have all known people who made public professions of faith in Christ, got involved in a church, showed signs of Christian growth and maturity, and yet ultimately fell away. They are not ignorant. They know who Christ is and what he offers, and they still reject him. In their departure, they were "recrucifying the Son of God and holding him up to contempt." To fall away from Christ is to pour contempt on him, which is equivalent to crucifying him all over again.

An Illustration of Apostasy

The concluding agricultural illustration helps explain this passage. The word *for* marks that an explanation is coming. This illustration about agricultural land receiving rainfall was common in the Old Testament.

For instance, Isaiah 5 uses the metaphor of rainfall causing crops in a field to grow. Isaiah makes clear that the field is Israel and the rain is the word of God. Isaiah 5 also warns that an unproductive field where rain has fallen is worthless. In Hebrews 6, the illustration begins positively. "For the ground that drinks the rain . . . produces vegetation." That is its purpose. It produces "vegetation useful to those for whom it is cultivated." This results in "a blessing from God." However, the illustration continues. "If it produces thorns and thistles, it is worthless." The phrase "thorns and thistles" brings to mind the curse on Adam in Genesis 3. Because of man's sin, the land no longer yields produce without cultivation and rigorous husbandry. Rather, the land naturally brings forth thorns and thistles. In Hebrews 6 a land that received rain but yielded weeds rather than a beneficial crop was to be burned.

Matthew 13 also informs our reading of this passage. There Jesus told a parable about a sower who scattered seed on four types of soil. These soil types represent four different patterns of response. The first represents hard-heartedness. The second represents the shallow heart. It produces immediate signs of life, but there is no root. When the afternoon sun comes, the plant withers and dies. The third soil represents the one who hears the word "but the worries of this age and the deceitfulness of wealth choke the word, and it becomes unfruitful" (Matt 13:22). The second and third soil types are the people warned about in Hebrews 6. They receive the word of God but ultimately produce thorns and thistles.

Through the author's choice to include this agricultural metaphor at the end of this warning, the Matthew 13 connection is apparent. More importantly, it reinforces the sobering warning Jesus gives in the parable of the Weeds. Under pressure, under persecution, or just when distracted by the allure of the world, many who once claimed Christ will go back to the world. Jesus is clear that these people never actually received salvation. John also affirms, "They went out from us, but they did not belong to us" (1 John 2:19). This is why Peter commands us "to confirm your calling and election" (2 Pet 1:10). Furthermore, blasphemy of the Holy Spirit, which is the final refusal of Christ, is a sin of which we cannot repent. Those who refuse the gospel will justly bear judgment for all eternity for their rejection of it.

For believers, Hebrews 6 is a humbling word that reminds us always to look to our own lives for the fruit of regeneration. Christ appeals to many for a time, but they reveal the true condition of their hearts when they go back into the world. As a pastor, the author of Hebrews is addressing this problem in his church. Sadly, it continues to be a common problem in the church today.

Happily, Hebrews does not end with this warning. The author assures believers that he had to write the warning for the unbelievers in the church needing to hear it. Pastorally, he is not seeking to put insecurity in the hearts of Christians. Believers who are faithfully following Christ's commands can be confident in their salvation. If we seek assurance of our faith, we will find it by doing the things faithful Christians do. We will grow out of the elementary things and into maturity.

Reflect and Discuss

1. Why is the temptation to try to earn our salvation through works so strong? Why do we still sometimes find ourselves returning to fruitless attempts to win God's favor through works even though we know better?

2. The author of Hebrews was encouraging his people not to divide their trust in Christ's righteousness with things that could not save them. In what elementary doctrines of the faith do you sometimes trust rather than resting in the righteousness secured for you in Christ?

3. What does it mean to recrucify the Son of God?

4. Why can't this warning be referring to true believers losing their salvation? Why can't the warning be merely hypothetical?

5. How can believers be confident that their salvation is secure? What are some of the marks of true conversion and genuine salvation? Can we actually ever be sure, this side of heaven, if someone is a genuine believer? Why or why not?

6. How does the tension between God's sovereignty and human responsibility play itself out in this passage? Are there other places in Scripture where you see this tension? If so, list them.

7. How does this author use God's sovereignty and "if God permits" in verse 3 to motivate his congregation into prayerful and obedient action?

8. How do other agricultural illustrations in the Bible inform our reading of this warning passage? What does the author want to enforce by using this illustration?

9. Why is it significant that the author concludes this warning with words of hope in Hebrews 6:9-10? How does this encourage you?

God's Certain Promise

HEBREWS 6:9-20

Main Idea: Though many will reject the gospel, those who respond with faith and patience until the end will inherit the promises God has made to them in Jesus Christ. Believers have an unshakable hope in the certainty of God's Word and a stable anchor for their souls in Christ. We can cling to these at all times and in every circumstance.

I. The Better Things Expected (6:9-12)
II. The Oath-Giving, Promise-Keeping God (6:13-18)
III. The Hope Behind the Curtain (6:19-20)

There are many different responses to the gospel. The point of Jesus's parable in Matthew 13 was not to plant doubt in the hearts of the disciples. Rather, Jesus was showing his disciples how many ways the human heart can respond to the good news. The author of Hebrews does something similar in Hebrews 6:1-8. He is showing his congregation the way that many unbelievers in the church rejected the gospel. In doing so, he pastorally exhorts believers in the church toward a faithful obedience and maturity in Christ.

Hebrews 6:9-20 displays the author's confidence in these remaining believers to endure until the end and to inherit the promises that belong to them. How will they accomplish this? With faith and patience, just as Abraham did. By trusting God and persevering until the end, Christians will hold on to the hope set before us. This is what the last half of Hebrews 6 is all about.

The Better Things Expected

HEBREWS 6:9-12

The warning the author began in 5:11 now draws to its conclusion in this passage. The severe and sobering word of admonition now ends with a word of assurance and comfort. The author is fully convinced that those to whom he is writing, unlike those who fell away, will not fall away.

For them, he is "confident of things that are better." He is certain that the good soil of their hearts will produce a good crop.

One of the "things" we encounter in the New Testament is those within the early church assisting and serving one another. This is what "by serving the saints" signals. The apostle Paul himself depended on the support of other churches for his own missionary ministry. The author of Hebrews could have been in a similar situation. Whatever the case, these Christians were showing their love for God by serving fellow brothers and sisters in practical ways. This love for other Christians solidified the author's confidence in them.

One of the most important catalysts of spiritual confidence is spiritual fruitfulness. Our faithful activity as Christians fuels our assurance. This is why the author longs for these Christians to show the same earnestness for the faith that they demonstrated when they first believed. As earnestness and diligence in their faith grows, so too will their fullness of hope until the last day.

The term *lazy* in verse 12 points back to the sluggishness that the author addressed in 5:11. There he was admonishing those who had become lazy and dull in their understanding. Now he is encouraging believers not to become sluggish but to instead pursue things that result in assurance. The author is pushing his people not to become like those whom he began admonishing in 5:11.

He encourages them to be imitators of those who through faith and perseverance inherit the promises. Throughout the book of Hebrews, the writer encourages believers to imitate saints from the Old Testament. In chapter 11, which 6:12 anticipates, we find an impressive list of Old Testament saints whose faith and patience is worthy of our emulation. The author charges his readers to face their difficulties with faith and perseverance, just as those saints who came before them faced theirs. Only earnestness in the faith until the end guarantees the reception of God's promises.

The Oath-Giving, Promise-Keeping God
HEBREWS 6:13-18

Oaths taken in ancient Israel were much different from oaths taken today. Oaths in ancient Israel's day were not contractual as they are now. They were not sealed with a signature. Ancient Israelites sealed their oaths by their personal word. This is the nature of God's oath with Abraham, which is the focus of this passage of Hebrews. God is an oath-giving God who seals his oaths with his own word and by his own name.

The context of verse 13 points to Genesis 22:16-17, where the Lord says to Abraham, "by myself I have sworn," and also promises to greatly bless and multiply him. God swears by himself because there is no one greater to swear by. This, in fact, is why humans invoke the name of God when they take an oath in court or an oath of office. Abraham believed the promise because God was the promisor. By swearing by his own name, God guaranteed the fulfillment of his promise, so Abraham waited patiently and obtained what was promised. God swore by his own name to declare publicly for all creation that he was making this pledge to Abraham and that he would keep it.

The first "heirs" of God's promise were Abraham and his descendants. In order to show the certainty and trustworthiness of his promise, God sealed his promise with an oath. But what does Abraham's promise have to do with the author's audience? For them, the heirs of the promise are those who have been adopted by faith in Christ as sons and daughters of God. As we have already seen in Hebrews 2:5-18, Jesus's brothers and sisters share in Abraham's promise.

The "two unchangeable things" the author mentions in verse 18 refer to the irrevocable nature of God's purpose and word, and the oath that he declared publicly. Because it is impossible for God to lie, God never deviates from the truth in these two unchangeable things. God would cease to be God if he could lie.

The author reinforces God's unchangeableness in order to encourage the church to once again hold firmly. The church is the refugee who must flee to God for rescue and who needs strong encouragement to seize the hope set before her. Because God's Word is true and it is impossible for him to lie, we have all the confidence in the world to take heart and trust God's promises just as Abraham did. The faithfulness of God and the certainty of his promises are not theoretical propositions. They are unchangeable realities. Like Abraham, we can stake our lives on God's promises because God is the One who has promised them. Our God is a promise-keeping God.

The Hope Behind the Curtain
HEBREWS 6:19-20

The author poignantly reminds his people of their need for "an anchor for the soul." The troubles and temptations of this world throw our souls around far too often. And yet, we have a sure and steadfast anchor that stabilizes our souls amidst the waves of this world. The promises of God are firm and secure enough to hold us steady in a storm. God's promise and oath anchor the hope that "enters the inner sanctuary behind the curtain," that is, the most holy place.

Once a year, on the Day of Atonement, the high priest went into the most holy place and offered the blood of an animal in order to turn God's wrath away from Israel. Jesus, as our high priest, entered the inner place behind the curtain and offered his own blood on our behalf. Our anchor, Jesus, has gone before us as our forerunner to accomplish all that God's justice required. As our great high priest, Jesus has purchased our salvation and assured us of the promises of God. Thus, Jesus's atoning work on the cross predicates the Christian's hope and anchors the Christian's soul.

Reflect and Discuss

1. How does the author's confidence in the believers addressed in Hebrews 6:9-20 complement the severe warning that precedes it? In other words, how does the author use his admonition to encourage believers in the certainty of their salvation?

2. What grounds the author's confidence in those who respond to the gospel in faith until the end? Why is the author so "confident of things that are better" for the believers in this church?

3. What are some practical ways that you and your church can serve and assist other like-minded, evangelical churches? How are you and your church currently serving and working with other churches? With individual Christians?

4. What are evidences of a heart receiving the gospel as opposed to one rejecting it? What does it mean to confirm your calling and election and to have earnestness in the faith? How is your earnestness in the gospel on display?

5. Name Old Testament saints other than Abraham who showed faith in God's promises and waited patiently for their fulfillment. How might you imitate their example?

6. How did the fact that God swore by himself encourage and equip Abraham to wait patiently for the promise? How should it encourage and equip us to wait for the fulfillment of God's promises to us?

7. How do God's promises to Abraham apply to believers today? What does it mean to be an heir with Abraham? How does being an heir of God's promise change your perspective on the promises of this world?

8. Think about the eschatological nature of this passage and God's promises. How does the future certainty of God's promises to believers equip our earnestness in the gospel and encourage us to hold on to our hope?

9. How does God's unchangeableness encourage you to flee to him in times of trouble or temptation? As you think about your experiences as a Christian, what are some tangible ways the truth of God's Word has anchored your soul and encouraged you to hold on to the hope set before you?

10. Consider the other passages in Hebrews in which the author talks about Jesus as our high priest. What implications does Christ entering the most holy place on our behalf have for us? What does it mean for Christ to be our forerunner?

Melchizedek the King-Priest

HEBREWS 7:1-10

Main Idea: The great king and priest Melchizedek is greater than Abraham, the greatest of the Jewish patriarchs, and is thus greater than the priesthood derived from the tribe of Levi.

I. **Melchizedek and Abraham (7:1-4)**
   A. Melchizedek, the king-priest of God Most High
   B. Melchizedek, the king-priest who blesses
   C. Melchizedek, the king-priest who endures
   D. Melchizedek, the king-priest who receives
II. **Melchizedek and Levi (7:5-10)**

Scripture is overflowing with names. Some of these names—like Matthew, Mark, Luke, John, David, and Daniel—resonate with most Christians because of their significance in the biblical storyline. In fact, many of these names are even recognizable to a number of non-Christians. Names like Sarah, Rachel, Mary, and Martha still connect with us because of the roles these figures played in salvation history. Some figures in biblical history are less familiar to us. For instance, Phinehas is not a name that sticks out to us in the Bible. Even those who study the Old Testament might easily forget about his small but important episode in Numbers 25.

As we consider names, certain biblical characters cannot be overlooked. Certain individuals in the biblical storyline play key roles in redemptive history. We must recognize and appreciate who they are in order to understand how Scripture unfolds salvation and leads us to the gospel. For example, we cannot fail to speak of Abraham, Moses, and David and the part these men played in bringing about the new covenant. In order to have a tighter grasp on the realities of the gospel, we need to know some names more than others.

If not for the book of Hebrews, the name Melchizedek might be left off the list of those we really need to know. As we saw in Hebrews 5, the author develops the priestly identity of Jesus by describing him as a great high priest according to the order of Melchizedek. Hebrews 7 unpacks the great significance behind what it means for Jesus to be a great high priest according to the order of Melchizedek. The first mention of Melchizedek occurs in Genesis 14, when Moses describes Abram's encounter with the man. Hebrews does not merely reference this encounter; it draws deep theological comparisons between Melchizedek and Jesus that inform how we understand Christ's identity as our great high priest. In other words, in order to understand who Jesus is more fully, we must understand who Melchizedek is. Melchizedek is a name we really need to know.

Melchizedek and Abraham
HEBREWS 7:1-4

The author of Hebrews uses the first few verses of the chapter to give important details about the identity and significance of Melchizedek for Christians.

Melchizedek, the King-Priest of God Most High

These verses begin with a description of the historical Melchizedek from Genesis 14. He is identified as a king over the region of Salem and as priest of "God Most High." Surprisingly, he has a coalesced ministry as a king and priest, which sets him apart from any other priest or king in Israel. While Melchizedek's kingship is important, the author primarily develops the significance of Melchizedek's priesthood and how it relates to Jesus.

Outside of Jesus and Melchizedek, Scripture identifies no one as both a king and priest. In fact, Israel markedly differentiated the roles of king and priest. No priest in the Old Testament could lawfully act as a king, and no king in the Old Testament could lawfully act as a priest. The opening verses of Isaiah 6 allude to this divide: "In the year that King Uzziah died, I saw the Lord seated on a high and lofty throne, and the hem of his robe filled the temple" (Isa 6:1). King Uzziah died in disrepute because he defied God's law by acting as a priest. As a consequence, God struck him with leprosy and cut him off from his people (2 Chr 26:16-21). Thus, the death of Uzziah demonstrates the divinely designed divide between the king and the priest in Israel. Yet Hebrews 7:1 tells us Melchizedek is the king of Salem and also priest of the Most High God. Shockingly, he is even from outside the tribe of Israel. This is an interesting character indeed.

The ancient pagan world had a plethora of different gods. The technical word for how the ancient Near East viewed this plurality of deities is not *polytheism,* but *henotheism.* Henotheism taught a hierarchy of gods; some were mid-range deities and others were high deities. Egyptians, Persians, and Sumerians ranked their deities according to this hierarchical pattern. Melchizedek's priesthood and worship of God Most High—a name God uses for himself—contrasts the typical priesthood and worship of the adherents of these ancient Near Eastern gods. Apologetically, asserting Melchizedek as a priest of God Most High makes a remarkable statement about the superiority of God, especially to a Jewish readership.

Melchizedek, the King-Priest Who Blesses

Hebrews 7:1 also recounts the meeting of Abram and Melchizedek. The context of Melchizedek's encounter with Abram, later called Abraham, is the termination of a war:

> *After Abram returned from defeating Chedorlaomer and the kings who were with him, the king of Sodom went out to meet him in the Shaveh Valley (that is, the King's Valley). Melchizedek, king of Salem, brought out bread and wine; he was a priest to God Most High. He blessed him and said:*
>
> > *Abram is blessed by God Most High,*
> > *Creator of heaven and earth,*
> > *and blessed be God Most High*
> > *who has handed over your enemies to you.*
>
> *And Abram gave him a tenth of everything.* (Gen 14:17-20)

After his victory over these kings, Abram, accompanied by Lot and his men of war, meets Melchizedek. Genesis tells us that the king of Sodom came out to negotiate with Abram, but that Melchizedek, king of Salem, came out to bless him with bread and wine.

Melchizedek's blessing of the patriarch is critical to the connection the author finds between Melchizedek and Christ. The coming verses teach that the greater one always blesses the lesser one. Thus, the fact that Melchizedek blesses Abraham, the head of the old covenant, is astounding. Is there a name in the Old Testament more exalted than Abraham, the great patriarch of Israel? Surely not! Yet Genesis 14 and the author of Hebrews show Melchizedek, a non-Israelite king, as a superior blessing an "inferior." During this triumphant moment of military victory in which Abram has functioned as the kinsman redeemer for Lot, this king of Salem blesses him. The situation presents Melchizedek, as the one doing the blessing, as the greater of the two figures.

In response to the blessing, Abram offers Melchizedek "a tenth of everything." Such a response is loaded with meaning, but the writer of Hebrews does not fully unpack the idea until later. What the author does tell us is the meaning of Melchizedek's name: "king of righteousness." The meaning of names meant more in Melchizedek's day than in our own. Although *Melchizedek* may seem like a strange name to us, those familiar with the Semitic language could hear the word for king (*mlk*) and the word for righteousness (*zdk*) as the constituent parts of his name. Thus, Melchizedek's name points to the fact that he is a righteous king. The writer of Hebrews also indicates that to say Melchizedek was the king of Salem was to say Melchizedek was the king of peace. In other words, Melchizedek's kingdom aligns with the realm of peace.

Melchizedek, the King-Priest Who Endures

It is possible to conclude from verse 3 that Melchizedek was somehow immortal. A closer reading of this text, however, reveals that the eternality of Melchizedek's personhood is not the subject of this verse. At issue is Melchizedek's priesthood. Melchizedek was not a priest because his father was a priest, nor was he a priest who had successors. By providing this familial background, the author is trying to communicate the unprecedented nature of Melchizedek's priesthood. Melchizedek is a priest of God Most High by divine ordination. Melchizedek enters into the Genesis story as if he has no mother, no father, and no sons. This kind of priesthood stands in stark contrast with the priesthood of Israel, which was entirely based on Levitical familial descent. The contrast will be highlighted for us in a later verse, but the author is using this verse to enforce that Melchizedek's priesthood had nothing to do with ancestry or descent. Divine designation predicates his appointment as priest. Thus it continues forever.

Melchizedek, the King-Priest Who Receives

In verse 4 the author of Hebrews leads the reader back to Abram's response to Melchizedek's blessing and gives more details about the tithe that the great patriarch gave to him. Abram gave Melchizedek "a tenth of the plunder." This is no small gift. Abram had just defeated a large number of kings and taken all of their possessions. One does not give a tithe to another without it being an obligation. Abram feels, as a matter of obligation to God Most High, that he should give this priest a tenth of everything he had obtained. This tithe would not have been a small tip but a large payment made by one of Israel's most important figures. Abram's tithe is one of the most unexpected and one of the most fascinating parts of the whole Old Testament.

Furthermore, that Abraham is addressed as a "patriarch" is another important detail in this verse. In the New Testament, the word *patriarch* does not appear many times, but it is a word of unique importance in the history of Israel. *Patriarch* denotes the highest level of honor in Jewish life. Men like Abraham, Isaac, and Jacob are considered some of Israel's most significant patriarchs. They were the foundation of Israel's identity. These patriarchs are recognized as figures through whom God acted in salvation history in order to set the stage for what he accomplished in Christ. Abraham is almost never specifically referred to as a patriarch, but he is in this passage because the writer of Hebrews is trying to emphasize his main point. By attaching this title of respect to Abraham, the author demonstrates the superiority of Melchizedek, even when compared to Abraham, the great patriarch. In other words, even Abraham, the great patriarch, pales in comparison to Melchizedek since he is the one that is blessed by this priest and is also the one who gives this priest a tenth of all his spoils.

Melchizedek and Levi
HEBREWS 7:5-10

In verse 5 the author reminds his audience that the Levites, who descend from Abraham, receive tithes from the other sons of Abraham on account of their priestly service. If Levi and his sons were to receive tithes, what is Abraham doing giving tithes to Melchizedek? This demonstrates that the priestly order of Melchizedek supersedes the priestly order of Levi because Abraham—the progenitor of the Levitical line—paid the tithe to Melchizedek. Since the Levitical priests descend from Abraham and Melchizedek surpasses Abraham, the Melchizedekian priesthood must be superior to the Levitical priesthood.

The author uses verse 6 to emphasize a second significant reality: Abraham "had the promises." These promises likely refer to the promises God made to him in Genesis 12:1-3. Yet Hebrews highlights the fact that Melchizedek gave a blessing even to the one who had the promises. This again testifies to the greatness of Melchizedek. He is of such importance that he can bless Abraham, even when Abraham appears to be the most blessed human being on the planet. Who can possibly bless Abraham? Abraham is the one who gives blessings! Yet in Genesis 14, Abraham pays tribute to Melchizedek and receives a blessing from him, and in so doing, demonstrates his own inferiority.

An understandable question confronts the reader about the greatness of Melchizedek: Why does the writer of Hebrews emphasize this point with such technical care? He wants the Hebrews to see that the Old Testament itself showed that the Levitical priesthood was always meant to give way to something greater. Thus the author, under the inspiration and authority of the Holy Spirit, weaves together a biblical-theological argument to convince his audience of this fact on the basis of Scripture.

Now we might think some parts of this argument are a bit strange, particularly the notion that Levi paid tithes to Melchizedek through his ancestor Abraham. But this kind of argumentation (principally seen in vv. 8-9) is not unprecedented in Jewish logic or in the Old Testament. In Deuteronomy 4 Moses is speaking to the children of Israel and essentially says, "You were there at Horeb when God spoke from the mountain and when I went up to the mountain and when I came down with the two tablets." But the Israelites Moses is speaking to in Deuteronomy 4 were not the same Israelites who were at Horeb! So how were they there? They were there biologically, in the loins of their fathers. This kind of corporate identity is not natural to our thinking, but it is essential to the Old Testament. Thus, the author of Hebrews closes his argument by using the concept of corporate identity to illustrate that Levi was biologically present when Abraham encountered Melchizedek. This is precisely why one might even say that Levi, who receives tithes, paid tithes through Abraham because he was in the loins of his ancestor Abraham when Melchizedek met him.

This section of Hebrews can seem biblically and theologically dense. But don't let that discourage you. As we continue on in Hebrews we will see how Jesus, the priest according to the order of Melchizedek, has done what the Levites never could do: he accomplished our salvation. Melchizedek may seem obscure to us, but by investing ourselves in passages like Genesis 14, Psalm 110, and Hebrews 7 we will find that we will develop a much richer appreciation for what Christ has done for us as our great high priest.

Reflect and Discuss

1. Why are we more familiar with some biblical characters than others? Why are some names more necessary to know than others? What names and characters are indispensable to the metanarrative of the Bible?

2. What role do individuals like Abraham, Moses, David, and Mary play in the history of Christianity? How are their lives connected to each other and to Jesus?

3. What did you know about Melchizedek before reading Hebrews 7? Read Genesis 14 and Psalm 110 and discuss what these two passages reveal about Melchizedek. How do the references to Melchizedek in these two passages relate to and inform the priesthood and kingship of Jesus Christ?

4. What were the roles of kings in the Old Testament? Read Deuteronomy 17:14-20. What were the roles of priests in the Old Testament? Read Exodus 28 and Leviticus 4.

5. Can you think of some important blessings given in Scripture? What are the blessings that have been granted to all Christians by their union with Christ (Eph 1:3)?

6. What does the author mean when he says that Melchizedek is without father, mother, or genealogy? How does this demonstrate Melchizedek's superiority to other priests?

7. What conclusion does the author draw from the fact that Abraham gave a tithe to Melchizedek? How does the author use the term *patriarch* in relation to Abraham to demonstrate Melchizedek's superiority?

8. How does the author argue that Melchizedek is greater than Levi?

9. Explain the corporate identity assumed by the author of Hebrews.

10. Why does the author of Hebrews choose to compare Melchizedek to Abraham? Why do you think he also chose to compare him to Levi?

Jesus the Priest-King

HEBREWS 7:11-22

Main Idea: Jesus Christ is the perfectly sufficient Priest-King who has made a final, effective atonement for his people.

I. The Perfect Priesthood of the Son (7:11-12)
   A. Putting the priesthood in context
   B. The need for a greater high priest
II. The Royal Priesthood of the Son (7:13-14)
III. The Eternal Priesthood of the Son (7:15-18)
   A. The permanence of the perfect priest
   B. The inability of the law
IV. A Better Hope in the Perfect Priest (7:19)
V. A Better Priest for a Better Covenant (7:20-22)

Imagine that a college student submits a paper to a professor in one of his classes. After reading the paper, the instructor decides that the paper should receive an A+. Is this paper truly as perfect as the grade implies? Even if you could not find a mistake on it, the paper is still not perfect because human beings, by definition, are not capable of perfection. The fall stains everything, even our greatest architectural designs or most amazing technological wonders. Nothing is impeccable. Nothing is perfect.

The word *perfect* is central to the meaning of this passage, but we must make sure that we are understanding the word in the way that the author of Hebrews is using it. Often we use the word *perfect* sloppily, sometimes even implying that we can reach a level of perfection this side of eternity. We describe people as being perfect. We describe certain achievements as being perfect. We use *perfect* much as we use *better* or *best*, as a comparative or superlative term instead of as a statement of objective fact.

The author of Hebrews, however, uses *perfect* according to the true sense of the word. Jesus is not simply a high priest who is more excellent in comparison to other high priests. He is the perfect high priest. When the author of Hebrews speaks about the perfection of Jesus (2:10; 5:9; 7:28), he does not mean that Jesus is merely better than previous high priests. Christ's perfection is not merely a superlative category. It is an intrinsic attribute. It means that Jesus Christ, the perfect high priest, is true perfection in a way that only one who is both fully divine and fully human can embody. Moreover, the intrinsic perfection of Christ is the defining characteristic of his priestly ministry. An A+ paper is not perfect in the way Jesus's priesthood is perfect. Christ's priesthood is perfect because he, the God-man, is actually and objectively perfect.

The Perfect Priesthood of the Son
HEBREWS 7:11-12

Putting the Priesthood in Context

This passage does not shock us like it should because we are so far removed from its original context. We need to understand what the writer is proclaiming in these verses. The author of Hebrews sets the superiority of Christ as our great high priest over the entire Levitical priesthood. He is proclaiming that Christ brings an end to the Levitical priesthood, the backbone of Jewish society and a major feature of God's covenant with Israel.

The priesthood defined the Jewish people. God established it through the male heirs of the tribe of Levi. These descendants of Jacob had certain priestly duties to perform. Due to the weighty responsibility entrusted to the Levites, other tribes actually took up contributions to feed and care for them.

The particularity and preservation of the line of Levi was paramount to Israelite society. As the mediators between Israel and God, the Levitical priests represented the people of Israel before Yahweh. They were the people's proxy. They also represented God back to the people through the fulfillment of their priestly duties. The writer of Hebrews declares that a greater priesthood exists than the one covenanted through the Levitical tribe. The priesthood of Jesus Christ is truly superior because Levi's priesthood did not achieve perfection. As right and righteous as Levi's priesthood was, it was imperfect. Thus, the Levitical priesthood could not accomplish the salvation of God's people.

The Need for a Greater High Priest

The fact that so much of the Mosaic law concerned the Levites reveals the significance of their priesthood. Yet even though the Levitical priests were central to the Mosaic system, they were not capable of truly accomplishing the task of mediating between God and men. Israel would not have been waiting for a great high priest if the Levitical priesthood had been sufficient. There was, however, a need all along for a great high priest to perform one final act atoning for sin. Levitical priests were not to blame for the insufficiency of their priesthood. The very conception of the Levitical priesthood demonstrated the cause of its insufficiency. If the Levitical priesthood itself could obtain perfection, there would have been no need for another one to come. Melchizedek would not have needed to appear in Genesis 14. Furthermore, the reference to Melchizedek in Psalm 110 would be stripped of its meaning. More importantly, there would have been no need for the Messiah to come and serve as mediator between God and his people. The insufficiencies of the Levitical priesthood as an entire system stand as shadows to the fully sufficient great high priest, Jesus Christ.

The people of Israel did not go and find this priest. They did not search the highways and hedges for a perfect priest. Israel did not intellectually ascend and discover that the Levitical priesthood was imperfect and thus know that they needed to find the priest or the priesthood that could establish perfection. Rather, God sovereignly and graciously initiated the sending of the great high priest to atone for the sins of the people. This great high priest, in his triumphal resurrection, arose according to the order of Melchizedek. Thus, Jesus Christ is without precedent and eternal. His priesthood is not patterned and perishable like the order of Aaron.

The Royal Priesthood of the Son
HEBREWS 7:13-14

Jesus is "the one these things are spoken about." Yet he is not of the tribe of Levi; he is of the tribe of Judah. And no descendant of that tribe ever served as a priest "at the altar" of God. The distinction between tribes and their societal functions in the nation of Israel must be understood. Distinct and definitive lines were strictly drawn in Israel between the roles of the priest and the king. The priest was not to be a king, and the king was not to be a priest. The tribe of Levi produced the priests, and the tribe of Judah, the tribe primarily remembered as the tribe of King David, produced the kings. Jesus Christ is not merely from the tribe of Judah, though. He is no ordinary member of the tribe. He is the Messiah who is going to reestablish David's throne. Nevertheless, the distinction remains: no king was ever to function as a priest and no priest was ever to function as a king.

The work of Christ in his threefold office—prophet, priest, and king—demonstrates a very different kind of perfection, one completely absent in the old covenant. No category for such a thing in the old covenant exists. In that covenant, different tribes performed the different societal responsibilities, and no tribe performed them eternally. Christ, on the other hand, performs all of these roles and does so singularly, continually, and eternally. The author of Hebrews demonstrates the newness of Christ's work by showing that even Moses knew nothing about a priest from the tribe of Judah serving at the altar of God. The writer of Hebrews deliberately references Moses because Moses was the final authority in these types of deliberations. Moses was the metaphorical trump card in Jewish debate. Yet in demonstration of the amazing new work that God has done in Christ, the author of Hebrews lays down a new trump card: the interweaving of priest and king in the person and work of Jesus Christ.

The Eternal Priesthood of the Son
HEBREWS 7:15-18

The author of Hebrews continues to tighten the cords of reasoning around his courtroom-like argument. The appearance of Jesus Christ as a high priest according to the order of Melchizedek should instantly reveal the limitations and inadequacy of the Levitical priesthood. The Aaronic priests were used by God to prepare his people for the coming of the Messiah who would achieve the final, complete atonement. God, when he sends Christ, establishes his Son as the final priest.

The Permanence of the Perfect Priest

As already noted, Christ does not descend from the tribe of Levi. Christ's priesthood is not predicated upon blood lineage—his priesthood runs much deeper. Christ's priesthood is founded on "the power of an indestructible life." This is one of the fundamental differences between Christ's priesthood and Aaron's priesthood. The Levitical priests died. Not one of them could fulfill the responsibilities in his mediating work as a priest forever. Yet the priest who arises according to the order of Melchizedek endures forever. This priest is not merely a priest because of lineage, but because his priesthood never ends—because it is predicated upon the power of an indestructible life.

The contrasts between the basis of the legal requirement and the power of an indestructible life are stark. Fulfilling the legal requirements of familial lineage does not render Jesus the great high priest. Something infinitely greater and eternally superior qualifies him for the position—namely, an indestructible life. This refers to the resurrection of Jesus Christ. "For it has been testified," the author of Hebrews notes, "You are a priest forever according to the order of Melchizedek" (Ps 110:4). The word *forever* is a weighty word. Our human minds, in their finitude, cannot grasp the reality of it. We cannot fathom what it means for something to never end. We can sing it, we can say it, we can read it, but we cannot fully grasp it. We can know, however, that it is *forever* that sets Christ apart from and above every Levitical and earthly priest. Christ is a priest *forever* according to the order of Melchizedek.

The Inability of the Law

The author of Hebrews then, following his assertion of Christ's eternality, tells his audience about the shortcomings of the former commandments and the former law, which they held in high regard. The writer is not alone in pointing out these shortcomings. Paul also points them out. In Romans Paul reminds the church that the law was powerless to do what Christ did for us. Jesus accomplished and effected our salvation, while the law was incapable of doing such a wonder. The law is perfect in the sense that it does all that God designed it to do, but it does not lead to salvation. Only Christ can do that.

The author combines two words in verse 18 that are incredibly powerful: *unprofitable* and *weak*. The law was not unprofitable in regard to its utility—it still adequately performed its given responsibilities. Paul tells us we should be grateful for the law since it exposes great need for a Savior. In Romans 7:7 Paul explains that he would not know he was a covetous person without the law. The law, therefore, is not unprofitable in the sense that it has no use at all but in the sense that obeying it does not provide any ultimate, eternal rewards. The law is used to condemn, but it can never be used to save. For effecting salvation, the law is unprofitable.

This is the heart of the law's weakness, as well. On the one hand, the law is so strong that it is stamped into the hearts and minds of every single human being in such a way that none are left untouched (Rom 2:15).

That's how powerful the law of God is. Yet on the other hand, it is not able to save. The law is weak in this regard. The law is weak and unprofitable where salvation is needed because God did not design it to save sinners.

A Better Hope in the Perfect Priest
HEBREWS 7:19

The author of Hebrews again makes a statement about perfection. This time he highlights the inability of the law to perfect anything. This contrasts with Christ the great high priest, who, through union with him by the working of the Holy Spirit, washes wretched rebels spotless before God. The law never made anyone perfect—it never produced a truly holy, perfect people, and it certainly never produced perfect individuals. The law reveals sin and the law kills—it certainly cannot save, for it was never intended to do such a thing. The former commandment is laid aside in order to give way to a better hope that is ours in Christ. In the old covenant, the law functioned in many ways the Israelites desperately needed, but it could not draw them closer to God. The law exposed the pervasive sinfulness of man and, as a result, the great need for a great Savior. Christ, however, does precisely what the law could never do. He saves. Jesus accomplished our salvation and gave us a new hope—a hope through which we now draw near to God.

A Better Priest for a Better Covenant
HEBREWS 7:20-22

These final verses once again highlight the fact that Jesus, the true and great high priest, is incomparably superior to the Levites. God may have established the Levitical priesthood, but he never swore an oath to them that their priesthood would continue into eternity. In fact, the fabric of their priestly responsibilities bore witness to their insufficiency.

But the author of Hebrews shows that in Psalm 110:4 God actually based Christ's priesthood and its eternality on an unchangeable oath. The author is adding layer upon layer to his case for the superiority of Christ over the old covenant. Christ's priesthood is rooted in the unshakable promises of God.

In verse 22 the author also connects priesthood to covenant. This is an idea that he will more fully explain in chapter 8. Yet for the time being, the author hints at the fact that not only is Jesus a better priest, but his priesthood is actually part of a better covenant, the "new covenant" spoken of in Jeremiah 31. Because Christ is the "guarantee" of this covenant, Christians can be assured that all the blessings of the new covenant will be infallibly applied to them. God's covenant promise cannot fail because God's priest, Jesus Christ, cannot fail.

Reflect and Discuss

1. How do modern notions and usages of the word *perfect* muddy the meaning of the word *perfect* in this passage? Describe a situation in which you heard Christ's perfection confused with that of created things.

2. Why is Christ's priesthood more perfect than other priesthoods? How does Christ's divine nature play into his perfection?

3. What does it mean that Christ is now, through his perfect work, the sufficient priest who mediates between God and man? How is Christ's final act of atonement superior to the Mosaic law?

4. What makes the concept of legalism and works-merited righteousness so enticing? Do you still find yourself slipping into a religiosity that denies Christ's sufficient, atoning death? Do you try to justify yourself by behaving morally and doing good rather than by faithfully following the new law inaugurated by Christ's death and resurrection? If you answered yes to one or both of the preceding, explain your reasoning.

5. How was the Old Testament law profitable and strong? How was it unprofitable and weak?

6. Why is the indestructible life of Christ so important to his work as the great high priest? How might his eternal ministry encourage us as Christians?

7. What does God's sending of his Son to be the perfect mediator reveal about God's nature and character?

8. How can you actively remind yourself of God's sovereign grace and redeeming love for you in Christ, the sufficient priest? How does our salvation and new hope in Christ enable us to draw near to God?

9. Why do we need Christ to fulfill the offices of prophet, priest, and king? In what ways does Christ fulfill these? How does this threefold office demonstrate Christ's perfection?

Jesus the Superior Priest

HEBREWS 7:23-28

Main Idea: Jesus Christ is superior to Levitical priests because his priesthood is both lasting and perfect. He intercedes for those who draw near to God, and the sacrifice of himself that he offers to God accomplishes all that is necessary for salvation.

I.   **The Permanent Priest (7:23-25)**
    A. The continuing nature of Christ's priesthood
    B. The intercessory nature of Christ's priesthood
II. **The Perfect Priest (7:26-28)**
    A. Christ's perfect nature
    B. A once-for-all-time sacrifice
    C. God's eternal plan

In Hebrews 7–10 the author majestically explains Jesus Christ as our great high priest. But the dominant issue for the original readers of this letter is missing from the mind of the modern reader. The sacrificial system, which was central to the experiences of the first audience of Hebrews, is a foreign subject for today's audience. Before the incarnation, God definitively met humanity in the temple and through the sacrificial system performed by the priests. While the priests offered both daily and annual sacrifices, those sacrifices could not effect the forgiveness of sins. If they had forgiven sins, there would have been no need for Christ. Instead, those sacrifices anticipated or foreshadowed the actual forgiveness of sin. Furthermore, when the high priest entered the most holy place on the Day of Atonement, he understood that the act pictured the satisfaction of the wrath of God against sin but did not actually accomplish it.

Throughout Hebrews the author argues that Jesus is superior to all who came before: the angels, Moses, Aaron, Joshua, and the entire priesthood. He concludes his argument in 7:22: "Jesus has also become the guarantee of a better covenant." That language likely does not shock today's Christian. Modern believers know that the covenant God enacted in Christ is a better covenant.

Yet the Jewish believers who originally received this letter would have heard that statement much differently. A better covenant would seem almost impossible to the Jewish mind. What could be better than the covenant God made with Abraham? The answer is simple: a covenant that saves. The Abrahamic covenant did not save, even though it bestowed many blessings. It created a covenant people who survived through God's providential care. They enjoyed the blessings of a sacrificial system, experienced the forbearance of sin, and tasted the forgiveness of sins. Nonetheless, that covenant could not save. Jesus is God's absolute assurance of the new covenant, and he functions in this new covenant as our great high priest.

The Permanent Priest
HEBREWS 7:23-25

Hebrews 7:23-25 explores the permanent nature of Christ's priesthood and its role in his power to save. Unlike previous priests, Christ as priest endures forever. His priesthood never ends and his priesthood saves, so as a result, his ministry of intercession for those who draw near to God through him never ends. Therefore, as the author argues, Christ is a superior priest.

The Continuing Nature of Christ's Priesthood

In Hebrews 7:1-22 the author completely redefines the priesthood, but that is not the end. He continues his argument by pinpointing specific ways Jesus as the great high priest supersedes the previous priesthood. Over the course of Israel's history, there were thousands from the tribe of Levi in the Aaronic priesthood. The priestly ministry needed to continue, yet they all died. As a result, every generation had to produce new priests. Christ, on the other hand, is a priest forever. There is now no need to produce any other priest. This great high priest is singular because he *continues*. Previously, the priesthood was a continual succession of many priests. Now it is a continual ministry of one priest: the great high priest, Jesus Christ.

On this basis, Christ "is able to save completely." It is helpful to picture a horizon when reading verse 25. As far as one can see, Christ has accomplished everything necessary for salvation. This horizon has at least two dimensions:

- Comprehensive
- Temporal

First, Christ saves in a comprehensive sense by accomplishing all that the sinner needs. The ground for salvation comes from no other source but Christ. Jesus completed every criterion necessary for the redemption of his people. The sinner seeking salvation does not have to appeal to any authority or person other than Christ. His priesthood leaves nothing undone.

Second, Christ saves in a temporal sense. Just as his priesthood is forever, so also the salvation he accomplishes is effective forever. The sinner does not need to look for anyone to come after Christ. He presently serves in his permanent priesthood, and Christ's eternal priesthood grounds our eternal salvation.

Israel knew it needed a continuing succession of priests. Indeed, an entire tribe was devoted to serving in that capacity. Even today believers desperately need a priest—a mediator, a liaison, an intermediary between us and God. Without a priest, no one is saved. The priest who saves the church is the great high priest, and he continues forever. Therefore, he is able to save to the uttermost those who draw near to God through him. That work is his priestly ministry. Jesus Christ draws sinners near to God through himself.

The Intercessory Nature of Christ's Priesthood

In the last half of Hebrews 7:25 the author shifts his focus from Jesus's past work on the cross and in the resurrection to the present intercessory work of his priesthood. Christians are dependent right now on the superior priesthood of Christ not only for his past death and resurrection but also for his present intercession at the right hand of the Father. Christians need an intercessor and mediator. Jesus obtains vastly different results from those of a conventional mediator, such as one helping to resolve a labor dispute. A federal mediator in a labor dispute would bring two opposing parties together and pursue a compromise. To accomplish this compromise, he would undoubtedly have to convince each party to relinquish some desire or demand. In other words, both parties must be willing to forfeit some of their demands in order for a true compromise to be reached. The divine mediator, however, achieves perfect peace. He in no way compromises the holiness of God. Instead, he fully satisfies the justice of God.

Christians need a priest who intercedes for sin and provides help in times of need. Jesus is able to sympathize with humanity because he was tempted in every way that we are yet he remained without sin (Heb 4:15). He represents us before the Father, intercedes for us, and speaks on our behalf so that those who have drawn near to the Father through him are now united to him. No other intercessor is needed. Christ lives to intercede for Christians, and Christians have direct access to him. He is the guarantee of a new and better covenant and remains the permanent high priest who intercedes for his people.

The Perfect Priest
HEBREWS 7:26-28

Permanence is not the only characteristic that distinguishes Christ's priesthood from previous ones. His priesthood is also perfect in every sense. In this passage, the author turns to the perfection of Christ both in his sinlessness and in the sacrifice he offers to God on behalf of the people. Jesus Christ is a superior priest because he is a perfect priest.

Christ's Perfect Nature

"Need" does not suggest that we deserved such a high priest. Instead, the author communicates that it was *necessary* to have such a high priest. Christ is the specific kind of priest we require because his priesthood provides the perfect answer to our need. He fulfills all the just requirements of the law. His priesthood is perfect because he himself is perfect. The old covenant made nothing perfect, but Christ is perfect.

His holiness bears witness to his perfection. Only a holy sacrifice could meet the just requirements of the law. He is also "innocent," for he was tempted in every way as we are yet remained without sin (Heb 4:15). He was "undefiled." The word is most often used regarding being defiled by the world. God calls Christians not to bear the stain of worldliness. Nonetheless, all people are stained. In one sense, Christ identifies with us in our humanity. In another sense, he remains "separated from sinners" because he did not sin. The Father exalted him "above the heavens," which can be said of no other human being. Christ, however, is no mere man. Christ is both fully human and fully divine. He is the God-man.

A Once-for-All-Time Sacrifice

The Levitical priests offered their sacrifices "every day" because their priesthood was temporary. Their sacrifices anticipated what would come, but their sacrifices were incomplete themselves. The priests needed to repeat both the daily sacrifices and the annual sacrifices. Christ, however, had no need to offer sacrifices repeatedly. He accomplished the full forgiveness of sins in his one and only sacrifice when he offered up himself on the cross.

Every previous priest had to perform his sacrifice first with reference to his own sin. Only after dealing with his own sins could he appropriately offer a sacrifice for the sins of the people. Christ, on the other hand, did not need to offer any sacrifice for his own sin because he had none. He is sinless, perfect, holy, undefiled, innocent, and separated from sinners. Jesus does not need to offer up sacrifices repeatedly because the cross and resurrection are not repeated events; they are "once for all time." Christ's sacrifice is not perpetual but historical. It was made once for all and is finished. Nothing can be added to it or taken from it. It was the perfect sacrifice, and it was completed all at once.

Jesus did not accomplish this perfect sacrifice by offering up the blood of another. Instead, he offered up himself. When the Levitical priest went into the most holy place, he carried blood with him. He took the blood from an appropriate animal for the corresponding sacrifice. As he carried in this blood, he was carrying blood that something else had shed. The priests had to cart off the sacrifice's carcass, serving as a clear sign of the costliness of sin and forgiveness. Without blood, there is no forgiveness of sins. When Christ offered his sacrifice, he offered the unthinkable. He gave himself and paid the penalty of sin with his own blood. Christ's offering of himself displays why his singular priesthood is definitive, permanent, perfect, continuous, and unrepeatable.

God's Eternal Plan

In Hebrews 7:28 the author stresses the difference between the lesser and the greater, a common theme in Hebrews. Christ is a superior great high priest because his priesthood came through an oath. This oath came later than the law, so it is superior to the law. In this new covenant, God "appoints a Son, who has been perfected forever." The sacrifice of an animal was not perfect even though it might appear so perfect. It was not fitting because it did not fulfill what was needed.

Even if a Levitical high priest had gone into the temple and spilled his own blood, it would still not have achieved our salvation. It would fail to accomplish atonement for our sins because the priest was not perfect. Only one without sin can atone perfectly for sins. This is precisely why we have Jesus Christ as the guarantee of a new and better covenant.

Scripture shows a seemingly innumerable succession of priests throughout Israel's history. This succession was important and vital, and it was under a covenant that faithfully pointed to its own inadequacies. Modern Christians can easily misunderstand these passages and the entire system of the priesthood within God's plan. It is tempting for Christians to believe that God had an initial plan and that this initial plan failed. This initial plan was the covenant that God made with Abraham. Since humanity was unable to meet the righteous demands of the old plan, God had to form a new plan in Christ. Scripture, however, teaches that this is not the correct understanding. God's plan from the beginning was Christ. He is the Lamb of God slain before the foundation of the earth (Rev 13:8). The old covenant was not an initial plan that failed. It succeeded gloriously. Its purpose was never to save; it was to demonstrate man's need for a Savior.

Under the old covenant, aging priests performed daily sacrifices knowing they would have to do so again and again. When God made the perfect sacrifice, Jesus uttered these fitting words: "It is finished." The old covenant faithfully demonstrated the forbearance of God until Christ came. It brought the conviction of sin and showed the need for a Savior. Without the law, man would not know of his need for a Savior. But now that Savior has come. And we understand that Savior as one who was witnessed to by the old covenant. Christ is a priest—a great high priest and the perfect high priest. We can only grasp the fullness of what that means when we see how Christ fulfills the expectations in the old covenant by being for us the great high priest of the new and better covenant.

Reflect and Discuss

1. What is the difference between the comprehensive and temporal aspects of the salvation Christ accomplished? Why are they necessary aspects?

2. What was the role of the priest in ancient Israel, and how does Christ fulfill this role?

3. In what ways is Christ's priesthood superior to the Aaronic and Levitical priesthoods? What was lacking in these previous priesthoods?

4. What are the two key characteristics of Christ's priesthood, and how do these characteristics have implications for our relationship with God?

5. How does Jesus Christ function as a mediator on our behalf? How should an understanding of Christ's intercessory role affect how we pray? How does it comfort you?

6. Why is it important that Jesus serves as a perfect priest? How does his perfect priesthood relate to both his divine and his human natures?

7. What features of Christ's sacrifice are superior to the sacrifices made by the Levitical priests? On what ground is Christ's sacrifice superior? Why did Christ need to be both human and divine for his sacrifice to be effective?

8. How does the sacrificial system demonstrate the costliness of sin? How does Christ's sacrifice demonstrate it? How does the biblical understanding of the penalties of sin compare to the secular world's understanding of sin's consequences?

9. What is the significance of Christ shedding his own blood instead of another's? How should this shape our understanding of Christ's death on the cross as it relates to us?

10. How do we know Jesus Christ was not the Father's backup plan? What does Jesus teach us in Luke 24:13-49 about the Old Testament and God's sovereign plan from the beginning? What are the problems associated with thinking that Christ was not the initial plan?

The Great High Priest of the New Covenant

HEBREWS 8:1-13

Main Idea: Jesus Christ ushers in a superior priesthood and a superior covenant, which the old covenant and its earthly priests anticipated.

I. The Superiority of the Great High Priest (8:1-5)
    A. The seat of the high priest
    B. The sanctuary of the high priest
II. The Superiority of the New Covenant (8:6-13)
    A. The better covenant mediated
    B. The better covenant fulfilled

God made a series of covenants with Adam, Noah, Abraham, Moses, and David. For a congregation of Greek-speaking Jews, these covenants were of utmost importance. But this author tells his audience that Israel's great covenantal history culminates with Christ, the guarantee of a superior covenant. For the writer's audience, it would have seemed virtually impossible that a covenant better than the covenant made with the patriarchs could exist. Yet the author shows them the need for a greater covenant by pointing to the need for a greater priest.

The Superiority of the Great High Priest
HEBREWS 8:1-5

Anyone who has ever translated a document from one language to another knows how difficult translation can be. In some sense, one reason modern day Christians think Hebrews is difficult to understand is because we constantly need to "translate" the author's and the audience's assumptions into our own day so that we can follow the argument better. At the beginning of Hebrews 8 the author greatly serves us by showing us the central thrust of his argument: "Now the main point of what is being said is this." In other words, the arguments and flow of thought in the first seven chapters may have been difficult to follow. But the author simplifies all of it to show us that "we have this kind of high priest." For the last seven chapters, he's told us what we've needed. Now he tells us we have exactly what we need. We need Jesus as a great high priest who mediates a new and better covenant.

The Seat of the High Priest

In verse 1 the author says Christ is seated "at the right hand of the throne of the Majesty in the heavens." This makes his priesthood completely different. The old priesthood was a terrestrial priesthood, which focused on the earthly calling of the priests. They became priests because they were born into the tribe of Levi. Priests from that tribe fulfilled this role over and over and from generation to generation.

But Christ, the great high priest, serves in an exalted status never occupied by those earthly priests. As such, he's seated at the right hand of God on high. Paul describes Christ's exalted position in Philippians 2. He writes that Christ humbled himself by taking on human form, even to the point of dying on a cross (v. 8). Because of this obedience, God has highly exalted Jesus and has given him a name that is above every name (v. 9). Christ's seat at the right hand of the Majesty—a title for God—demonstrates his exalted status. This imagery of "sitting at the right hand" is from the ancient world when kings would surround themselves with powerful nobles. The person to the right of the king was the most powerful and the most prestigious noble in the royal court. Thus, Christ's place at the right hand of God is a supremely exalted position.

From his seat at the right hand, Christ continues his work as Redeemer. Too many Christians think Jesus has already done all that he's going to do for us. We look back to the cross and the resurrection and assume this is where his work ends. But two very important aspects of his work aren't finished. For starters, Christ didn't accomplish in his earthly ministry all the Messiah was foretold to accomplish. This didn't make his mission a failure. Rather, Revelation tells us a spectacular fulfillment is coming. We're still waiting for Christ to vindicate his church and judge the nations, so this aspect of his work is yet to be finished.

Additionally, Christ is not done mediating for his people. While Christ's atoning work is finished, his advocating work is not. This mediatory work is the primary occupation of Christ in heaven. As Jesus sits at his Father's right hand, he intercedes for us. What a tremendous encouragement to reflect on Christ's active and ongoing work for his people!

The Sanctuary of the High Priest

In verse 2 the author mentions the "sanctuary" of the high priest. "The true tabernacle that was set up by the Lord and not man" isn't just poetic language; it's very specific and exceedingly important. The word *tabernacle* is rarely used in modern American vocabulary, and it often sounds like some sort of spiritual buzzword. At its most basic, a tabernacle is the same as a tent. More specifically, *tabernacle* refers to the tent where God met with his people after the exodus from Egypt. Israel needed a tent as a place of meeting for several reasons. The most important reason was that they were wandering in the wilderness in those days. God had not yet commanded them to build the temple because they weren't in Jerusalem yet. Thus, the tabernacle provided a mobile place to meet with God.

Hebrews tells us Christ fulfills his ministry in a tabernacle that the Lord set up. It's not a tabernacle on earth; it's a superior tabernacle in heaven. The tabernacle on earth was real, but it wasn't the place where full salvation was won. Full salvation takes place in the true tabernacle in heaven. Man does not make it. Only the Lord does.

Verses 3 to 5 detail the priest's duties in the tabernacle. It's here the author's argument gets really interesting. When the priest went into the tabernacle, he didn't go empty-handed; he took a sacrifice. He had to "have something to offer." But Christ didn't fit the mold of a typical Levitical priest. The law stipulated that the high priest was to come through the Aaronic line, through the tribe of Levi. But Jesus is from the tribe of Judah, not Levi. He's not an earthly priest from the line of Levi that brings his offering to an earthly tabernacle. He ministers in the heavenly tabernacle, so Jesus brings a superior offering. This is what verses 4 and 5 are saying. The priests on earth, Levitical priests, "serve as a copy and shadow of the heavenly things" (8:5).

Since the author wrote to Jewish Christians immersed in Greek culture, it's important to note the language of *shadow*. His audience probably would have been familiar with Plato's parable of the cave. Plato (ca. 429–347 BC) argued that our knowledge is like that of a man who is kept in a fire-lit cave and only sees the shadows of real objects when he looks at the cave's walls. Plato believed we only know things as shadows of the original; the real object cast the shadow in the firelight.

The Old Testament never presents the tabernacle as a shadow of something more real. The New Testament, however, emphasizes its shadowy nature. Repeatedly the author of Hebrews shows us how to read the Old Testament. In this instance, he's showing us how to understand the Old Testament tabernacle. Like the Levitical priesthood, the tabernacle of old was inadequate. It displayed dimly the glory of God while pointing to something greater.

Verse 5b notes that a careful reading of Exodus reveals a "pattern" for building the tabernacle. This pattern helps us see that the earthly tabernacle was modeled after something else—namely, the heavenly tabernacle. God commanded the building of a tabernacle in which he would dwell among his people. Moses was to build the tabernacle in exactly the way God showed him (Exod 25:9,40). In Exodus 26 God issues remarkably detailed plans for the tabernacle. By using the language of shadows and copies, the author of Hebrews shows us that these detailed plans and specifications were meant to reflect deeper realities. The plans laid out in Exodus 26 were like plans for a replica of the real thing, which is the heavenly temple. As such, the earthly tabernacle was like a shadow dancing on the wall of a cave. But we have a great high priest who does not offer sacrifices in a shadow. Jesus ministers in the true tent that the Lord set up. The heavenly temple is his sanctuary.

The Superiority of the New Covenant
HEBREWS 8:6-13

As the writer will soon show us, Christ's work allows us to directly and confidently enjoy God's presence. We no longer have to come before God in a tabernacle made by human hands. Because Christ has fulfilled the tabernacle's purpose, we can draw near to the very throne of God. Heaven is God's true tabernacle. This great truth permeates the pages of the Old Testament. The King who ransoms his people from their iniquities and brings them peace with God has ushered in the new covenant by his blood. And that covenant is of far greater excellence than the first.

The Better Covenant Mediated

The old covenant wasn't without fault. Its faultiness wasn't like a machine in need of repair, though. Its faultiness was rooted in its incompleteness. The old covenant was faulty because it was not final. If it were the final covenant, there would have been no need for a better covenant.

Further, the old covenant came up short because it could not provide a priest who would make ultimate and full atonement for the sins of

God's people. The old covenant's fault and failure to provide a final sacrifice for sin should have been obvious. After all, under the old covenant there remained an unrelenting need for constant sacrifices. This endless repetition of sacrifices demonstrated the covenant's incompleteness and its inability to deal with sin once for all time. This makes Christ's statement on the cross all the more breathtaking. When he cried, "It is finished" (John 19:30), he was announcing that the wrath of God toward the sin of his people was finally paid in full. Never again would there be a need for animal sacrifice, for Jesus paid it all.

Furthermore, even the high priest of the old covenant had to make unrelenting sacrifices for his own sins before he could make a sacrifice for the sin of his countrymen. In the light of the new covenant, that's no gospel. But the author of Hebrews is now declaring that the final priest has come, not to atone for his own sins, but to save his people. Indeed, a better priest with a better ministry has come to mediate a better covenant enacted on better promises. Jesus's ministry of inaugurating the new covenant is "superior" precisely because of these "better promises." In the new covenant God will write his law on the hearts of his people (rather than on tablets of stone). As a result, all covenant members will know the Lord, and sins will be dealt with completely.

The Better Covenant Fulfilled

The new covenant promise is laid out in Jeremiah 31:31-34. The author of Hebrews leads his readers to this text in verses 8-12. Jeremiah wrote to show that the Lord had long ago foretold the day when his final priest would come. The covenant community should have inferred from the sacrifices of old that a final sacrifice and a final priest—who would not have to sacrifice repeatedly—were coming. Thus the author of Hebrews uses Jeremiah 31:31-34 to ask his readers, "Were we not told? Why did you not see?" This is similar to the way he uses Genesis 14 and Psalm 110 to show them they should have been anticipating a priest according to the order of Melchizedek. God spoke through Jeremiah to announce the need for and the coming of a new and better covenant.

The picture Jeremiah paints is one of eschatological peace. This peace would come through the mediator of a new and better covenant. The terms of this new and better covenant would bring a peace infinitely greater than what the old covenant could produce. The extraordinary promise of the new covenant was not that God would dismiss the old covenant but that he would be merciful toward our iniquities and remember our sins no more (Jer 31:34).

Our greatest problem is sin, for it severs us from the presence of God. Our sin and his holiness are incompatible, yet God promised to reconcile sinful people to himself through the mediator who would inaugurate the new covenant. He chose to do this through his Son, Jesus Christ, the mediator who established the new covenant in his blood (Luke 22:20). In him, the extraordinary promises and the better covenant were fulfilled. The Lord is merciful to his people because Christ suffered and died in their place, and they are now hidden in him forever by virtue of their faith and repentance. In Jesus all the new covenant promises belong to God's people.

Reflect and Discuss

1. What main point has the author been making up until now? How does Hebrews 8, particularly verse 1, connect to the previous chapters and summarize the author's main point?

2. How do the old covenant and the earthly priesthood anticipate the new covenant and a superior priest? Why do we need a superior covenant and priest?

3. Where is our great high priest now located? What makes that seat so significant? How does Christ's position help you persevere in your faith, particularly in times of trial and suffering?

4. Did Christ's work for us end with his death and resurrection? If not, then in what ways is Christ still at work? How is his current work significant for your life?

5. How does the author of Hebrews use the language of "copy and shadow"? Why is that language important? How does it relate to a heavenly tabernacle? What deeper realities do the earthly tabernacle and the contents of Exodus 26 communicate?

6. Explain the differences between the earthly tabernacle and the heavenly tabernacle. Why is it significant that one is made by earthly hands and the other is set up by the Lord? Why is the work of Jesus in the heavenly tabernacle superior to the work of priests in the earthly one?

7. What does it mean that the old covenant is not "faultless"? Where else in Hebrews have we seen the author point to the old covenant's faultiness?

8. In what ways is the priesthood of Jesus Christ better than the earthly priesthood? Why is it important that he's better? What makes the new covenant "much more excellent"?

9. Look at the promises of Jeremiah 31:31-34. List ways the new covenant is better than the old. In what ways did Christ fulfill each of these promises? How does the new covenant deal with our greatest problem once and for all?

The Tabernacle and the New Covenant

HEBREWS 9:1-10

Main Idea: The old covenant laid the foundation for the new covenant inaugurated by the person and work of Jesus Christ. The external acts of worship in the tabernacle foreshadowed the day Christ would purify the consciences of his people and dwell among them.

I. **The New Covenant Worship of God Foreshadowed (9:1-5)**
   A. Old regulations for worship
   B. The tabernacle
II. **The End of Mediated Access to God (9:6-10)**
   A. The ministry of the priests
   B. What the Holy Spirit was indicating
   C. Imperfect offerings

Humans tend to place greater trust in things they can see with their own eyes and touch with their own hands. This was one of the reasons the Israelites held the old covenant in such high regard. Not only did God initiate his plan to redeem his people through the old covenant, but following it also provided the people the chance to get their hands dirty and to see its inner workings with their own eyes. Israel was able to participate in the physical process of offering a sacrifice, thereby reckoning its temporary atonement more certain. When the animals were slaughtered, an external act performed something visible and tangible—the shedding of blood for sin.

The shedding of blood happened most graphically on the Day of Atonement in the earthly tabernacle. Christ, however, entered a heavenly temple to offer his sacrifice for sin. The author is determined throughout Hebrews to show how Jesus's work in the heavenly temple is fundamentally superior to the work done by priests in the earthly tabernacle. His spiritual work is of far greater value than the work accomplished in the earthly tabernacle because it fully and finally satisfies God's wrath. In order to continue drawing out this contrast, the author turns his attention to the regulations for worship and for the earthly tabernacle. The imperfections of the earthly tabernacle and our tendency to trust things we can see and touch set the stage for Hebrews 9:1-10. In this passage the author removes the hope Israel puts in their participation in the sacrifices and shows them how they should think about the old covenant practices in light of Christ.

The New Covenant Worship of God Foreshadowed
HEBREWS 9:1-5

The author reminds his readers of the tabernacle, which served as God's temporary dwelling place amidst the Israelites after the exodus. The exacting detail of the commands given in Exodus 25–30 demonstrates that Israel was not to worship like the pagans. While their pagan neighbors devised new ways to portray whatever false deity they honored (as seen in Jer 10), Israel was not to speculate, innovate, or experiment with what kind of house or what kinds of objects for worship God preferred.

Old Regulations for Worship

In verse 1 the author reminds his readers that the old covenant had particular regulations concerning worship. God, through Moses, prescribed specific covenantal duties and a precise place in which to perform them. Unlike the pagans, the Israelites were not to worship God however they wanted. The one true and living God specifically told Israel how and where to worship him. His regulations for worship were expressly authorized by his word. A failure to abide by them led to grave consequences (Lev 10:1).

The tabernacle stood as the epicenter of old covenant worship. This is why the author refers to it with the phrase "earthly sanctuary." The tabernacle was the place where Israel offered sacrifices and where the priests interceded on behalf of the people. Because the tabernacle was so central to the old covenant, Israel was intensely focused on what happened inside it. The new covenant, however, shifts our focus away from the tabernacle. Under the new covenant, a central location of worship required by God no longer exists. Since the Spirit unites us to Christ by faith, Christians now worship the Father "in Spirit and in truth," not in a tabernacle (John 4:24). Furthermore, Christ now dwells in the midst of his people (Matt 18:20). John even describes Christ's incarnation in language similar to that applied to the tabernacle: "The Word became flesh and *dwelt among us*" (John 1:14, emphasis added). The epicenter of new covenant worship is not in a place, it's in a person: Jesus Christ.

The Tabernacle

In verses 2-5 the author outlines God's specific commands for how Israel's men of skill were to construct the tabernacle (Exod 25–31, 35–40). The tent reflected the holiness of God. It communicated his transcendence, perfection, and righteousness. It was also a vibrant reminder of the covenant God made with Israel at Sinai. Within the tent were the holy place and the most holy place. Regarding the holy place, the author mentions the lampstand (Exod 25:31-40; 37:17-24), the table (Exod 25:23-29; 37:10-16), and the presentation loaves (the Bread of the Presence; Exod 25:30). From there the author moves on to consider the furniture in the most holy place: the gold altar of incense, the ark of the covenant, a gold jar containing manna, Aaron's staff that budded, and the tablets of the covenant. All of these items broadly demonstrated God's great acts of redemption, covenant faithfulness, and holiness. They each communicated specific things as well.

Aaron's staff served as a reminder of how God kept his people alive in the wilderness and of how God chose Aaron for the priesthood (Num 17:1-13). The tablets reminded the people of God's covenant with them and of their responsibility to uphold that covenant by obeying the law. The golden urn holding manna served as a constant testimony to God's sustaining care of Israel for forty years in the wilderness (Exod 16:31-34). And the ark attested to God's covenant love for Israel and his steadfast faithfulness toward them.

But why does the author mention the altar of incense? Doesn't Exodus 30:6 say that the altar is in front of the curtain, in the holy place? Given that the author has repeatedly shown his great familiarity with Jewish tradition throughout the letter, such a statement shouldn't lead us to think the author is confused. Instead, he is deliberately associating the altar of incense with the presence of God in the most holy place. He probably does this because the burning of incense was such a key feature on the Day of Atonement (Lev 16:12-13).

The author also notes the presence of the cherubim and the prominence of gold in the most holy place. The cherubim were heavenly creatures to whom God gave specific tasks (Gen 3:24). Verse 5 teaches us the cherubim of glory overshadowed the mercy seat and were tasked with guarding the presence of God. Gold in the ancient world was effectively priceless. It was the most valuable commodity known. The golden composition of these items demonstrates the infinite value of heaven and heavenly worship.

The Jewish Christians to whom the author was writing would have understood the holy place and the most holy place to be inextricably linked to the way God met with his people. They would have been tempted to imagine the sights, sounds, and smells of the tabernacle and think of them as "the real." The problem with this, of course, is that the new covenant makes the old covenant obsolete (Heb 8:13). Nevertheless, the author doesn't degrade these representative objects of the old covenant. He dignifies them and shows how their placement in the tabernacle demonstrated deeper realities.

The End of Mediated Access to God
HEBREWS 9:6-10

This passage shifts from a focus on the arrangement of the furniture in the tabernacle to the ministry of the priests in the tabernacle. As he makes the switch, the author outlines the stipulations for priests in the holy places and the deficiencies in their work.

The Ministry of the Priests

The priests regularly performed their ritual duties of sacrifice in the first section, the holy place, but only the high priest could go into the second section, the most holy place, to intercede for the people. Even then, entering the most holy place only happened once a year on the Day of Atonement. The high priest carried blood with him into the most holy place because blood was necessary for the atonement of his own sins and for the sins of the people (Lev 16). The priests who served in the holy place, however, regularly performed their duties. They ministered every day within the holy place.

What does the author mean by "the sins the people had committed in ignorance"? Christians tend to think of sin in two categories. First, we think of sin as deliberately wrong acts. We call these "sins of commission." The Bible certainly teaches that disobedient acts—doing what we ought not to do—are sinful. Second, we think of sin as failing to do what we ought to do. We call these "sins of omission." Failure to do what God commands us to do is no less sinful than doing what he has commanded us not to do.

Yet the author identifies a third category of sin Christians often miss: sins committed in ignorance or unintentionally. Unintentional sins are those we commit without realizing we are committing them.

Due to the pervasive and insidious effects of sin on our entire beings, we can't even recognize the times we're unaware we're sinning. It's these unintentional sins of the people that precipitated the high priest's ministry and made it necessary for him to offer a blood sacrifice.

What the Holy Spirit Was Indicating

Notice that the high priest only went in to offer sacrifices once a year for the unintentional sins of the people. Yet the author says the Holy Spirit was speaking through this repetition. When you read the words "the Holy Spirit was making it clear that the way into the most holy place had not yet been disclosed while the first tabernacle was still standing," remember the distinction between the holy place and the most holy place. In the holy place, the regular offering described in the sacrificial system was presented. The high priest only entered the most holy place, the holy of holies, on the Day of Atonement to sprinkle blood on the mercy seat of the ark of the covenant.

The infrequent nature of the high priest's offering and the structure of the tabernacle demonstrated that sinful men could not approach a holy God. Even when provision was made for that approach to take place through sacrifice, it was only allowed once a year. Furthermore, the repetitive nature of the Day of Atonement (the fact that it happened *every* year) highlighted that the priestly work of the sons of Aaron would only come to an end when something final arrived. This is why the author says the Holy Spirit was indicating something through the architecture of the tabernacle: even he was crying out for the day when the final sacrifice would come. As long as there was a curtain between the holy place and the most holy place, the people were not fully in the presence of God. They could not draw near to God with confidence. Thus, the veil between the most holy place and the holy place indicated incompleteness and an inability to approach God.

Under the new covenant, we no longer need to make the distinction between the holy place and the most holy place. When Christ cried, "It is finished," and the veil separating the most holy place and the holy place tore from top to bottom, God was announcing to the world that people could indeed come into his presence through faith in the finished and final work of Jesus Christ. We don't need a high priest to meet with God now. We now have direct access to his throne room through Christ.

Imperfect Offerings

The gifts and sacrifices that were offered to the Lord mattered. They were necessary for holding back the wrath of God. We learn from verse 9, though, that they could not perfect the conscience of the worshiper. They could not plumb his depths and change his heart. The external acts of worship that took place in the tabernacle were purely external. They only dealt with external things like food and drink, various washings, and regulations for the body. But Israel needed acts of worship that dealt with the internal issues of the heart.

The author of Hebrews shows that not even the highest of all sacrifices—the sacrifice made by the high priest on the Day of Atonement in the most holy place—could cleanse the conscience of the worshiper. Even it couldn't bring about newness of life. This is why gifts and sacrifices continued to be offered in Israel. They had to be offered because there was never final purification from sin. As soon as an Israelite finished offering one sacrifice for sin, he needed to offer another.

The contrast could not be clearer. While the old covenant required incessant and imperfect offerings that could not purify the depths of the human heart, Christ accomplished final and full purification. Jesus is the hope of the new covenant. When he appeared as high priest (Heb 9:11), everything changed.

Reflect and Discuss

1. What does it mean for Christians to approach God? How does this passage inform our understanding of worshiping God? Where does Scripture command us to approach and worship God?

2. Why is it significant that a central tabernacle in which God is to be worshiped no longer remains? What does this mean for individual Christians and for the corporate gathering of Christians in the local church?

3. Explain how God's commands concerning regulations for worship in verse 1 are fatherly and loving. How does God's kingly reign affect your life, especially as you go about day-to-day business? What are some ways we can joyfully demonstrate God's loving reign in our lives?

4. Look at verses 2-5 again. To what deeper realities do each of these objects in the tabernacle point? What do they tell us about God, the new covenant, Jesus Christ, and ourselves?

5. What are sins committed in ignorance? How do unintentional sins reveal the pervasive and insidious effects of sin? In what ways do this kind of sin affect your life and your relationships with other people?

6. What does the most holy place communicate about the character of God? What does it mean that Christ's work on the cross eliminates the division between the most holy place and the holy place? Why does this matter for Christians?

7. Explain how the contents of verse 8 foretold the coming of the new covenant. What did the infrequent nature of the high priest's work communicate? What role did the Holy Spirit play in this?

8. How did the continuous nature of the gifts and offerings in the old covenant demonstrate their insufficiency? What does this tell us about Christ's offering in the new covenant? How should this affect our confidence and encourage us to endure?

9. What were the gifts and sacrifices offered under the old covenant good for if they couldn't perfect the conscience of the worshiper? How does this help draw out the contrast between the covenants?

10. What does the author mean by reference to "the time of the new order" in verse 10? Why does he call it this?

The Superiority of Redemption in Christ

HEBREWS 9:11-22

Main Idea: The blood of Christ, our great high priest, is superior to the animal sacrifices of the old covenant since his blood accomplishes a once-for-all-time redemption, secures an eternal inheritance for us, cleanses our consciences, and makes him the mediator of a new and better covenant.

I. The Superiority of Christ to the Levitical Priests (9:11-12)
II. The Superiority of Christ to the Levitical Sacrifices (9:13-14)
III. The Superiority of Christ as Mediator of the New Covenant (9:15)
IV. The Better Blood of the New Covenant (9:16-22)

One of the most effective teachers in my life was the woman who taught my literature class in the eleventh grade. She was a remarkable teacher and helped me develop a deep love and appreciation for good literature. Perhaps the most formative assignment she gave the class was something that I never would have tried on my own. She required us to write a one-page summary of every book we read. Initially, composing a one-page summary didn't seem too difficult a task. However, I soon discovered that even though I really enjoyed reading the books, I really hated writing the summaries. Great novels seem to defy being reduced to one page. However, the assignment taught me that writing a short summary is one of the most effective ways to remember what I have read and to increase my comprehension. Given that we tend to forget more than we remember, we desperately need summaries.

This is one reason why Scripture employs so many summaries. Paul does this quite often. In Romans 3:9-20; 5:1; 8:1; and 12:1 we see Paul concisely summarizing previous arguments. This is similar to the way in which the sermons of Moses in Deuteronomy summarize large portions of the Pentateuch. Likewise, we might say that Hebrews 9–10 functions as a summary of all that has gone before. Thus, it is imperative that we understand Hebrews 9:11-22 within the context of what the author has already said in his letter.

The Superiority of Christ to Levitical Priests
HEBREWS 9:11-12

The beginning word *but* is very important. Hebrews 9:1-10 discusses the old covenant and the Levitical priesthood, which were characterized by the temple and its regular practice of sacrifices that were unable to "perfect the worshiper's conscience" (v. 9). "But" Christ's priestly work starkly contrasts with these Levitical practices, since his priesthood actually accomplishes the salvation to which the old covenant could only point. In contrast to the old covenant priests, our new covenant priest fully and finally atones for the sins of his people and ushers in the "good things" of redemption for which they had always hoped.

The word *appeared* is also important because it highlights the fact that God's plan of salvation has now been made visible in Christ. Christ's appearance as high priest signals the dawning of the eschatological promises—promises that have in some sense already arrived in Christ, but that will not be complete until he arrives again. This is why the author identifies Jesus as the high priest of the "good things that have come." Even though aspects of our redemption—life with God in heaven, glorification, and full sanctification—are still future, we are inheritors of these good things in the present. What are these "good things"? They are the fruits of Christ's atonement that culminates in our "eternal redemption" (v. 12).

The author of Hebrews also indicates that Christ's priestly work occurs as he passes through the "greater and more perfect tabernacle" into "the most holy place." This, of course, is not the earthly tabernacle. The writer of Hebrews has already explained that the earthly tabernacle (or tent) was actually patterned after the heavenly dwelling place of God. The most holy place in the tabernacle on earth was therefore a picture of the realities of heaven. Whereas the Levitical high priest could only go as far as the earthly most holy place by means of the blood of animal sacrifice, Christ entered the eternal and heavenly most holy place by means of his own blood.

This entrance into the most holy place is "once for all time." This emphasizes the completeness and eternality of Christ's sacrifice as opposed to the repetitive sacrifices of the Levites. They continually had to offer up sacrifices to God; Christ only offered up one. In doing so, he secured an eternal redemption for us and demonstrated the sufficiency of his atonement for those who obey him. This eternal security and sufficiency grounds our confidence in Christ and the author's exhortation to endure. Once we are redeemed, we cannot be lost. Jesus's atonement was once for all time, accepted unconditionally by the Father, and presented in the heavenly sanctuary. Certainly we can see now how these verses so succinctly and spectacularly summarize the mission of Christ.

The Superiority of Christ to the Levitical Sacrifices
HEBREWS 9:13-14

To approach God under the old covenant required becoming ritually clean. This was even necessary for the high priest before he could enter the most holy place to perform the Day of Atonement sacrifices. Becoming ritually clean is what the author means by "purification of the flesh." The old covenant priests engaged in these ceremonies so that they might be rendered externally, outwardly clean and thus go into the holy place and sacrifice for the people—even if it was just for the briefest of moments. But these ceremonies and sacrifices could not cleanse the inner person or the conscience.

Christ, however, is decisively different. He did not need to purify himself by means of blood sacrifices and external washings as the priests of the old covenant did. Jesus did not need ritual cleansing because he was already clean. He offered himself not through ceremonial rituals that purify the flesh, but as One without blemish "through the eternal Spirit." The phrase *eternal Spirit* suggests a reference to the Holy Spirit. There follows an even greater contrast between Christ and the priests of old. Whereas they had to be externally purified just to engage in sacrifice, Christ's sacrifice of himself internally cleanses those for whom he died. He purifies our consciences.

Finally, the last words of verse 14 read, "from dead works so that we can serve the living God." What does it mean for our consciences to be cleansed "from dead works"? Anyone under the old covenant who recognized the pervasiveness of his sin would know he would need another sacrifice as soon as the Day of Atonement was over. This is why they repeated the Day of Atonement every year. These are "dead works" because they amount to nothing, just as many of us through our own efforts have tried to earn God's favor through "dead" moral and religious works. But Christ's atonement fully cleanses our consciences such that we now no longer have the weight of our sin condemning us before God. Christ's work on the cross fully removes our guilt, thereby rendering our consciences clean.

Because of this internal cleansing, we can now serve the living God without fear. Hebrews remarkably captures the balance of the Christian life. Redeemed people serve God and find fulfillment and joy in doing the very things that we did out of obligation and frantic determination to try to justify ourselves before Christ came. The completed work of Christ rescues us from this foolish attempt and saves us from dead works.

The Superiority of Christ as Mediator of the New Covenant
HEBREWS 9:15

Because Christ is the high priest who has secured our redemption through offering himself, the author of Hebrews says Jesus is "the mediator of a new covenant." *Mediator* is a dangerous word for many of us because we *think* we know what it means. We assume that a mediator is someone who gets two opposing sides together and tries to effect a compromise or an agreement between them. For example, if you have conflict in the Middle East, you'll bring in diplomats and mediators to try and effect some kind of compromise—an arbitration in which two parties try to find some common ground by means of a mediator.

But there is no common ground between a holy God and sinful humanity. Therefore, Christ, as mediator, doesn't find a compromise between the two because God's holiness cannot be compromised. Far from suggesting a compromise between two opposing positions, Christ agrees with the Father that we deserve the infinite outpouring of his wrath. He agrees with the Father about the ugliness of our sin. He agrees with the Father about the necessity of a sacrifice. And as our mediator, he agrees to be that sacrifice even as the Father sends him for that task. In this mediatory work, Christ procures an eternal inheritance for his church (i.e., the "called"), an inheritance simply synonymous with all of the present and future benefits of Christ's salvific work. This "eternal inheritance" is comparable to the "eternal redemption" in 9:12.

Again the author of Hebrews highlights that it is specifically Christ's death that accomplishes what the sacrifices under the first covenant could not—namely, eternal redemption and forgiveness. The animal sacrifices of the old covenant could not secure redemption eternally. They were temporary and needed to be repeated. Christ's death, on the other hand, secures redemption forever. His death wins forgiveness from all of the transgressions committed under the first covenant. Furthermore, the old covenant could not secure redemption sufficiently for the people. It could not repair man's severed relationship with God, for the old covenant anticipated and depended on the new covenant. The animal sacrifices offered for sin and purification under the old covenant foreshadowed the fully sufficient sacrifice in the new: Jesus Christ. He mediated a better covenant and offered up a better sacrifice, one that was efficient to redeem people from the transgressions committed under the first covenant. In doing so, Christ secured an eternal inheritance for those who are called.

The Better Blood of the New Covenant
HEBREWS 9:16-22

The church today is often impoverished by truncated, reductionistic articulations of the gospel. We often talk about how someone can come to know the Lord Jesus Christ and be saved from their sins, but we often have no idea what took place in order for that promise to be true. Hebrews demonstrates that it is the Father's will that his people understand not only *what* Christ has done for us but *how* he did it. The reason is because *how* Christ achieves our redemption more fully demonstrates the glory of God. We can't honor, appreciate, and worship God for what he has done for us unless we understand what it cost to achieve our salvation.

Verses 16-22 begin to unveil *how* Christ achieved our redemption. The author explains that the covenant is like a last will and testament. Just as a last will and testament bequeaths gifts to others after the death of the testator, so also the death of Christ results in the giving of gifts to members of the new covenant community. The account of the inauguration of the first covenant in verse 18 draws the reader back to Exodus 24:4-8. In this covenant-initiation ceremony the sprinkling of the people with the blood of animals signified that the punishment for covenant disobedience was death. However, the deaths of these animals also signified that God provided a substitute to stand in the place of covenant breakers. Covenant breakers could only be forgiven by the shedding of blood. Moreover, the shedding of blood was the inauguration sign of the covenants. The shedding of blood—that is, the death of a substitute—inaugurated both the old and the new covenant. This is what the author means in Hebrews 9:18. Thus, the shedding of blood represented the beginning of a covenant and the forgiveness of sins. This is the theological heart of verse 22. Just as the first covenant was inaugurated with the death of animals and the purification of the tabernacle by their blood, so Christ has inaugurated a new covenant with his blood and has thereby accomplished the forgiveness of sins.

Why blood atonement? In the Old Testament, God tells his people, "The life . . . is in the blood" (Lev 17:11). You don't have to know very much about anatomy and physiology to know that's true. Just try losing too much of it and see how well you do! Without blood, there is no life. The Israelites would remember this every time they cut the throat of an ox or a lamb in sacrifice. When they watched an animal's blood drain out, they watched its life drain out as well.

So if we think theologically about the sacrificial system, we can see the connection between blood, death, covenant, and atonement. The act of sin brings about the covenantal consequence of death. The demand for the transgressor's death is essentially the same thing as the demand for the transgressor's blood. The substitutionary animal sacrifices in the old covenant were vivid reminders that transgressors deserved death. Yet, through these substitutionary blood sacrifices, God made a way to atone for sin. Therefore, blood is symbolic in the sacrificial system under the old covenant because it demonstrates the costliness of sin. It graphically illustrates that with sin comes death.

The events on Calvary are the most vivid depiction of this reality. Christ—the One who was fully God and fully man, who was tempted in every way as we are yet remained without sin—shed his own blood. When he shed his own blood, he became the mediator of a new and better covenant. By that blood, and that blood alone, all who are called and endure receive a redemption and inheritance that lasts forever.

Reflect and Discuss

1. In what ways is Jesus's priesthood starkly different from and superior to the priesthood of the Levites in the Old Testament? In what ways did the Levitical sacrifices point to Christ's ultimate sacrifice? How does Jesus's death fulfill animal deaths that happened under the old covenant?

2. Why is Jesus the perfect sacrifice for your sins? Since Jesus did not need to ritually cleanse himself as the Levitical high priest did, how does this affect the security of your salvation?

3. How does Jesus's "once for all time" atonement affect the way that you view your relationship with him? How does this truth anchor

our hope in the security of our salvation and help us endure until the end?

4. In what ways does Jesus's example of unconditional atonement defy our culture's understanding of forgiveness and love?

5. What does it mean for your conscience to be cleansed "from dead works"? How does this cleansing free you to genuinely worship God and joyfully serve him in your local church?

6. How does Christ's role as our mediator differ from our culture's understanding of a mediator? Explain the folly of trying to strike a compromise with God.

7. How is your motivation to share the gospel strengthened by the knowledge that Jesus's death secures redemption for every person who is called? Does this knowledge refine your definition of "success" in evangelism? Explain your answer.

8. Why was it necessary for Jesus to be born as a man and die for our sins? What does this necessity teach you about the costliness of your salvation? What does it teach about God's love for you?

9. What are some of the good gifts that Jesus's priesthood has secured for you in the future? What good gifts has he secured for you in the present? Explain how you can be the benefactor and recipient of these good gifts, even the future ones, right now.

10. Does your local church promote a truncated, reductionistic articulation of the gospel? If so, in what ways? How might you lead the people in your church to understand and embrace the full gospel of Jesus Christ?

The Sufficient and Final Sacrifice of Christ

HEBREWS 9:23-28

Main Idea: Christ's sacrificial death was sufficient to end the need to make continual offerings and to put away sin forever. Salvation in him will ultimately culminate in blessing when he returns.

I. **The Superlative Sacrifice of Christ (9:23-26)**
II. **Judgment and the Second Coming (9:27-28)**
   A. Man's appointed death
   B. Christ's imminent return

Hebrews 9 teaches that Christ is the great high priest who secures an eternal redemption for his people by shedding his own blood. As a result, Jesus is the mediator of a new and better covenant. As we saw in Hebrews 9:22, almost everything under the law is purified with blood; and without the shedding of blood, there is no forgiveness of sins. This blood of ceremonial animals ultimately foreshadowed the blood Jesus shed on the cross when he was crucified. As we will see in the chapter's final verses, Jesus's blood also purified the heavenly places, put aside sin forever, and guarantees final salvation for those who endure in him.

The Superlative Sacrifice of Christ
HEBREWS 9:23-26

The copies of the heavenly things in the earthly tent needed to be purified with blood. Such cleansing was necessary even though they merely represented the greater realities in heaven. Because there could be no forgiveness without the shedding of blood, it was vital to purify these copies with blood. But the heavenly realities, which the copies symbolized, needed greater sacrifices. They required better sacrifices because they represented greater realities.

This reference to purifying the heavenly things does not mean the heavenly places needed cleansing because they were somehow defiled by human sin. Rather, it speaks to the effectiveness and superiority of

Christ's sacrifice. The author's use of heavenly language corresponds with his use of superlative language in relation to Christ. Jesus's sacrifice is better because it is associated with heaven itself—the place of God's very presence.

Verse 24 continues drawing out verse 23. Jesus did not enter an earthly tabernacle to offer himself; he went into the very presence of God. Again, we should not think in terms of location or spatiality. The language is symbolic and points to the superior nature of Christ's sacrifice, just as it does in verse 23. We can endure in Christ because he appeared in the presence of God—in heaven itself—to make his sacrifice on our behalf. His sacrifice is a better sacrifice, indeed.

Christ's death as a singular event is central to the Christian faith. This is the reality Hebrews 9:25-26 expounds. Christ does not need to be sacrificed daily, which is one of the reasons Christians stress his resurrection. Jesus appeared once for all at the end of the ages to put away sin by the sacrifice of himself. His offering is so superior it doesn't need to be repeated year after year, and it renders all further offerings obsolete. This is yet another way Jesus supersedes the priests of old.

It's important to fully understand what the author means by saying Christ appeared "one time." This calls to mind the phrase "once for all time" that occurs three times in Hebrews (7:27; 9:12; 10:10; cf. Rom 6:10). Once again, the author is reinforcing the sufficiency, singularity, and effectiveness of Christ's sacrifice. His supreme sacrifice does not need repeating. All previous sacrifices, earthly priests, and Days of Atonement were meant to make us anticipate and long for Christ. Now, once for all and at the end of the ages, the fulfillment of all these things has finally arrived to put away sin forever by the sacrifice of himself.

Christ's incarnation is an unprecedented moment in time. He has appeared in history—"at the end of the ages" (cf. Heb 1:2)—once for all time to put away sin. Paul speaks with the same outlook on time in Galatians 4:4. "The removal of sin" means judging and condemning sin. The Son's superior sacrifice dispenses sin, exiles it, places it under judgment, and ultimately defeats it. Though this phrase might be common in modern evangelical vernacular, the idea of the Messiah removing sin by sacrificing himself was truly revolutionary in the first century. Christ's radical self-sacrifice is the means by which sin is finally overcome.

Judgment and the Second Coming
HEBREWS 9:27-28

In the final two verses of this passage, the author brings new material into the conversation: man's appointed judgment and Christ's second coming. As the text makes clear, Christ comes a second time not for the sake of addressing sin but to save those who are eagerly waiting for him.

Man's Appointed Death

In verse 27 the author considers man's looming death and judgment as they relate to the work of Jesus. The reason for our appointment with death and judgment takes us back to the garden of Eden. God told Adam and Eve they would die if they ate the forbidden tree's fruit. He "appointed" their death in the event of their disobedience. And in their moment of rebellion, mortality entered the human experience. By virtue of our corporate union with Adam, our forefather's sin, and his experience of death became part of our experience.

This emphasizes the finality in human existence. Life is lived one time, and then there is death and judgment—just as there was for Adam and Eve. Man will die and then God will judge him. This directly relates to the work of Christ. He too was appointed to die once. He died one time, and his death need never be repeated. And because he has died once, he will not come again to act as a sacrifice. Rather, he will come to bring final salvation for his people.

This focus on death and judgment refutes the notion that death is some kind of cosmic accident. Death is not just some natural process in the world. It is part of the divine judgment on sin. Death is a verdict. But this is not the end of the story. Because of the gospel, there is hope. It's this hope to which the author turns in verse 28.

Christ's Imminent Return

The message found in verse 28 is that life comes after death for those who trust in Jesus until the end. Christ was delivered up to be crucified in accordance with the definite plan of God (Acts 2:22-24). As is the case for all men, Jesus's death was appointed. But unlike all other men, Jesus will return again. And as we consider the future with the knowledge that Christ is coming back, we must remember he's not coming back to repeat his sacrifice. He's not coming back to forgive sin; he's coming back to save those who are eagerly expecting him. This is *great* news!

Christ is returning to rescue those he's saved and to claim his church solely for himself. For those who eagerly await Jesus, sweet salvation is coming.

The word *waiting* points to the fact that believers should be longing for Christ's return. We who are alive should be consciously and readily anticipating his second coming. Those who are saved and share in the hope of Christ's return are safe. Even though earthly struggles and toils still pervade our lives, Christians can and must hold to the hope that we are eternally secure in Christ right now. Again, this is part of the already/not yet tension the author has been highlighting throughout the letter. We are absolutely saved now, but Jesus is coming again to complete our salvation experience.

Our salvation is a past, present, and future salvation. It is past in the sense that what Christ accomplished by his blood happened long ago. It is present in the sense that we are saved and united with Christ right now. And it is future in the sense that we will be saved out of this broken world into eternal communion, peace, and freedom from sin when Christ returns. So, as we eagerly wait in the present, we rejoice in the past and anticipate the new heaven and a new, restored earth in the future. Every generation of Christians has been waiting for the coming kingdom. This is true of our generation as well. So as long as we are living, we are waiting. We must do so eagerly.

Reflect and Discuss

1. Why does the author use the language of the "heavens" to explain the sacrifice of Christ? What point is he trying to stress? How does it display the superlative nature of Christ's sacrifice?

2. Why is Christ's death as a singular event central to the Christian faith? How does his sacrifice differ from old covenant sacrifices? What makes it the superior sacrifice?

3. Why did God originally command repeated sacrifices in the old covenant? What did they anticipate? What does it mean for Jesus to be the last sacrifice "at the end of the ages"?

4. According to this passage, what was Jesus's mission in his first coming? What does it mean for Jesus to remove sin? Summarize the key differences between his first and second coming.

5. Why does the author draw a comparison between man's death and that of Christ? How is his death different from ours?

6. Consider your own death and judgment. How do they connect to the garden in Genesis? What does Adam's experience tell you about your own? How does the looming prospect of your death and judgment before God motivate you to persevere in the faith?

7. How does Christ's first coming help you endure in the faith? How does the promise of his second coming help you endure? In what ways do you see the already-not yet tension working in this passage?

8. Since Christians are promised hope for the future, how should the church prepare today for eternity? How can Christians prepare both corporately and individually?

9. What would you expect to see in the life of someone who is eagerly waiting for Christ's return?

10. Explain, in your own words, how your salvation is a past, present, and future salvation.

The Sufficiency of Christ's Once-for-All-Time Sacrifice

HEBREWS 10:1-18

Main Idea: Whereas old covenant sacrifices were unable to completely atone for sin, Jesus's sacrifice puts aside old covenant practices and secures total forgiveness and sanctification for God's people.

I. **Insufficient Sacrifices (10:1)**
   A. Key contrasts
   B. Shadows and the Son
II. **A Sacrifice Sufficient to Take Away Sin (10:2-4)**
III. **A Sacrifice Sufficient to Supplant Old Testament Sacrifices (10:5-10)**
   A. Jesus and Psalm 40
   B. Jesus and the last sacrifice
IV. **A Sacrifice Sufficient to Bring Perfection (10:11-14)**
   A. The priest who sits
   B. The priest who sits in power
V. **A Sacrifice Sufficient to Bring Forgiveness (10:15-18)**

As we begin the tenth chapter of Hebrews, we face one of the most important issues in biblical interpretation: understanding the contrast between the old and the new covenant. When Christians talk about the differences between these covenants, we almost habitually fall into a mindset that views the old covenant as bad and the new covenant as good. We are tempted to consider the old covenant negatively because we know it could not save us. The author of Hebrews, however, does not see the contrast in this way. Although he draws necessary and sharp distinctions between the covenants, he does not want his readers to despise the old covenant. Rather, he contrasts the two covenants to show how the old one cries out for and finds fulfillment in the new one. The old covenant prepares the way and ultimately reveals our need for the new.

Insufficient Sacrifices
HEBREWS 10:1

These verses pinpoint some of the key deficiencies of the old covenant sacrifices. As the author makes clear in these verses, old covenant sacrifices were merely shadows of better things to come. They were offered year after year but could never save and could not perfect those drawing near to God.

Key Contrasts

In verse 1 the author uses descriptive language to demonstrate that the law pointed to "the good things to come." The phrase "the good things to come" sums up everything Christ purchased and accomplished for us by virtue of his life, death, and resurrection. The greatest of these good things is the forgiveness of sins. The writer already made this point clear in 9:11-12.

The eternal redemption accomplished by Christ is the key contrast between the old and the new covenant. While the new covenant brings permanent redemption through Christ, the old covenant only temporarily suspended the judgment of God. As we look back on the old covenant sacrifices through the lens of Hebrews 9:22, we can see that old covenant sacrifices could not achieve the forgiveness of even one sin. Instead, we see that these sacrifices *pointed* to the forgiveness of all sin.

What, then, was the immediate effect of old covenant sacrifices? According to Romans 3:21-26, those sacrifices held back the wrath of God for a time. For instance, on the night when the angel of death struck the firstborn of Egypt, the firstborn sons of Israel were saved because the Israelites acted in faith and put the blood of the Passover lamb across their doorposts as God commanded. While Israel's firstborns would eventually die because of their sin, they did not expire on that horrible day of God's judgment against the Egyptians. God delayed his justice and judgment on account of the sacrifice offered in faith. Similarly, when the high priest went into the most holy place on the Day of Atonement and sprinkled the blood of the animal on the mercy seat, God withheld his wrath for another year. Thus, God received every sacrifice that preceded Christ's sacrifice as a means of suspending his wrath against sin.

Shadows and the Son

The author of Hebrews uses the image of a "shadow" to draw the contrast between Christ's sacrifice and the old covenant sacrifices. When Christ died on the cross, he did not shed the blood of another; he shed his own blood. Nor did he enter the tabernacle by making a sacrifice for his own sin first; he was sinless. Nor did he enter the manmade tabernacle; he entered the heavenly tabernacle. Then, after he accomplished atonement for us, he accomplished an eternal redemption once for all time, which brings true forgiveness of sins. All those animals died as shadows pointing to these realities accomplished through the cross of Christ. There Christ perfectly fulfilled all these things.

When the author uses the word *law*, he refers to the totality of the old covenant. The law, that is, the old covenant, "has only a shadow of the good things to come." Under the old covenant, Israel merely saw the shape of what was to come. The shadow left them crying out for the real thing. As a shadow, the old covenant is insufficient. It could not perfect those who draw near.

Only Jesus can accomplish that. God is satisfied with the sacrifice of Christ and imputes the righteousness of his Son to us because nothing less than a perfect righteousness will meet God's standard. We are woefully and infinitely short of perfect righteousness on our own. Only the righteousness of Christ will suffice for sin. Only Christ can bring atonement for sin and secure eternal redemption.

A Sacrifice Sufficient to Take Away Sin
HEBREWS 10:2-4

In verse 2 the author asks a rhetorical question to draw out the insufficiency of the old covenant sacrifices. "Consciousness of sins" points to the part of the human person that remained untouched and unaffected by the old covenant sacrifices. Although the high priest went into the most holy place on the Day of Atonement to cleanse the people of sin, nothing could cleanse the consciences of the people for the sins they would commit right after the sacrifice. The law could do nothing to alleviate the guilt of the human conscience. The logic of verse 2 is that if old covenant sacrifices had sufficiently delivered all the promises of God, the priests would have stopped offering them. But they did not stop offering them. Sacrifices were made daily, weekly, and yearly. Israel's sacrifices could not keep up with the people's sinfulness.

Verse 3 reveals that these recurring sacrifices served as reminders of sin. They annually reminded the people of their guilt and disobedience and that the sacrifices could not ultimately purify them. "Year after year" clearly links these sacrifices to the Day of Atonement. That day was essentially an annual and graphic event that reminded the people they were unable to perfectly obey the commands of the law and desperately needed a priest to mediate on their behalf.

Verse 4 establishes an essential gospel point: it is impossible for the blood of animals to wash away sin. This claim is interesting, especially when we consider that the author says there is no forgiveness for sin without the shedding of blood (9:22). Nevertheless, the old covenant sacrifices, in all their bloodiness, could not take away sin. Instead, they pointed to the one sacrifice that could bring forgiveness of sin: Jesus Christ. His perfect sacrifice happened once and never needs to be repeated. His blood, unlike that of animals, washes sins away forever.

A Sacrifice Sufficient to Supplant Old Testament Sacrifices
HEBREWS 10:5-10

In these verses the author continues to draw out the distinctions between Christ's sacrifice and old covenant sacrifices. He continues to highlight the inadequacy of the sacrifices made by the high priests under the old covenant when compared to the superiority of the sacrifice made by the great high priest, Jesus Christ. Here the author particularly explains what Christ came into the world to accomplish and shows the necessity of his death. To this end, the author leans heavily on Psalm 40.

Jesus and Psalm 40

The writer of Hebrews attributes Psalm 40:6-8 to Christ at his incarnation. He says Christ spoke these words. This should not surprise us since the author believes that the triune God is the author of Scripture. By asserting this, the writer demonstrates to his readers how to see Jesus in the Old Testament correctly. The author shows us that he didn't believe this psalm should *only* be read historically, but that it should also be read typologically.

Jesus came into the world to do his Father's will. This required laying down his life as a sacrifice for sins. This is what verses 5-7 teach.

When Christ entered the world, he knew his body would be the sacrifice that pleased God and satisfied his wrath. Old covnenant sacrifices and offerings could not ultimately bring the forgiveness of sins. Even worse, for many who made the offerings, the sacrifices represented nothing more than mere religious ritual. Those people no longer offered up sacrifices in faith and obedience. They were just going through the motions.

The Father did not ask his Son to offer sacrifices. He prepared a body for him and asked him to be the sacrifice. In doing so, the Father was asking the Son for obedience. The Father's will and the Son's obedience are precisely what we see described in Isaiah 53. God delights in obedience, not in burnt offerings and sin offerings (1 Sam 15:22-23). This does not mean the old covenant offerings contradicted the will of God in any way. It simply means God is not interested in religious ritual if it is not driven by faith and obedience. Works without faith are meaningless in God's eyes.

In verse 8 the author of Hebrews gives a brief commentary on the words he attributes to Jesus. He further explains that God did not delight in the sacrifices of the Levitical cult "offered according to the law." Once again, this highlights the temporary and inadequate nature of the old covenant sacrifices. A greater sacrifice was still to come—a sacrifice in which God would be permanently pleased.

Jesus and the Last Sacrifice

Verse 9 tells us Jesus did away with the old covenant in order to establish the new. This is what Jesus was announcing when he said, "See, I have come to do your will." These words took away the first and established the second. Therefore, the Old Testament sacrificial system is completed. The author actually uses the Greek word for "abolish" to punctuate the termination of the Old Testament sacrificial system as forcefully as he can. The era of the law is over. Jesus abolishes it. He is why we no longer need to sacrifice bulls and goats. This is good news for bulls and goats, and it is far better news for us.

Verse 10 expands on the supremacy of the second and final sacrifice. In doing so, the author returns to the language of Jesus's body. Jesus did the will of the Father by offering his body as a once-for-all-time substitute for sin. His willing sacrifice is the final and fully effective one that abolishes the old sacrifices and inaugurates the new covenant. By virtue of their union with Christ and on account of his sacrifice, believers are now in the realm of the holy and purified. They "have been sanctified."

"Once for all time" is one of the most important phrases in Hebrews. It announces loud and clear that Christ's sacrifice is definitive and sufficient. No sacrifice ever needs to be made again. God is pleased with Christ's. The author is speaking emphatically: not just once, but *once for all time*.

A Sacrifice Sufficient to Bring Perfection
HEBREWS 10:11-14

The Priest Who Sits

At the heart of these distinctions are two kinds of priests: priests who stand and the priest who sits. Verse 11 details the inadequacy of priests who stand. Under the old covenant, priests stood daily at God's service, offering the same sacrifices repeatedly. The sacrifices could never take away sins (10:4), yet they continued to offer them. They stood every day because their work was never completed, nor did their work progress. This is why the priests stood each day offering the "same" sacrifices. Their ministry had to be repeated over and over again, generation by generation, and it could not save a single sinner.

Verse 12 details the priest who sits: Jesus Christ. Once Jesus offered a single sacrifice for sins that was sufficient for all time, he sat down at the right hand of God. This is known as the Session of Christ. It means Jesus is seated in authority and power at the right hand of the Father and carries out the ministry of intercession for God's people there, waiting for the day his enemies are made a footstool for his feet. The priests who stand offer many sacrifices repeatedly. Jesus, however, only offers one sacrifice. His is sufficient to take away sins forever, and its benefits never end. Jesus sits because there's no need for him to keep standing. His atoning work is complete, and now he intercedes for us.

The Priest Who Sits in Power

The anticipation of the time when Jesus's enemies are made his footrest brings us back to the words of Psalm 110. The psalmist tells us that the Messiah will make his enemies a footstool. This is a reference to Jesus's second coming. The author of Hebrews has already alluded to the second coming in the previous chapter (9:28). This shows us the return of

Christ is at the forefront of the author's mind. Jesus will return, but he will not come to offer another sacrifice. The priest who sits will return to judge his enemies. Jesus is the priest who sits in power.

Verse 14 reiterates the effectiveness of Jesus's single offering. By the priestly offering of his own body, Jesus has perfected—not just improved—those who are being sanctified. How many times and in how many ways can the author make this point? Evidently one time is not enough. We need to see this beautiful reality emphasized repeatedly. Jesus has perfected, for all time, those who are being sanctified. His work perfects believers forever. Their perfection is an objective and eschatological reality that will never end.

A Sacrifice Sufficient to Bring Forgiveness
HEBREWS 10:15-18

The author makes another appeal to the Old Testament in verses 15-18. Here he turns to Jeremiah 31:31-34 and the revelation of the new covenant. The Lord promises to put his laws in the hearts of his people and to write them on their minds. Jesus's final and supreme sacrifice brings the full forgiveness of sins, so an offering for sin is no longer necessary. The new covenant brings a new heart.

The author once again attributes the words of the Old Testament to the Holy Spirit. We have already seen him say the Holy Spirit speaks through the Old Testament in Hebrews 3:7 and 9:8. The new covenant was new, but it was not a new revelation. Jesus's sacrifice was the fulfillment of an old revelation, the one promised by the prophet Jeremiah through the witness of the Holy Spirit. Notice that the promise was not Jeremiah's; it was God's. Through Jeremiah's prophetic word, the Holy Spirit bears witness to this new covenant.

We have already seen the author reference Jeremiah 31:31-34 in Hebrews 8:8-12. He cites these verses again to tell his readers this new covenant has been made with them, which suggests the author may be conceiving of his readers as the new Israel. Whatever the case, the writer is expressing that the readers of his letter are also the recipients of the new covenant. One of the key features of this new covenant is God's sovereign grace. God himself writes his laws on the hearts and minds of his people. Their obedience is a result of his sovereign and gracious inscription. The old sacrifices could never accomplish this—only Christ could.

"I will never again remember their sins and their lawless acts" was not a reality under the old covenant. The people of Israel cried out in the knowledge of their sin, especially on the Day of Atonement. God still remembered their sin, even though he did not pour his wrath out on it immediately. But now that Christ has mediated a new and better covenant, God no longer remembers our sins and our lawless deeds. The blood of Jesus blots them out forever.

Verse 18 gives another important component of the forgiveness won by Jesus in the new covenant. If Christ's blood has truly granted the forgiveness of sins forever, then "there is no longer an offering for sin." This is why there's a table for the Lord's Supper and not an altar for sacrificing animals at the front of our church auditoriums. Christ accomplished everything necessary for the forgiveness of our sins. Because Jesus's offering for sin was sufficient to forgive our sins once for all time, his offering was sufficient to end all other offerings.

Reflect and Discuss

1. This section of Scripture deals with how the old covenant points to the new. How would you explain the old covenant? How did the old covenant point to the new? What is the new covenant? What Bible passages are helpful in defining and explaining the two covenants.
2. Explain the relationship between the old covenant and sacrifices. Why did God institute the sacrificial system? If sacrifices were ultimately insufficient, what was their effect?
3. The first thing the author wants to emphasize about the old covenant sacrifices is that they are unable to perfect those who offer them. What is the first line of argument that the writer uses to show that this was the case? Why does this characteristic about the sacrificial system show its insufficiency?
4. Why does the author note that rather than bringing forgiveness of sin, the sacrificial system actually brought a reminder of sin? What is the conclusion the author draws about the blood of bulls and goats that were sacrificed?
5. In Hebrews 10:5 the author attributes a quotation to Christ that is found nowhere in the gospels. Instead, it is a citation from one of the psalms of David. Explain how the author can rightly attribute the psalm to Jesus.
6. In Hebrews 10:11, the author explicitly begins to contrast the sacrifices of the old covenant with the death of Jesus. What exactly does

he compare? What about Jesus's sacrifice does he emphasize in contrast to the ancient sacrifices? How do these aspects reflect the insufficiency of old covenant sacrifices and the sufficiency of Christ's?

7. The author of Hebrews connects the sacrifice of Christ to his coming judgment. How does he do this? Why is this an important connection to make about the role of Jesus in Scripture?

8. Hebrews 10:14 says, "By one offering he has perfected forever those who are being sanctified." How are both the perfection and the sanctification the author refers to here related to the work of Jesus? Explain the already-not yet tension at work in this verse.

9. What foundational difference between the old and the new covenant does the author of Hebrews make by quoting Jeremiah 31? Why is this so important for new covenant Christians?

10. What glorious conclusion does the author draw about the sin of those for whom Jesus has offered a sacrifice? How does the language of "once for all time" relate to the forgiveness of sins and the end of offerings for sin?

A Confident Confession of Christ

HEBREWS 10:19-25

Main Idea: We have confidence to approach God through Jesus Christ's priestly work. Because of this confidence, we can encourage one another to grow in assurance as we anticipate Christ's return.

I.   **Confidence in Christ (10:19-22)**
  A. Entering through the blood
  B. Entering through the priest
  C. Entering with a true heart and full assurance
  D. Entering with clean hearts
II. **Holding On to the Confession (10:23-25)**
  A. God's faithfulness to past promises
  B. Present assurance through Christian fellowship
  C. Anticipation for Christ's future return

When the author sets out the structure and substance of the gospel in Hebrews, he continually reviews its meaning. He will often repeat the same truth, but will do so by emphasizing a slightly different aspect to get the attention of his readers. After considering the "once for all time" aspect of the gospel in Hebrews 10:1-18, the writer turns his attention to another implication of the gospel in Hebrews 10:19-25. He is once again going to summarize its various aspects in order to help his readers remember the glorious realities Jesus's work accomplishes for his people. Additionally, he will exhort his people to action on the basis of these glorious realities.

Confidence in Christ
HEBREWS 10:19-22

The word *therefore* at the beginning of verse 19 marks a new section and leads us into several implications that are grounded in the truths the author has just finished discussing. The exhortations given by the writer are anchored in the priestly work of Jesus and reinforce just how truly remarkable his work is.

Entering through the Blood

Notice these words: "since we have boldness to enter the sanctuary through the blood of Jesus." Christian readers can pass over these words without even realizing it, but we must slow down and digest them. "The sanctuary" refers to the most holy place in the tabernacle. No one could enter it except the high priest, who could only go inside it once a year under the strictest supervision. If anyone besides the high priest entered the most holy place without permission, they died. Now, however, on account of Christ's work on the cross, believers can enter the most holy place with confidence. This does not mean they enter a physical sanctuary, only that they can now enter the very presence of God with confidence in Christ's work. By God's grace, the door to his presence is now wide open. That is nothing less than revolutionary.

Some individuals have sought to rid Christianity of blood language, speaking only about Jesus's love instead. The blood of Christ, however, is integral to Christian theology. His blood divides the sheep from the goats, but unites those it saves. If we lose the language of blood, we lose the gospel. The hymn "There Is a Fountain Filled with Blood" by William Cowper captures the role of Christ's blood beautifully:

> There is a fountain filled with blood
> drawn from Immanuel's veins,
> and sinners plunged beneath that flood
> lose all their guilty stains.

Those words have full biblical warrant.

Hebrews shows that Christians have access to God precisely because the blood of Jesus Christ has made it possible. Without Christ's blood there is no access to God. There is no remission of sins without the shedding of blood. Just as the old covenant required blood sacrifices, so too does the new covenant require a blood sacrifice. The final and effective blood sacrifice, however, came not through the blood of an animal shed on an altar, but through the blood of God's own Son shed on the cross. In his perfect and sinless blood, we have boldness to enter the sanctuary.

Entering through the Priest

Verse 20 continues explaining the way Christ opened the door to the presence of God. The author calls this "a new and living way," words that once again highlight the superiority of the new covenant. Jesus is a better priest of a new covenant, and one who intercedes for his people forever (7:25).

This new and living way is opened "through the curtain." The curtain in this instance refers to "his flesh": Christ's body, broken and bloodied for us on the cross. In the tabernacle, the curtain (or veil) separated the holy place from the most holy place. Christ, by dying on the cross, opened the way to God's presence. This is represented in the tearing of the temple curtain at the time of Jesus's death (Matt 27:51). By virtue of Jesus's priestly work and sacrifice, we no longer enter God's presence through a curtain. We enter through Jesus, our great high priest over the house of God.

Entering with a True Heart and Full Assurance

On account of all Christ's work as priest, the author confidently claims that God's people are to "draw near with a true heart in full assurance of faith." To whom can we draw near? To the Father. And in what manner can we draw near to him? With a true heart in full assurance. In other words, we can now stand before God certain that our sins are forgiven by virtue of our faith in Jesus.

Full assurance of faith has been a matter of Christian turmoil and some controversy throughout the centuries of the church. Many Christians struggle with the certainty of their salvation. But the New Testament exhorts Christians to know they are saved. God grants assurance, not on the basis of man's faith, but on the basis of Christ's faithfulness. The apostle John writes in 1 John 5:13, "I have written these things to you who believe in the name of the Son of God so that you may know that you have eternal life." And Romans 10:9,13 promise that the one who calls on the name of the Lord will be saved. Thus, the believer is to have full confidence, not in self or in personal faithfulness, but in the object of the faith, Jesus Christ. At the same time, believers must heed the numerous warnings the author of Hebrews gives through his letter. A believer necessarily produces fruit. If a faith is fruitless, it will not save.

Entering with Clean Hearts

The language of sprinkling alludes to the sacrificial system in the Old Testament. On the Day of Atonement, the priest would sprinkle the blood of the sacrifice on the mercy seat of God, resulting in propitiation (Lev 16:14). Consequently, God would alter his disposition toward Israel from wrath to acceptance. Just as the blood spilled and sprinkled purified God's people under the old covenant, Christ's blood purifies us under the new covenant. Jesus's blood, however, cleanses us with superior power and efficiency. His blood, unlike that of bulls and goats, purifies the conscience. It cleanses us from sin at our cores and perfects our hearts.

The washing with "pure water" also points back to the Old Testament, where washings of the body were required for cleanliness. These washings were unable to truly cleanse the people, though. A washing that truly purifies seems to be the type the author of Hebrews has in mind here. This pure water washes us completely clean from sin. It is a comprehensive cleansing that purifies us internally, not just externally. The language of washing also suggests a beautiful image pointing to baptism as a picture of salvation. In baptism we are graphically buried with Christ and beautifully raised with him in newness of life. It is the external symbol of the internal work accomplished by Christ.

Holding On to Our Confession
HEBREWS 10:23-25

In this passage the author of Hebrews brilliantly addresses all aspects of time:

- Past: God's Faithfulness to Past Promises in Christ
- Present: Assurance through Christian Fellowship
- Future: Anticipation of Christ's Return

He first comments on the past by mentioning God's faithfulness to his promises. He addresses the need for Christian fellowship and encouragement in the present. He also extends his exhortations into the future, recognizing the approaching day of the Lord.

God's Faithfulness to Past Promises

On the grounds of confidence and full assurance, the author of Hebrews implores his readers to "hold on to the confession of our hope." The confession demonstrates faith. It is the verbal verification of repentant hearts. What is the confession of Christian hope? Jesus is Lord and Jesus saves. The writer of Hebrews is not referencing a lengthy doctrinal statement. The confession on his mind is the central confession that Jesus saves sinners. Christians must never waver or stray from that confession in any capacity. Like the author's audience, we must hold on to the confession in which we initially place our hope.

The Christian holds on not by his own tenacity, but by God's faithfulness. We will persevere until the end because God does not abandon his children. God has proved faithful to his promises throughout Scripture. Jesus affirmed the Father's faithfulness in John 6:37: "Everyone the Father gives me will come to me, and the one who comes to me I will never cast out." No one who comes to Christ can ever be snatched out of his hand (John 10:28). God's power guards his children. Man can do nothing by his own power to keep himself. The security of God's protection and provision allows the church to hold the confession without wavering.

Present Assurance through Christian Fellowship

The author shifts to the present in verse 24. Here he stresses Christian fellowship and the church's role in helping believers persevere until the end. We cannot have confidence and full assurance of faith apart from the church. We cannot endure in isolation. Each Christian desperately needs the body of believers for encouragement. To obtain assurance, we need continual reminding from other saints.

Christ calls his followers to bring out the best in each other. Believers must actively and verbally stir up one another to love and good works. An unhealthy church fails to do this. Unfortunately, some churches bring out the worst in their attendees rather than the best. The hymn "Blest Be the Tie That Binds" beautifully echoes the fellowship in the Lord Jesus Christ and the value of bearing one another's burdens.

Christians must not neglect gathering together for corporate worship and for times of prayer and encouragement. Verses 24 and 25 are strong words of judgment against those who are in the habit of neglecting other believers. Those who neglect assembling together cut themselves off from the very means whereby Christ feeds, assures, and protects his people. To say, "I can do this alone," is to defy the very command of Christ. Some may claim that they can hear better preaching on the Internet or that they are too busy to attend church, but these excuses reveal the reality of a disobedient heart. Instead of searching for an excuse, Christians should be doing everything within their power to meet together. Not only because they need to be fed by the preaching of God's Word but also because it is part of the faith to stir up fellow believers to love and good works.

Anticipation for Christ's Future Return

Finally, the author turns his focus on the future. Many English translations capitalize the word *day* because it refers to a specific day in history. It refers to the day of Christ's return and God's judgment (2 Pet 3:10). Christ will call together his church on that day, and he will judge those who do not belong to it.

Faithful anticipation should characterize the church's daily life. The nearness of Christ's return makes our encouragement of one another and our gathering together all the more urgent and all the more significant. As time moves toward the Day of the Lord, the author expects the church to grow in faithful commitment. No one knows when that day will come, but God's Word confirms that the day is imminent. We must remain ready.

Reflect and Discuss

1. Identify the purpose and result of the author's summaries in Hebrews, particularly in the passage studied above.
2. Why is the blood of Christ an important doctrine for Christians? What would Christianity lose if the blood language were removed? What does Christ's blood make possible for us? Why?
3. What does the author of Hebrews mean when he says that Christ has opened "a new and living way through the curtain"? How do we enter the presence of God now? Explain the role Christ's priestly work and sacrifice play in this new and living way.
4. Why are we able to draw near to the Father with a true heart and full assurance? How does Scripture affirm that Christians can have full assurance in their salvation? Give examples.
5. How is Christ's sprinkling of his blood related to the sprinkling of blood in the Old Testament? How is Christ's sprinkling superior to the sprinkling of old covenant sacrifices? What does this sprinkling symbolize and accomplish for the believer?
6. How is the washing with water mentioned in verse 22 superior to the washings mentioned in the Old Testament? How do these washings link to baptism? What is the role of baptism in salvation? How significant is baptism for our sanctification? Explain.
7. What is the confession of our hope? Why is it imperative that we not lose this confession? What role does God's faithfulness play in our holding on to our confession? What role do God's promises play in

encouraging believers? Where in Scripture do you see God fulfilling his promises? How do these instances encourage you to hold on?

8. Why does a Christian need the church? What does the church offer to an individual believer that he cannot get elsewhere or on his own? How does the local church help us endure in the faith and hold on to our confession?

9. What role does discipleship in the local church play in the command the author gives in verses 24 and 25? How can Christians help their brothers and sisters with building confidence in salvation? What are some practical ways that believers can encourage one another to have assurance?

10. How might a church better emphasize living in anticipation of Christ's coming? How does eschatology influence daily life? How does it affect your daily life? How should it affect our discipleship and church life?

The Obedience of the Faithful

HEBREWS 10:26-39

Main Idea: A true Christian not only lives a life of obedience to God but also endures and is faithful in the midst of persecution. The one who places his faith in Christ will ultimately have reason for confidence in the promise of hope at his return.

I. **A Fearful Warning (10:26-27)**
II. **The Judgment of God (10:28-31)**
    A. Disregarding the law of Moses
    B. Three marks of apostasy
    C. In the hands of the living God
III. **The Faith of Those Who Endure (10:32-39)**
    A. Recall the earlier days
    B. Those who do not draw back

The Bible's hard passages help us grasp a fuller understanding of the whole counsel of God. If we skip over challenging passages, we will become biblically impoverished. Consequently, when our Bible reading is impoverished, so too is our growth in godliness. We must seek to understand the Bible's difficult parts by reference to its clearer parts. As the Reformers taught us, Scripture interprets Scripture. Difficult passages become clearer when we set them within the context of the entire canon. Reading Hebrews 10:26-39 requires this approach.

Hebrews 10:26-39 is one of three warning passages in Hebrews. Its admonitions are some of the most severe found in the Bible. They are sobering and haunting, and they ought to drive us toward faithfulness. As the author of Hebrews will soon show, the perils of abandoning the faith are too costly to bear.

A Fearful Warning
HEBREWS 10:26-27

The writer concludes his section of assurance with a warning. The Greek word translated "deliberately" is actually at the beginning of the sentence. He uses this structure to emphasize a specific point for his readers: do not remain in sin. The warning against sinning "deliberately" does not mean that all sin we commit nullifies Jesus's sacrifice for us. Rather, it means that if you continue in sin and definitely refuse to repent, then you essentially reject the gospel and willingly walk the path that leads to destruction. In that sense, there no longer remains a sacrifice for your sins because you rejected the only valid sacrifice and turned your back on the only One who can justify you before God. There is no forgiveness for a person who has made that decision.

What does the author mean by "receiving the knowledge of the truth"? This refers to those who hear and know the gospel and still deliberately and definitely reject it, even though they understand its truthfulness. The author also has in mind those who at one time embraced the Christian faith but have since apostatized. At one time they claimed to be believers, but their profession proved false. Rather than enduring in the faith, they abandoned it to pursue sin (most likely when under persecution). There can be no forgiveness for those who apostatize.

Jesus warns about such people in Matthew 13. He spoke of the gospel seed falling in shallow soil and showing immediate signs of life but dying out when persecution came. The initial sign of life does not describe regeneration, only spiritual interest. The regenerated life, by contrast, is transformed, bears new fruit, and has a lasting eternal impact. This parable, like Hebrews 10:26, is a sobering reminder that hell is full of people who have a clear understanding of the gospel but never bowed the knee to Christ as King. The apostle John also warns us that there will be those who identify with God's people but eventually abandon his church (1 John 2:19). We have been warned. The Bible is clear. Those who go on sinning willfully and deliberately after receiving the knowledge of truth will not find forgiveness in the end.

Verse 28 tells us what is in store for those who go on sinning deliberately. Rather than receiving merciful forgiveness for their sins, they receive justice for them. They await God's coming judgment because they have rejected the Son. Instead of aligning with God's people, the church, they have chosen to identify with his adversaries. The judgment here refers to God's final judgment when he will condemn all of his enemies once and for all. The language of verse 27 also recalls Isaiah 26:11, which details the day God will judge his adversaries with fire. As we will see in a later verse, our God is a consuming fire. Those who reject Christ make themselves enemies of God and will be subject to his wrath. This is a sobering reminder.

The Judgment of God
HEBREWS 10:28-31

The author of Hebrews continues his argument by appealing to the Old Testament again. In this passage he once more compares the Mosaic law with the new covenant. Additionally, he highlights the severity of falling into God's hands on account of one's rejection of Jesus. These are weighty warnings against apostasy. We must not treat them lightly.

Disregarding the Law of Moses

Disregarding the law of Moses primarily refers to breaking the first commandment, which forbids idolatry. The phrase is shorthand for a total rejection of the whole Old Testament law God gave to Israel through Moses. Those who disregard the law of Moses forfeit the right to become children of Israel.

Disregarding the law of Moses, then, should not be thought of in terms of merely ignoring the law. It refers to an egregious and high-handed rebellion against God himself. Thus, those who violated the law in this manner, based on the witness of two or three people, were put to death without mercy. This punishment for committing idolatry makes the words of Hebrews 10:29 that much more severe.

Three Marks of Apostasy

Verse 29 shows that those who trample the Son of God, regard as profane the blood of the covenant, and outrage the Holy Spirit will have an even more severe punishment than that found in the Old Testament. Those who disregarded the law of Moses received an earthly punishment; those who disregard the revelation of Jesus Christ receive a worse punishment. The author of Hebrews employs a rhetorical question to demonstrate just how seriously apostasy will be judged. The offense is threefold: (1) trampling underfoot the Son of God, (2) regarding as profane the blood of the covenant, and (3) insulting the Holy Spirit.

The first offense, trampling underfoot the Son of God, describes those who reject the identity of Christ. Jesus extrapolates this idea in John 14 when he says that if a person rejects the Son, he rejects the

Father. This is a crucial point. Those who reject the divinity of Christ and his sonship reject the Father and no longer have a sacrifice for sins.

The second offense, regarding as profane the blood of the covenant, evokes the Old Testament and the respect for holy things in the tabernacle and the temple. To touch any holy object without being purified was to invite instant destruction. Hebrews 10:29 shows treating the blood of the covenant—that is, the blood of the covenant sacrifice, Jesus Christ—like it was profane is even more egregious than denigrating or belittling the holy objects in the temple (see 1 Sam 2:17). To treat the blood of the covenant as profane essentially means not to believe that the blood of Christ can effect purification for sins. We have already seen the centrality and power of his blood throughout the letter (9:12,14,25-26; 10:19), and verse 29 is no different. We are told that the blood of the covenant sanctifies us. To disregard Christ's blood is to spurn the purification it accomplishes.

The third offense, insulting the Spirit of grace, refers to disparaging the Holy Spirit, which is the equivalent of blaspheming the Spirit (Matt 12:31-32). Because the Father gives the Holy Spirit through Jesus to comfort and help believers (John 16:7), those who reject Jesus also reject the Spirit. Those who apostatize essentially make themselves an enemy of the Holy Spirit, for the Spirit is insulted by those who transgress against Christ.

In the Hands of the Living God

The author quotes from Deuteronomy 32:35-36 in verse 30. Moses spoke these words just before the Israelites entered the promised land. The author uses these citations to anchor his argument that those who sin deliberately deserve worse punishment. The quotations leave little doubt that God will indeed judge those who reject him. His divine vengeance and justice await those who trample the Son, regard his blood as profane, and insult the Spirit. Earthly justice is often inadequate, but the Lord's justice will be perfectly administered. We must not fall into his hands the way Israel did.

This should strike real fear into the hearts of those who disregard Christ. God's final judgment is a matter of eternal horror. We must not trifle with God. Apostasy is no game to be played. It truly is a terrible thing to fall into the hands of the living God, the very God who is a "consuming fire" (12:29). Those who reject the Son have every reason to fear the Father.

The Faith of Those Who Endure
HEBREWS 10:32-39

This passage continues to encourage readers to persevere. The author has encouraged them, warned them, and now exhorts them to endure whatever comes their way. Here the author essentially echoes the words of Jesus in John 16:33. Troubles will come for Christians in this world, but we must take heart; Jesus has overcome the world.

Recall the Earlier Days

In verses 32-34, the author calls these believers to remember the earlier days, which most likely means the years just after their conversion. They should remember their strong zeal for the Lord and how they handled the difficulties they experienced on account of following Christ in a world opposed to him. They endured sufferings for their faith then, so they can endure suffering in their present situation.

The specifics of their sufferings in the earlier days are identified in verses 33 and 34. They were publicly exposed to reproach and affliction. This means that they were not ashamed to make their faith in Jesus public and were insulted and mistreated when they did. They chose to identify with Christ in a fallen world, so society shamed them. Not only did they receive this kind of abuse themselves, but they also chose to identify with others bearing this reproach.

As Christians, we must be willing to endure the same persecution. Identifying with Jesus in a world that does not want him as King will mean becoming victims of verbal abuse, mockery, and shame in the public square. Nevertheless, those who stand with Christ cannot be those who assimilate with the winds of culture.

Verse 34 further develops the experience of these Christians in their earlier days. They had sympathy on those in prison and joyfully accepted the confiscation of their property. "Those in prison" refers to Christians who had been incarcerated for their faith. In the early days of their faith, these Christians showed tender compassion to their brothers and sisters in chains. Though they were not in prison themselves, they chose to identify with those who were persecuted in that way.

Additionally, they endured the plundering of their property with joy. What is remarkable is not that they lost their possessions because they identified with Jesus, but that they responded "with joy" to such persecution. Why were they able to respond in such a remarkable way?

Because they knew they had "a better and enduring possession." They knew a heavenly kingdom with heavenly possessions awaited those who rejoiced when persecuted (Matt 5:12). These believers understood that "better" possessions were in store for those who persevered in the midst of persecution, so they continued to align with Christ—even when it cost them in earthly matters. Moreover, they knew the possession that awaited them was "enduring." They knew their possession in heaven was an everlasting possession that would not be taken away from them and would never expire. This knowledge helped them endure early in their faith, so the author exhorts his readers to recall those days to help them endure in their present circumstances.

We may lose everything for the sake of Christ, but, in an eternal sense, we lose nothing. We may lose possessions, friends, family, and the comforts of this life, but we have a better and abiding possession waiting for us in our heavenly city. As with the believers in the book of Hebrews, what we gain when we endure persecution can never be taken away from us.

Those Who Do Not Draw Back

Verses 35-39 remind these believers of the confidence they now possess in Christ and of the eschatological reward that belongs to them, so long as they continue to endure. The boldness that believers now have on account of their union with Christ is a central theme in the letter. The author again highlights this reality in verse 35. To abandon the faith is to throw away the confidence that belongs to Christians to approach the throne of God. If the readers apostatize, they will lose that confidence and the great reward of eternal life that comes with it.

Verse 36 tells us of our need for endurance and of the promised inheritance that awaits those who persevere. We demonstrate our endurance in the faith if we do the will of God. As long as we obey the Lord and faithfully do his will, we will receive the eternal inheritance he has promised to believers (9:15). This promise may not be fulfilled in our lifetimes, but it will be fulfilled soon, as the next verses indicate. Our inheritance is not an earthly inheritance; it is a heavenly inheritance, a promise fulfilled eschatologically.

The author quotes from Habakkuk 2:3-4 to support this reality. Habakkuk speaks of God's coming judgment on Judah for refusing to do the will of God. The author of Hebrews picks this up typologically to point to the final judgment that is coming at Christ's return. In other words, Habakkuk speaks of God's coming, which the author of Hebrews sees fulfilled in the future coming of Christ. His coming is soon, so we must continue to do the will of God and not draw back in our faith. As verse 38 indicates, the Lord will find no pleasure in us when he returns if we do not go on living by faith.

In verse 39 the author expresses his utmost confidence in his readers by reminding them of their identity and strength as God's people. He proclaims that they will not draw back in their faith and thus will prove their allegiance to Christ until the very end. Destruction awaits those who do draw back, but not those who press on and preserve their souls. They will obtain the life promised to those who endure. In every sense of the word, they will be saved. This is what it means to be a follower of Christ.

These warning passages keep the believer from spiritual complacency. Before learning from and appreciating the faithful examples the author identifies in Hebrews 11, these believers must be reminded to persevere in the faith. Before they can associate themselves with those listed in the following chapter, they must make every effort not to draw away from Christ. It is with this final warning that the author reminds all believers to hold true to the faith and thus to associate with the saints throughout the centuries.

Reflect and Discuss

1. What does the author mean by sinning "deliberately"? How does this kind of sin in particular nullify the sacrifice for sins? How should we think of those who sin deliberately "after receiving the knowledge of the truth"? What does the author mean by this phrase?

2. How does the writer use the law of Moses to anchor his argument against falling away? What does it mean to "disregard" the law of Moses? How does this compare to disregarding the new covenant? How does the punishment for disregarding the Mosaic law compare to the punishment for disregarding the new covenant?

3. To what does "trampl[ing] on the Son of God" refer? What is so shocking/ironic about rejecting the Son of God? How is rejecting Christ's identity related to a rejection of the Father?

4. What does it mean to regard the blood of the covenant as profane? What is so significant about the blood of the new covenant? Consider the many times Jesus's blood is referenced throughout

the book of Hebrews to help you form your answer. How do these verses/passages help inform your understanding of this offense?

5. What does it mean to insult the Spirit? In what way is insulting the Spirit equivalent to insulting the Father and the Son? How do those who apostatize make themselves enemies of the Holy Spirit?

6. How does the author use the two Old Testament quotations in verse 30 in relation to the three marks of apostasy? How does the warning of verses 30-31 discourage you from apostasy and spur you on toward faithful obedience?

7. Recall the early days of your Christianity. What were they like? How was your zeal different then from what it is now? What specific sufferings have you experienced in the past that can help you endure in your present trials?

8. In what ways do you see culture mistreating and misrepresenting Christians in the public square? In what situations have you seen Christians being shamed for identifying with Christ in a fallen world? How have you experienced that?

9. Why were the Christians referenced in the book of Hebrews able to endure their sufferings? Why were they able to respond joyfully at the plundering of their property? What can we learn from their response to such persecution?

10. What is our confidence, especially in the midst of persecution and suffering? How does Christ's impending return charge this confidence? What is the reward for remaining confident? How is our confidence related to our endurance?

11. How are we "saved" by our endurance in the faith? What does the author mean by this? How does this particular warning passage keep you from spiritual complacency?

The Hall of Faith

HEBREWS 11:1-10

Main Idea: Our Old Testament forefathers received the salvific blessings of God by faith. New covenant believers receive these blessings by faith as well and so must emulate the faith of those who came before.

I. **An Invested Assurance (11:1-2)**
II. **Abel's Faith (11:3-4)**
   A. Walking by faith
   B. A faith that still speaks
III. **Enoch's Faith (11:5-6)**
   A. Enoch's example
   B. Faith's impossibilities
   C. Reason for faith
IV. **Noah's Faith (11:7)**
   A. Noah's reverence
   B. Justified by faith
V. **Abraham's Faith (11:8-10)**
   A. Faith of a foreigner
   B. Faithful living for a promised future

Hebrews 11 is one of the most familiar passages in the entire Bible; it's the so-called hall of faith. While familiarity with certain passages in Scripture is wonderful, it can also be dangerous. We may become so accustomed to the words of a chapter that we lose sight of their meaning and function within the section's larger context.

Hebrews 11 comes after a repeated series of warnings to the original audience. The author has been reminding his congregation not to take the gospel lightly and not to have a superficial understanding of sin (10:31). Indeed, he even warns them what is in store for those who spurn the Son of God and set aside the gospel (10:29).

Hebrews 10:32-39 connects the admonitions and exhortations of chapter 10 to chapter 11. "Remember the earlier days when, after you had been enlightened, you endured a hard struggle with sufferings" (10:32). These are words we need to remember as we enter into chapter

11. We must remember the "hard struggle" that the audience is called to endure in the midst of persecutions and trials. As the author reminds them, "We are not those who draw back and are destroyed, but those who have faith and are saved" (10:39). Notice the theme here: perseverance. Perseverance is the demonstration of faith. Faith is grounded in what God has done for us in Christ. The author expresses confidence that his audience's endurance of persecution for the sake of Christ is a demonstration of their faith. This leads us right into the main subject of Hebrews 11.

Additionally, as I have already mentioned many times, one of the author's primary goals is to teach us how to read the Old Testament. Christians must read the Old Testament *Christologically*. God embedded in the history of redemption types and shadows that pointed forward to Jesus Christ. Thus, from Genesis to Revelation the Bible tells one story—the story of the grace of God found only in Jesus Christ.

Yet, we must also remember that reading the Old Testament Christologically does not mean we are imposing something on the Old Testament that is not already there. In fact, one of the most important hermeneutical observations we can glean from Hebrews 11 is that the true people of God in the Old Testament (those with circumcised hearts) understood that the old covenant and all of its attendant features pointed forward to a Messiah. This was something they received *by faith*. In other words, just as by faith we look back to the cross of Christ and his resurrection to receive the salvific grace of God, so too did the Old Testament saints look forward, through the types and shadows of the old covenant, to the Messiah. They thereby received the salvific blessings of God by faith.

An Invested Assurance
HEBREWS 11:1-2

"Approval" does not just refer to temporary material blessings. Rather, this is the final eschatological approval—an eternal commendation instead of an eternal condemnation. It is important to remember that these are the only two options: commendation or condemnation. There is no third alternative. On the day of judgment, we will either be approved in Christ or we will be condemned without him.

How did the people of old win God's approval? In other words, why were the patriarchs and matriarchs of Israel commended? This is not just an important question theologically; it is a particularly important question for the writer and for the original audience. In light of what has come before in this epistle, it would be natural for these Jewish Christians to be thinking, *So what about Abraham? What about Moses? How were they included in this story of God's grace to us in Christ?* The author plainly answers that these men and women received their approval because they exercised faith.

Paul makes this same point in Romans 4:1-12. Abraham was counted righteous before God because of his faith (see Gen 15:6). These passages demonstrate the consistent and clear New Testament teaching that the redeemed from Israel who lived before the death and resurrection of Christ were saved because they trusted God to be faithful to his promises. Their faith was a messianic faith. They had an assurance that they invested in the promises of God. They hoped in things yet unseen, in a deliverer that had been promised but had not yet come.

Abel's Faith
HEBREWS 11:3-4

In verse 3 the author indicates that just as we begin our Christian lives by faith, we also embrace the Christian worldview through faith in the Word of God. We were not eyewitnesses to creation. Simply put, we were not there to experience it. We affirm the divine creation of the cosmos because by faith we receive it from Scripture and affirm with Scripture that everything exists to display God's glory. Even more, as Calvin reminds us, creation is the theater of God's glory in the drama of redemption. We know this by faith.

Walking by Faith

Hebrews 11:4 begins the catalog of biblical characters who function as exemplars of faith. This catalog is interesting on numerous accounts, if nothing else because it provides a great deal of information that we would not know merely by reading the Old Testament. The introductory words *by faith* not only introduce the main theological point of the chapter but also structure the text and provide a powerful rhetorical device for getting our attention.

Furthermore, repeating *by faith* also teaches us to avoid the error of moralizing the Old Testament stories. This happens quite often among evangelicals, particularly in children's Sunday school curricula: "Be like Moses, not like Pharaoh." While the Old Testament narratives do indeed contain moral lessons we ought to learn, the author reminds us that these moral lessons are not the main point. We must remember that the moral lessons of the Old Testament come within the context of the storyline of the gospel. The writer draws some hortatory applications from these individuals, but he does so while reminding us that the reason these men lived as they did was because they walked *by faith*— looking to a Redeemer.

A Faith that Still Speaks

The first "by faith" story mentioned is that of Abel. In Genesis 4 Moses indicates that Abel offered a sacrifice from his flock whereas Cain brought to the Lord an offering of the fruit of the ground. There is of course nothing wrong with offering a sacrifice from a harvest. As a matter of fact, God demanded the firstfruits of the harvest in his statutes given to Israel later in the Old Testament. So why did God accept Abel's sacrifice but not Cain's offering? Genesis does not answer that question. The rest of the Old Testament, however, provides a few hints as to why Abel's offering was accepted. For example, earlier in Hebrews we saw that "without the shedding of blood there is no forgiveness" (Heb 9:22). We see then that Abel's sacrifice was in some sense foreshadowing the entire sacrificial system of the Old Testament and thus the sacrifice of Christ. Abel understood that his greatest problem was that he was under divine judgment, and he needed a propitiatory sacrifice. His blood sacrifice pointed to his own sin and to his hope in God's provision of a sacrificial Savior. This is why Abel's sacrifice was "acceptable" to God: it was offered "by faith" in God's promises (Gen 4:4).

The final statement, "even though he is dead, he still speaks through his faith," is both tremendously interesting and encouraging. Think about it this way: what will be said at your funeral? What words are going to make up the content of your eulogy? How will your life be summarized in fifteen minutes of reflection? Hopefully, we will all leave the type of testimony left by Abel: though he was dead, his life bore witness to the grace and mercy found only in a substitutionary sacrifice. Christians should aspire to leave behind a legacy of faith. They should aspire to leave their eulogists a wealth of material that testifies to the saving power of Jesus Christ, just as Abel did. His faith testified to the greatness of Christ even beyond the extent of his life.

Enoch's Faith
HEBREWS 11:5-6

The Old Testament characters the author chooses to highlight in this chapter are remarkable. We would expect to find many of them. Noah, Abraham, Isaac, Jacob, Joseph, and many of the other Old Testament figures mentioned are major Old Testament characters. But sometimes the author of Hebrews highlights a minor character, someone we might never expect to see in the Bible's own "hall of faith." This is certainly the case when we read about Enoch in verse 5.

Enoch's Example

We know little about Enoch. In fact, he is mentioned in only a few verses in Genesis:

> *Enoch was 65 years old when he fathered Methuselah. And after*
> *he fathered Methuselah, Enoch walked with God 300 years and*
> *fathered other sons and daughters. So Enoch's life lasted 365 years.*
> *Enoch walked with God; then he was not there because God took him.*
> (Gen 5:21-24)

The account of God "taking" Enoch is not very descriptive. In other words, here we have recorded a remarkable end to the life of Enoch, yet we know almost nothing about him and the extraordinary event that ended his life. The only other time in the Old Testament where something similar happens is with the case of Elijah, who was taken to heaven by a fiery chariot.

The author does, however, tell us something important about Enoch: the miraculous end to his life here on earth was a result of his faith. Enoch's faith honored God; thus, God commended Enoch so that "he did not experience death." Faith honors God and God honors faith. Enoch is the prime example of this reality. His faith was a pleasing aroma before God.

Faith's Impossibilities

The author uses Enoch and Abel as his Old Testament proofs of the theological assertion found in verse 6: "without faith it is impossible to please God." These words teach us two important theological truths. First, without faith it is impossible to be *commended*. While works of external righteousness and general morality may commend us before men, these things are not sufficient to commend us before God. Humanitarianism, religiosity, morality, and following the most scrupulous personal ethical codes cannot bring us God's approval on the day of judgment. Without faith it is impossible to please God. There is no divine commendation for anyone who walks uprightly (by the world's standards) without placing faith in Jesus Christ.

Second, with faith it is impossible to be *condemned*. This, of course, is the glory of the gospel. The righteousness of Christ is credited to us such that even our worst sins and most atrocious deeds cannot separate us from the love of God. By faith in Christ's substitutionary sacrifice and resurrection, we can have confidence that we cannot be condemned. As Paul says in Romans 8:38-39,

> *I am persuaded that neither death nor life, nor angels nor rulers, nor things present nor things to come, nor powers, nor height nor depth, nor any other created thing will be able to separate us from the love of God that is in Christ Jesus our Lord.*

Reason for Faith

This leads us directly to the final clause of verse 6: "the one who draws near to him must believe that he exists and that he rewards those who seek him." Faith is that which unites us to the blessings of God. It trusts the promises of God and recognizes that he is not a greedy miser; God is a gracious giver, a "rewarder" of those who trust in his goodness.

This clause makes two primary affirmations: first, we accept the existence of God by faith, and second, we accept the promises of God by faith. Of course, to say that we accept the existence of God by faith is not to claim that we accept the reality of God's existence *against* reason. As the history of theology and philosophy has shown, there are many good reasons to believe in the existence of God and even more reasons *not* to be an atheist. Some of the best and most time-tested arguments for theism are what we call the "classical proofs" for God's existence (the teleological argument, the moral argument, the cosmological argument, and so on). Yet the author of Hebrews reminds us that the ultimate reason we accept the existence of God is because we believe that he has revealed himself in Jesus Christ and that he has spoken in Scripture (1:1-2).

This should not scare Christians. All convictions on ultimate authority are based on faith commitments. Norman Geisler and Frank Turek hint at this in the title of their book, *I Don't Have Enough Faith to Be an Atheist*. In other words, it is not that Christians are people of faith and atheists are people of reason. Everyone has an ultimate intellectual start-ing place, a system of beliefs that are basic to their worldview. Atheists operate from a worldview that is based on a set of assumptions and pre-suppositions that they have received by faith: secular naturalism and materialism. The Christian, however, accepts the biblical worldview as his ultimate intellectual starting point—again, not against evidence and reason but in concert with them.

The second assertion, "that he rewards those who seek him," reminds us of the grace of the gospel. God is a "rewarder" because he gives grace and mercy to those who *trust* in his promises. In the gospel, God makes promises of salvation and declarations about the goodness of his character. When we trust those promises and believe those dec-larations, he fulfills his word and rewards us with his kindness. What a glorious truth! How does one enjoy the blessings of God? By believing that God will make good on his word to shower us with grace if we come to him with the empty hands of faith.

Noah's Faith
HEBREWS 11:7

Noah exemplifies the theological assertion in the final clause of verse 6. How did Noah survive the judgment of God? The answer is not sim-ply that he built a big boat. What motivated the construction of the ark? Noah *believed* the word of God. His actions flowed from the fountain of faith.

Excursus: Theological Observations about Noah

For some reason, many evangelicals underestimate the importance of the story of Noah in redemptive history. Perhaps the reason is because we have often only encountered this story as it is trivially retold in litera-ture designed for little children. Or it might be the case that we simply lose the importance of the flood because it stands between the two theo-logical mountains of the creation and fall narrative (Gen 1–3) and the Abrahamic covenant (Gen 12; 15; 17).

In light of this reality, it is important that we pause to make a few theological observations about the Noah story. First, the Bible is abso-lutely clear that this was a universal flood. The biblical text clearly indi-cates that the flood was a global judgment on all of humanity. Further, the geological features of the earth testify to this reality—from remnants of marine life in the middle of Colorado to the formation of the Grand Canyon.

Second, the flood's origin is divine, not natural. In other words, this was not just a natural disaster like any other. Noah's flood was a divinely orchestrated, supernatural judgment on humanity.

Third, the story of the flood is an essential element of biblical theology. The flood is the archetypal example of God's judgment and the catastrophe of human sin. In fact, throughout Scripture we see that the flood typologically points to God's final eschatological judgment.

Noah's Reverence

With this in mind, let's consider what the author of Hebrews tells us about Noah. First, Noah believed God's warning of a coming flood—an event "not yet seen." This highlights once again the nature of true faith by reminding us of verse 1 (emphasis added): "Faith is the reality of what is hoped for, *the proof of what is not seen.*" In other words, Noah believed divine revelation even in matters of predictive prophecy.

This passage also tells us that Noah constructed the ark "motivated by godly fear." Noah recognized the holiness of God. He knew, as Hebrews states, that "God is a consuming fire" (Heb 12:29). Reverent fear is the only appropriate response to the justice of God. He is wonderfully gracious, but that grace is only truly known against the dark backdrop of his justice and wrath against sin.

"By faith he condemned the world." How did Noah condemn the world? It's not that Noah sat in an official capacity as judge over the antediluvian people. Rather, whenever an individual lives in obedience to God against the immorality of the world, that individual condemns the rest of the world in its unrighteousness. Think of it this way: What happens when you put a light in a dark room? The light stands out from the darkness, and what had previously been unseen is revealed for what it truly is. Often we do not even recognize how dark our environment has become until someone shines a light in it. By the same token, the obedience of a righteous man both reveals and condemns the disobedience of the world.

Justified by Faith

The final phrase of verse 7 is quite remarkable: "By faith he . . . became an heir of the righteousness that comes by faith." We find then in the last phrase of 11:7 the glorious doctrine of justification by faith alone. This phrase shows us that the Old Testament saints were imputed the righteousness of Christ (retroactively) when they believed (see Gen 15:6), just as Christians receive that same righteousness by faith alone.

From a biblical-theological perspective, the ark and those in it stand as a picture of the church. Noah is the exemplar who exercises faith and is saved from God's watery judgment. Even in the midst of the Old Testament's most horrific display of God's wrath, we find an extraordinary display of the grace of God. Noah and his family are saved, not because they are more righteous than others, but simply because "Noah . . . found favor [i.e., *grace*] with the Lord" (Gen 6:8).

Abraham's Faith
HEBREWS 11:8-10

The inclusion of Abraham in the hall of faith is expected but nonetheless significant. Abel, Enoch, and Noah are figures who come before the formation of the nation of Israel. In other words, they are just as much a part of the story of all humanity as they are a part of Israel's story. But Abraham is the fountainhead of the nation. If Abraham lived by faith in the promises of God and in a coming Messiah, then the implication is that all Jews should do the same. If the readers of Hebrews think that to reject Christ is to embrace Abraham, they are mistaken. Embracing Christ is, in fact, to walk in accord with Abraham.

Faith of a Foreigner

Verse 8 can seem fairly complex on first reading, but the point of the sentence is rather straightforward. Abraham's faith is seen in the fact that he left his home country of Haran in Mesopotamia in obedience to God, even though at the time he had no idea exactly where he was going. Of course, this may not strike us as a remarkable act of faith, but that simply proves how unfamiliar we are with the culture of the ancient Near East. The Mesopotamian world could be quite dangerous. Physical protection was often the result of being closely knit to one's kin and community. Travel was particularly hazardous since it separated a person from his place of protection and exposed him to marauders and thieves. In this light, the fact that Abraham left Haran and traveled to a land that he did not know is indeed a remarkable act of trust in God.

Verse 9 indicates that even though the Lord promised to make
Abraham a great nation and that his descendants would possess the
land, Abraham himself lived his entire life as a foreigner in the land of
Canaan; he was not a resident. By faith he beheld something that was
coming, but he never saw the fulfillment of those promises of fruitful
land and vast descendants. This verse also indicates that the covenant
promises were passed through Abraham to Isaac and Jacob. These three
individuals form the patriarchal foundation of the nation of Israel. They
too were "coheirs [with Abraham] of the same promise."

Verse 10 explains the content of Abraham's faith and the motivation for his obedience. "He was looking forward to the city that has
foundations, whose architect and builder is God." The imagery of a
"city" in contrast to Abraham's nomadic experiences is quite powerful.
Abraham lived in tents. Tents do not rest on "foundations." Foundations
imply permanence.

Faithful Living for a Promised Future

There are two important points in this passage. First, the city that God
builds is an eternal city. The city that God builds will not be like the cities of Mesopotamia, Egypt, or even ancient Rome, which once called
itself "the eternal city." These places have come and gone. They have
been sacked, marauded, plundered, and pillaged. All that now remains
of them are ruins. But the city that God is building is truly the eternal
city. It is entirely secure, unshakable, and cannot be destroyed. By trac-
ing the theme of "city" through Scripture, we find that this promised
city is the "new Jerusalem" described in Revelation 21:9-27.

Second, Abraham walked in faith *by* setting his hope on the fact that
God would act and bring about eschatological salvation. Abraham was
not just looking forward to inheriting the land of Canaan; he was looking beyond Canaan to what it foreshadowed—the city of heaven coming
to earth and God's restoration of creation. Abraham framed his entire
existence by living in anticipation of the fact that God would be faithful to his promises. In other words, Abraham was faithful *in the present*
because of his confidence in what God would do *in the future.*

Let's be candid. If you do not have any assurance of joy in the life to
come, then it makes sense to pursue all the pleasure you can in this life.
As Paul says in 1 Corinthians 15:32, "Let us eat and drink, for tomorrow
we die." As Christians, however, we cannot place our ultimate satisfaction and hope in the promises and pleasures that *this* world has to offer.

We must live *by faith*, recognizing that one day we will experience a joy that is greater than any joy we can know here in this life. The joys of this world are fleeting and passing. But the joys of heaven are eternal, abundant, and never-fading. If we live for those joys, we will set our affections on eternity, live meaningful lives for Christ, and endure suffering in his name as we look for the joy that awaits us in God's heavenly city.

Our cities, our homes, and the comforts of this life are fleeting. This is not an eternal city, but Christians know that there is a city where Christ is King. Faith in Christ is what grants us citizenship in that city. Abraham saw that city even while he was a wandering tribesman in the middle of the desert; that is what faith looks like. We may not be wandering tribesman in the desert, but all Christians are pilgrims in land that is not our own. The sandcastles of this world must not distract us from the heavenly city that awaits. In that city we put our hope.

Reflect and Discuss

1. How does the end of Hebrews 10 connect to Hebrews 11? What does perseverance have to do with faith? How does faith motivate our perseverance?

2. How does the author once again teach us in Hebrews 11:1-10 how to read the Old Testament? How did people in the Old Testament look forward to the Messiah and receive salvation from God?

3. Explain in your own words how the people of old received their commendation or approval from God. In what did they place their faith? How is their faith the same as our faith? How is it different?

4. What is the danger of merely moralizing the characters we encounter in the Old Testament? How does the phrase *by faith* help us avoid the error of moralizing Old Testament stories?

5. How does Abel still speak, though he is dead? After considering the manner of your life right now, what would be said about you in your eulogy? What might you need to change so that your faith continues to speak even after you've passed?

6. Why shouldn't Christians fear placing faith in the biblical worldview? How do all worldviews—whether atheistic or theistic—necessitate some degree of "faith"? How does this passage help us see that faith and reason are not opposed to one another, but actually work in concert? What is the ultimate reason Christians accept the existence of God?

7. In what way(s) does Noah demonstrate the assertion the author makes about faith in verses 1 and 6? What does God's holiness have to do with our reverence for him? How does Noah's faith "condemn the world"?

8. How does Noah's faith demonstrate the doctrine of justification by faith? How does this demonstrate the similarity between Old Testament saints and new covenant believers? How does the ark picture the church?

9. How does the certain reality of a future and everlasting kingdom encourage you to press on by faith? How did this reality motivate or encourage Abraham? How does our present faithfulness relate to God's future faithfulness?

10. In what ways can this world and all that it offers interfere with our faith in God and his future promises? What comfort do you find in knowing this world is not our home? How can you, like Abraham, frame your life in a way that anticipates the fact that God will be faithful to his future promises?

The Faith of Abraham, Sarah, and Those Who Died in Faith

HEBREWS 11:11-19

Main Idea: Sarah and Abraham characterize true faith by believing in God's promises in difficult circumstances and trials.

I. The Faith of Sarah in Childbearing (11:11-12)
II. The Faith of Those Who Died in Faith (11:13-16)
III. The Faith of Abraham in Child Sacrificing (11:17-19)

In the previous section the author focused on Abraham's faith. By faith Abraham obeyed and followed God's command to go to Canaan, even though it seemed God was calling him to nowhere. Yet this "nowhere" was the very land God would promise to give to Abraham. From that place God would bless the nations through Abraham. The letter's attention to the man demonstrates his pivotal role in salvation history and his place in the annals of those who endured in the faith. Now the author continues to focus on Abraham's faith but also includes that of another: Abraham's wife, Sarah.

The Faith of Sarah in Childbearing
HEBREWS 11:11-12

As we saw in the previous passage, the people of old received their commendation *by faith*. What is Sarah's commendation? She "considered that the one who had promised was faithful." These verses emphasize the power of trusting in God. By faith this woman trusted God to be faithful to his word, so she "received power to conceive offspring."

When most of us consider the process of conception, we don't think of a woman necessarily *receiving* power to conceive. As a matter of fact, most people never stop to consider the theological implications behind the reality that each and every conception of a baby is the inauguration of a new human life, a new image-bearer of God. The Bible tells us that conception is not merely an act of biology, which conveys two important implications we need to consider. First, there are no accidental births.

Every human being is made in the image of God and comes to life because God says, "Let there be life." Second, there are no naturalistic births. Scripture speaks of God opening the womb. God is ultimately sovereign, even over the conception of children.

Sarah was praying for the ability to have a son, which is referred to here as the "power to conceive offspring." Furthermore, she was not praying for conception because she desperately wanted children. She was praying because she wanted to be in line with the promises God made to her husband. She was very much aware that Abraham was to father a great nation, implying she was to mother a great nation. To understand this, we must understand Genesis 15.

Even though God made great promises to him, Abraham lacked an immediate heir; his only heir was one of his slaves, Eliezer of Damascus. Abraham was an old man who despaired that his seed would ever receive God's promises. Yet despite Abraham's wavering, he is still counted among the faithful because he "believed the LORD, and he credited it to him as righteousness" (Gen 15:6). Faith, even faith that is wavering as was Abraham's, can qualify a person as "faithful." Abraham believed that the Lord is faithful to his promises. Sarah also believed that "the one who had promised was faithful" (Heb 11:11), and for that faith she was credited and rewarded. God reaffirmed his promise to Abraham's family: "I will bless her; indeed, I will give you a son by her. I will bless her, and she will produce nations; kings of peoples will come from her" (Gen 17:16). In the context of Genesis, Abraham and Sarah are in the middle of nowhere with a bunch of sheep. Their little entourage doesn't look like a nation. In response to God's renewed promise, "Abraham fell facedown. Then he laughed and said to himself, 'Can a child be born to a hundred-year-old man? Can Sarah, a ninety-year-old woman, give birth?'" (Gen 17:17). In the continuing narrative, a child is born, and this child, Isaac, becomes the heir of promise. The Lord does exactly as he had promised. "The LORD *came* to Sarah as he had said, and the LORD *did* for Sarah what he had promised" (Gen 21:1; emphasis added).

Hebrews 11 summarizes these events in Genesis, and Sarah is commended because of her faith: "Sarah herself . . . received power to conceive offspring, even though she was past the age." Sarah was ninety—not even close to the age for bearing children. But in his sovereignty, God chose a ninety-year-old woman in order to make a point about his power to fulfill his promises. "She considered that the one who had promised was faithful." There's the essence of the faith that saves. "Therefore from one man—in fact, from one as good as dead—came offspring as numerous as the stars of the sky and as innumerable as the grains of sand along the seashore" (Heb 11:12). The writer of Hebrews wants to communicate to his readers what faith looks like. Faith looks like a one-hundred-year-old man and a ninety-year-old woman believing that God will fulfill his promises, even when the fulfillment of those promises seems impossible according to human reason.

The Faith of Those Who Died In Faith
HEBREWS 11:13-16

Verse 13 takes us back as far as Abel in verse 4. Those listed in Hebrews 11—all of these Old Testament figures—died in faith. They lived trusting in God to keep his promises and died according to those promises. They saw the promises of God, but did not see them fulfilled. Abraham died before seeing the children of Israel march into the promised land. But he died in faith. It's one thing to live in faith, but it's an entirely different thing to be facing your own death and still trust God to fulfill his promises. This is exactly what the patriarchs listed in Hebrews 11 did. They saw God's power and faithfulness with eyes of faith, and thus they saw what their physical eyes never saw: God's future fulfillment of his promises. They knew God was faithful, so they never stopped believing.

The author describes their journey of faith in terms of a pilgrimage to a city. As the patriarchs got closer, they saw the city's glow, but they knew they were not going to make it there in their lifetimes. Still, they endured in their faith having "confessed that they were foreigners and temporary residents on the earth." As exiles and strangers on the earth, the patriarchs—and ultimately all who endure in the faith—were seeking a different city. This is exactly what Peter says of Christians when he calls them "those chosen, living as exiles" (1 Pet 1:1) and "strangers" (1 Pet 2:11). Paul echoes this sentiment when he tells us "our citizenship is in heaven" (Phil 3:20). Like the saints of old, we long for a home that is heavenly.

By both their words and their actions the patriarchs demonstrated that they were foreigners and resident aliens on this earth. This is what verses 14-15 make clear. The author suggests that if the patriarchs had kept looking backward, they would not have maintained their faith until death. Nothing prevented Abraham from going back to Haran—nothing except faith in God's promise. The people of God don't look backward. They look forward because they are absolutely convinced God's promises are true.

As we have seen multiple times throughout this letter, the word *better* is vital to the argument of the author, and in verse 16 he uses this word again. The patriarchs looked for a *better* city. They looked for a *better* country. Following the writer's logic, everything is infinitely *better* in Christ. Grounding themselves in the faithfulness of God and in the certainty of his promises, the patriarchs didn't just long for earthly fulfillment; they longed for a heavenly reality of these promises.

As a result of the enduring faith of our forefathers, God was not ashamed to be called their God. The implication of this is that God is ashamed of some people—namely, those who did not die in faith. God was ashamed of those who did not demonstrate belief that he could do what he promised. But for those of whom he is not ashamed, he has prepared a city. God promises a heavenly city—a heavenly kingdom—to those who endure in faith, even unto death. We are guaranteed this city in Christ.

The Faith of Abraham in Child Sacrificing
HEBREWS 11:17-19

In Genesis 21 God told Abraham that the covenant promises would continue through Isaac, not Ishmael. In Genesis 22, when Isaac was probably around the age of twelve or thirteen, Abraham faced an excruciating test:

> *God tested Abraham and said to him, "Abraham!"*
> *"Here I am," he answered.*
> *"Take your son," he said, "your only son Isaac, whom you love, go to the land of Moriah, and offer him there as a burnt offering on one of the mountains I will tell you about.* (Gen 22:1-2)

Genesis 22 is one of the most important and also one of the most infamous passages in all of Scripture. God tells Abraham to take Isaac—the son he loves and the son who will continue the line of promise—up to the land of Moriah and to sacrifice him there as a burnt offering. We know what a burnt offering is. A burnt offering happens when an animal is slain, its blood is drained, and its carcass is burned. Any father told to do this to his son would be tested beyond anything he could possibly imagine, and this is how Abraham was tested.

Remarkably, the text tells us Abraham obeyed the Lord:

> *So Abraham got up early in the morning, saddled his donkey, and took with him two of his young men and his son Isaac. He split wood for a burnt offering and set out to go to the place God had told him about. On the third day Abraham looked up and saw the place in the distance.* (Gen 22:3-4)

Though the Lord's instructions seemed to run counter to his promise to Abraham, the man did as God commanded.

Yet in the end we see that God's command did not run counter to his promise. Abraham believed God was able to raise Isaac from the dead if he was sacrificed. This is the commentary the author provides in verse 19. Abraham's own words in Genesis 22:5 show that he believed Isaac would return alive: "Stay here with the donkey. The boy and I will go over there to worship; then we'll come back to you." Therefore, because Abraham responded in faith to God's command, God reiterated his promise to Abraham: "I will indeed bless you and make your offspring as numerous as the stars of the sky and the sand on the seashore. Your offspring will possess the city gates of their enemies" (Gen 22:17).

In a sense, Isaac did die. This is what the second half of Hebrews 11:19 points out. He didn't die physically, but he did die in a figurative sense. He was taken right up to the point of death and then brought back to life. So in a sense we can say that Isaac died and was resurrected. In this way, this story and Isaac's role in particular anticipate the death and resurrection of Jesus Christ, our great high priest.

Abraham passed God's test because he was committed to God's promises. He showed faith in God through his willingness to obey God's command and sacrifice his son. He trusted God to deliver Isaac, and he may have even perceived that doing so would be the greatest display of God's glory. That's the story of the gospel. God has determined to save sinners and has done so in a way that brings him the greatest glory possible. This explains why God, who loves his Son to an even greater degree than Abraham loved Isaac, sent his Son to die for us. God's word is true and his promises always come to pass, even when we can't envision how he will do what he has promised. Nevertheless, we are called to obey him and follow him—*by faith.*

Reflect and Discuss

1. How did Sarah demonstrate her faith? Why is this considered faith? What makes the promises of God—no matter how absurd they may sound or seem to us—so worthy of our trust and obedience?

2. How is Sarah's prayer for the "power to conceive offspring" tied to the promises God made to Abraham? What is the author using the example of Sarah and Abraham to communicate to his readers?

3. What does God's promise to Sarah teach us about the process of conception? How does this differ from what today's culture is telling us about birth and childbearing?

4. Who are the "all" in Hebrews 11:13? How did they die "in faith"? What didn't they see? Why is the author describing their journey in terms of a "city"? How is this important?

5. How was Abraham a foreigner and a temporary resident? What does this language communicate to you? Why are these appropriate words for describing Christians? What can we learn and apply to our own lives from Abraham and the other patriarchs living as resident aliens?

6. Why is Abraham's testing significant? Explain how God's command to Abraham did not run counter to his promise to Abraham. What did Abraham believe God would do through the sacrifice, and how does the author use Genesis 22:5 to display this in Hebrews 11:19?

7. In what sense did Isaac die in the land of Moriah? How do Isaac's role in Genesis 22 and the author's commentary in the second part of verse 19 anticipate the death and resurrection of Jesus Christ?

8. See Genesis 22:10-14. What did God provide in place of Isaac? How does God's provision of a substitute sacrifice point to Jesus as the ultimate sacrifice? How do the story of Isaac's sacrifice and the story of the gospel bring God the greatest glory possible?

9. Why do you think the author of Hebrews holds up Abraham and Sarah in particular as examples of faith in this passage? How is Isaac an example of faith?

Faith in the Faithfulness of God

HEBREWS 11:20-40

Main Idea: Life within the covenant family of God is marked by faith and trust in his covenant promises.

I. The Future-Looking Faith of Isaac, Jacob, and Joseph (11:20-22)
II. Moses's Faith-Fueled Obedience (11:23-27)
   A. Faith fixed on the worth of God
   B. Faith bearing witness to Jesus
   C. Faith trusting in the unseen
III. Surprising Faith in the Covenant-Keeping God (11:28-31)
IV. Final Examples of Faith (11:32-40)
   A. Flawed lives marked by remarkable faith
   B. Old promises fulfilled in a new covenant

In this passage the author gives us a glimpse of the spiritual ancestors who went before us, those through whom God initiated his work of redemption. Though they were not perfect, Scripture holds them up as examples of faith from whom we ought to learn. They serve as paradigms of what it means to live faithfully, trusting in God and his promises. They did not throw away their confidence, and therefore they did the will of God and received what was promised (10:35-36). As we read this passage, we need to remember that it isn't merely a summary of Old Testament history; it's part of every Christian's story. These examples are not merely Israel's patriarchs, matriarchs, and heroes of the faith. They are also ours. We are members of the same family under the headship of the Lord Christ.

The Future-Looking Faith of Isaac, Jacob, and Joseph
HEBREWS 11:20-22

Isaac was the son through whom God would fulfill his promise to Abraham, yet the building of the nation would ultimately take place through his sons, Jacob and Esau. Isaac passed the promises he had received from his father to his sons (Gen 27:27-29,39-40). This demonstrated his trust in God's promise that through Abraham's heir his offspring would be as numerous as the stars (Gen 15:1-6; Gal 3:29). Isaac looked to the future and believed God would fulfill his covenant promise to Abraham.

Like his father, Jacob also trusted God to keep his promise. Even as he neared death, he blessed his sons and anticipated what God would do in the future (Gen 48:1-22). His faith was future oriented and fixed on God's faithfulness.

Similarly, Joseph looked forward in faith and trusted that God would redeem his people from Egypt. As the text says, he anticipated the day he would return to Israel (Gen 50:24-25). That would only happen when God led Israel out of Egypt and into the land of promise. For Joseph to look forward to the exodus and to communicate that to his sons is almost as shocking as Abraham saying to Sarah, "We are going to have a child." Nevertheless, Joseph demonstrated remarkable trust in God's plan. He believed God would not leave or forsake Israel in a foreign land. That is faith—the kind of faith we are to emulate.

Moses's Faith-Fueled Obedience
HEBREWS 11:23-28

Faith Fixed on the Worth of God

The author continues exploring the exemplary faith of Israel's patriarchs. Here he particularly concentrates on the faith Moses displayed during the events of the exodus. When the author says Moses was hidden because he was "beautiful," he is not saying Moses was hidden because he was a cute baby. Rather, Moses's beauty alludes to his particular destiny. Moses was a beautiful child because he was set apart for a specific task by God: leading Israel out of Egypt and into Canaan. Therefore, his parents were not afraid to disobey the king's edict that every son born to the Hebrews be cast into the Nile but every daughter be allowed to live (Exod 1:22). Instead of acting in fear, Moses's parents saw the exquisite quality of their son and trusted in God.

In verse 24 the spotlight shifts from the faith of Moses's parents to Moses's own faith. If Moses had not rejected sonship to Pharaoh's daughter, he would have been choosing the fleeting pleasure of sin. The choice before him was ultimately this: comfort and privilege in the house of Egypt or persecution and suffering with the people of Israel.

Making the former choice is faithlessness; the latter is faithfulness. Moses chose the latter. Rather than laying claim to stature, he aligned himself with Israel because he trusted the Lord and knew Egypt was not his home. Moses recognized the vanity of Pharaoh's house and the all-surpassing worth of obedience to God.

Faith Bearing Witness to Jesus

Verse 26 raises an interesting question: What does Christ have to do with Moses's rejection of Egypt? The storyline of Scripture rests squarely on the promise of a coming Messiah. The author of Hebrews demonstrates that Moses's mistreatment ultimately pointed to Jesus, the very Messiah who would come to redeem his people. Moses himself wrote that a prophet would come who was greater than he and who would fulfill God's promises (Deut 18:15-22). The covenant promises, in which these Old Testament saints believed, all find fulfillment in Jesus (2 Cor 1:20). Moses, therefore, was looking for the One who would redeem Israel, and the reproach he endured because he identified with the Israelites bore witness to the reproach Christ would bear for his people.

By choosing persecution instead of the fleeting pleasures of sin, Moses acted in accordance with his faith in God's promise. The reward for trusting in God and his promise rather than in the wealth of man is greater than everything this world can offer. Indulging in sin will bring great pleasure, but that pleasure is temporary. Joining Jesus in his reproach, like Moses did, brings an everlasting reward and unending joy.

Faith Trusting in the Unseen

Moses also demonstrated his faith in God by leaving Egypt. Note the parallel with Joseph. Moses, like Joseph, knew that Egypt was not his home; it was not the promised land. He left because he believed God's promises to Israel. Verse 27 is a reminder of a basic biblical principle: we must decide whose anger we fear more—the anger of the world and its governing authorities, or the anger of the Lord, the One who will judge the living and the dead. Moses clearly understands who God is: the Lord, sovereign over all. Thus, Moses did not fear Pharaoh. Instead, he followed God.

Though it may seem odd, the author's point that God is invisible is very important. Recall the first verse of this chapter: "Faith is the reality of what is hoped for, the proof of what is *not seen*" (emphasis added). Not only is this truth—God is invisible—the essence of theism (we do not look to an idol), it is also connected to the trust displayed by those mentioned in this chapter. Their trust in promises was intimately connected to their trust in God. As they trusted in the unseen God, so they trusted in the unseen fulfillment of his promises. This is the very essence of faith.

Verse 28 identifies Moses's faith in keeping the Passover. The substitution pictured in the Passover foreshadowed the final perfect Lamb who would be slain for the forgiveness of those who put his blood on the doorpost of their hearts by faith (Isa 53:7; Matt 27:14; Acts 8:26-40). Led by Moses, the Israelites kept the Passover, not doubting that God would keep his promise to them. The death of the firstborn son would have ended the covenant promise to Abraham. But Israel's firstborn were protected. Why? Because Moses did not waver in availing himself of the substitutionary sacrifice God provided. He trusted God to be faithful.

Surprising Faith in the Covenant-Keeping God
HEBREWS 11:29-31

Verse 29 mentions one of God's most extraordinary and miraculous displays of his lordship: the parting of the Red Sea. It was a foretaste of the redemption that would come when Jesus liberated sinners. The author of Hebrews, an inspired interpreter of the Old Testament, makes explicit what is implicit in Exodus: it took faith in the trustworthiness of God to walk across the seafloor as one would on dry land. What held the water back? God, in his providence, keeping his covenant promise to Israel. This is why, when the Egyptian army tried to cross, the water was released and they were drowned.

Verse 30 moves us from the exodus to the battle of Jericho (Josh 6). It is rather curious that the author would draw our attention to faith demonstrated by Israel at Jericho. After all, Joshua does not record anything about the people's faith. Nevertheless, the writer says that they obeyed the Lord's battle plan in faith.

In verse 31 the author takes us from Jericho to the story of Rahab, which at first seems like a dramatic shift in content. Until this point, the author has identified people we naturally assume would be set forth as examples of faith. *Rahab*, however, is not a name we expect to find on this illustrious list. A prostitute is not one typically described as faithful to God. Still, he puts Rahab forward as an example to emulate. How did she trust God and why is her faith commendable, despite her occupation? Rahab hid Israel's spies and informed them how they could escape (Josh 2). As a result, Rahab and all her household were spared (Josh 6:22-25). She was not motivated by courage, self-protection, or some political calculation. She was motivated by faith. Rahab trusted in the God of Israel not only to fulfill his promise to his people but also to protect her from the destruction of Jericho. In a time of danger, she identified herself with the people of Yahweh and believed his promises, even though she was not an Israelite. Hers is truly a faith worth emulating.

Final Examples of Faith
HEBREWS 11:32-40

As we come to the chapter's end, it is as if we have experienced a great symphony. There has been expansive movement across many portions of the Old Testament. And now the list of characters culminates in a crescendo of final examples. Even though we may be less familiar with them, the central message intended is the same: the individuals were marked by an astonishing faith in God. The same should mark us.

Flawed Lives Marked by Remarkable Faith

The lives of those mentioned in this passage serve as examples for us. Were they perfect examples? No. Luther's dying words, which underscore our need, apply to them: "We are beggars. This is true." Gideon demanded signs from God and led Israel to sin when he made an ephod (Judg 6:36-40; 8:24-27); Samson was sexually promiscuous and broke his covenant with God (Judg 13–16); Jephthah vowed to sacrifice his own daughter (Judg 11:30-31,34-40); David committed adultery with a woman and tried to cover it up by arranging the death of her husband (2 Sam 11). Even so, the author does not remember them for their flaws. He commends them for their faith. Though they sinned, their lives were ultimately marked by their faith in God, which the author highlights in verses 33 and 34. They failed yet accomplished each of these feats by faith, so they serve as examples of remarkable trust in God.

Verses 35-38 shift our attention to those who suffered for the sake of Christ by faith. The women receiving back their dead is probably a reference to the work of Elijah in 1 Kings 17:17-23 and the work of Elisha in 2 Kings 4:18-36. These women trusted God and so received back their dead. Those who experienced the terrible suffering the author details did not fail in their faith, even in the midst of their persecution. They believed God would not fail to give them the promised land and trusted he would raise them to life on the last day. Though they were counted righteous by their faith, they were despised by the world for their devotion to God, so "the world was not worthy of them."

The author is not calling us to die like they did, but he is calling us to trust in the covenant Lord like they did—even if that means suffering a death like theirs. Justin Martyr, an early church father, echoed this same kind of faith. When beholding the very place where he and his congregation would be martyred, Justin said, "Remember brothers and sisters, they can kill us, but they can't hurt us." This is the kind of devotion that marked these Old Testament saints, and it's the kind of devotion we should display in our own lives.

Old Promises Fulfilled in a New Covenant

The author ends the symphony of chapter 11 by taking his readers back to its beginning, namely the theme of 11:2. These saints only had preliminary glimpses of God's wondrous fulfillment of his promises. They did not live to see the coronation of King Jesus on the cross of Calvary. Still, they are commended for their extraordinary faith in God's promise. They did not receive the ultimate fulfillment of that promise, but they recognized that they would experience it eschatologically. Their faith, like that of those the author discussed earlier, was a future-looking faith.

This again highlights the supreme significance of the new covenant. It was only in the establishment of the new covenant by the blood of Jesus that the old covenant promises could be fulfilled. This is what the author means in verse 40. Apart from the new covenant, there is no hope of perfect, unmitigated fellowship with God on the last day.

Reflect and Discuss

1. Do you actively remind yourself of the promises God has made to you as a member of the new covenant? How does remembering the promises of God affect the way you live? How do they help you fight sin and strive for holiness?

2. Are you feeling at home in this world? Do you long for comfort in the culture in which you live? How can you better prepare for the day when Christ will return and you will be home in every sense of the word? How can you fight against feeling at home in this world?

3. How did Isaac, Jacob, and Joseph demonstrate faith in the covenant promise of God? How did Joseph's faith in particular point to the exodus?

4. What does it say of Moses's parents that they hid him in spite of the possibility of retribution from the government? In what ways might we be forced to practice similar acts of faith in our own cultural context? Is your life marked by the same lack of fear of man that Moses's parents displayed? If not, why?

5. What things did Moses do that demonstrated his faith? How did his actions reveal the worth of God? Does your life say the same—namely, that the worth of God is all-surpassing and the pleasures of this earth are fleeting? In what way can you actively demonstrate the worth of God in your own context?

6. In your own words, explain what the author means by mentioning reproach for the sake of Christ in relation to Moses. How do the events of the exodus point to Jesus?

7. Does the inclusion of Rahab the prostitute in this list surprise you? What does this tell us about God's character toward sinners who put their faith in him?

8. How should God's faithfulness affect how we understand our circumstances? How do those who suffered for their faith encourage you to endure?

9. What does it mean to have a future-looking faith? How did all of the examples in this chapter demonstrate a future-oriented faith? In what ways might new covenant believers do so?

10. What does the author mean when he says that these saints "would not be made perfect without us"? What does the new covenant have to do with their perfection?

Run the Race

HEBREWS 12:1-11

Main Idea: Christians ought to look to Jesus, who endured the full weight of suffering, and trust in the Father's benevolent providence through all trials and hardship.

I. Run the Race (12:1-3)
   A. The spiritual race
   B. The source and perfecter
   C. Consider Jesus
II. The Father's Discipline (12:4-11)
   A. The place of the Lord's discipline
   B. The purpose of the Lord's discipline

The author of Hebrews provides a list of faithful examples in chapter 11. He then uses these examples as a basis for urging his readers to remain faithful. But the point of this passage is not to look to our earthly fathers but to look to Jesus, our ultimate source for finding strength and for obtaining a proper understanding of the heavenly Father's discipline. Believers look to Christ because he endured suffering for the church's salvation. The hostility he bore was the hostility his people deserved. None of the Old Testament figures suffered or acted for the elect in the way Christ did by substituting himself. Christ, therefore, is the key focus.

Run the Race

HEBREWS 12:1-3

The New Testament is full of metaphors. Jesus frequently uses agrarian metaphors, such as the parable of the Wheat and the Weeds. We also find many military and athletic metaphors in Paul's epistles. Here the writer of Hebrews employs a clear athletic metaphor, which again indicates that he was probably writing to a congregation of Hellenized Christians in one of the great cities of the empire. The athletic metaphors would make the most sense where the games were most prominent, in a city like Alexandria, for instance. Thus, the author calls us to a great race. This great race is one that takes place in a stadium filled with Old Testament saints. This is not merely a coliseum of spectators; it's a coliseum of enduring saints who have already finished running.

The Spiritual Race

The last four chapters of Hebrews contain the author's spiritual exhortation to endure. He begins chapter 12 with the word *therefore*, which is his hinge from examples of Old Testament saints to application in the life of the believer. No athlete would intentionally run a race carrying weights, so believers must "lay aside every hindrance." One of the most horrifying truths about sin is that it clings to the sinner. Christians would like to say that once we have come to faith in Christ, sin assaults us no more. Unfortunately, it's not easily shed. God's Word never says that sin will stop assaulting or enticing us after conversion. Instead, Scripture gives warnings and examples, as Paul does in Romans 7. Sin is a real threat with which Christians must constantly contend. This is why the author commands us to throw it off and lay it aside. If we don't, we won't endure.

We must also run the race "with endurance." In typical races the vast majority of people only watch. Very few actually run. In the Christian life, the starting pistol has been fired. From the moment of our salvation until the moment of our death, all are running a race. Paul tells Timothy, "I have finished the race" (2 Tim 4:7). All believers want to be able to say the same. Finishing the race is the product of endurance. God's elect endure to the end and finish the race set before them.

No believer runs with endurance by his own strength. We are beset with weaknesses. What endurance we run with is entirely of Christ. We only endure because we belong to him. As 1 Peter 1:5 teaches, we are being guarded by God's power. But this does not mean that we passively endure. God does not honor the saints of the Old Testament because they were passive. They were actively faithful. Likewise, God calls us today to a race that requires active faithfulness.

The Source and Perfecter

What will be the key to our strength? The author just took us through the catalog of the faithful in Hebrews 11. It begins with Abel and ends with those unnamed who were stoned, sawn in two, killed with the sword, or otherwise afflicted and mistreated. The world was not worthy of these, forcing some of them to wander about in deserts and mountains, to live in dens and caves. At this point the reader might assume that he would be told to look to that great host of witnesses. But that is not what the author states! Verse 2 tells the church to look to "Jesus, the source and perfecter of our faith."

Christianity is not a cult of hero worship. It is centered on the singularity of Jesus Christ. We are not here because of Abel, Moses, Abraham, or even those who were sawn in two or those who wandered the earth living in caves. The church exists because Jesus died and rose again, and the only way to endure is by looking to him. This great cloud of witnesses encourages and inspires us, but the One who keeps us in the race is Christ alone.

Verse 2 describes Jesus in two ways:

- Source
- Perfecter

The meaning of the word *source* is clear. Jesus is the One on whom our faith is founded. He is both the cornerstone and the capstone. He is the unshakable ground on which our hope and salvation rest. Without him, our faith is futile and we have no basis for belief. If Jesus is not who he says he is, then our faith is in vain (1 Cor 15:14-15). It is not an overstatement to say that the entire Christian faith rests on the validity of Christ's person and work.

He is also the *perfecter* of our faith. Does that mean that he alone perfectly lived the Christian life? Although that's true, that's not the author's point. That would be superficial. By perfecter he means "finisher" or "the One who completed it." Christ's work was perfect when he said, "It is finished," and when the Father honored his obedience by raising him from the dead. Christ's work is still perfect today. As the author has made abundantly clear, Jesus continues to act as our mediator and will succeed in bringing his people home. In other words, Christ has done all things necessary to secure our salvation, and he will see his work through to the end.

This passage is exhilarating for Christians even without the context. But the context of the athletic games adds a further layer of depth that's not there without it. Athletes competed in the games to win the prize at the end. In the ancient Greek and Roman games, the prize at the end generally was a laurel crown. It was not worth much itself, but earning it brought considerable fame. In the ancient world, fame was difficult to acquire. People were typically famous due to noble birth, inherited wealth, or military genius and prowess. Through athletics, people could become well-known, improve their standing, and enter a new realm of life as the champion. After those games, the winner was granted the honor of sitting with royalty. This is how the author describes Christ at the end of his race. Christ endured the cross for us, not because he was looking for monetary or societal gain or because he wanted to wear a laurel crown. Instead, he despised the shame, refusing to see it as shame, and wore the crown of thorns for our good and his Father's glory.

Consider Jesus

The writer again reminds his people to consider Jesus in verse 3. The author isn't asking them to merely take Christ under consideration. By *consider*, he means to hold up Christ as a model and to constantly look to him for inspiration and encouragement. Jesus shows his followers how to be found faithful in the end. This is not a new argument in Hebrews. The writer is echoing his exhortation from chapter 3. The only way to endure and stand firm is to consider Jesus. He endured great hostility in the race.

It doesn't take much pain to get our attention or much hostility for us to feel persecuted. There are persons right now enduring vehement physical persecution because of their faith in Jesus Christ. There are people being flogged, beaten, imprisoned, separated from their families, and even martyred in his name. I was in the Middle East several years ago, and I met an Iranian pastor who had scars on his back from being beaten by the secret police with chains. It was an unforgettable sight. This is the kind of hostility the author of Hebrews is talking about.

While the increasing secularization occurring in the West may marginalize and malign Christians, this passage specifically speaks of physical persecution and the shedding of blood. This is a reality for many Christians around the world, which evokes the extreme persecution first and second century Christians experienced. Thinking of physical hostility, the writer of Hebrews reminds us that our Redeemer was tortured. Jesus was flogged, whipped, and endured this hostility against himself. Considering what Jesus Christ endured will help us endure in a world that continues to grow more and more hostile and opposed to Christianity. We must fix our eyes on him if we are going to persevere.

The Father's Discipline
HEBREWS 12:4-11

The struggle is not just against persecution. It's also a struggle against sin. In other words, the author is saying that resisting the temptation to fall away can also be described in terms of resisting the temptation to fall into sin. The temptation to avoid persecution or to abandon the faith is ultimately the temptation to submit to sin.

The "not yet" in verse 4 is critical. Although some Christians might not yet have experienced physical persecution, it remains a real possibility for all of us. We must always remember that the comfort we know now is not guaranteed to last forever. Things can change quickly, and in many parts of the world they do. Almost instantly, countries change regimes, constitutions, or law enforcement approaches. Persecution of Christians can happen anywhere at any time, and it can quickly lead to the shedding of blood.

The Place of the Lord's Discipline

Recall that the author is writing to a Jewish congregation. His readers are Jewish converts. They are familiar with *torah* and with the Old Testament. They know the Wisdom literature of the Old Testament, including Proverbs, which is cited in verse 5. In Proverbs 3:11-12, Solomon was warning his son not to make light of the Lord's discipline. He does not want him to scorn God's discipline because discipline is a sign of sonship. The very presence of the Lord's discipline in a person's life is evidence that the person is loved by God. This concept is something that the readers are intended to understand instinctively. The concept actually works backward to a confused and generally undisciplined generation such as our own, but this is exactly the truth Solomon was trying to communicate to his son.

Administering discipline is a parent's job. No one disciplines someone else's children. The one who disciplines is treating the recipient like a son or daughter. When Solomon writes to his own son, whom he disciplined, he essentially says, "You should take the Lord's discipline as the sign of how much he loves you, in the same way that I discipline you because I love you." The writer of Hebrews assumes that discipline is an act of love by the righteous parent who understands his child's need.

The Purpose of the Lord's Discipline

Discipline is by nature unpleasant. It is painful, but it has a purpose. Parents know what they're doing. Children don't always know why they're being disciplined or how the discipline is an act of love, but it's not necessary that children understand these things at every point. If children understood all this in advance, they would not have done whatever it was that required the discipline. Certain lessons can only be learned by discipline.

The author continues his discussion and reveals the purpose of discipline. It is to bring "the peaceful fruit of righteousness" into the child's life. Because the parent loves the child, he always disciplines in a reasonable, firm, authoritative, and yet loving and righteous way. A father shows his son that he loves him through his discipline. If he did not love him, he would let him run wild. But he wants this son to know the peaceful fruits of righteousness. To show him this, the father's love must sometimes take the form of discipline.

People tend to think that things happen to them by chance. The truth is that things come into our lives by the sovereign intentions and purposes of the Lord. Not all things are good, but all things are for the good and edification of those who love God. Sometimes Christians have to keep faith when things do not seem to be for our good.

In Romans 8 Paul describes that God is working in all things for the good of believers. This doesn't mean we need to be thankful for the development of tumors or other tragic things that happen. These aren't things for which we would ask or pray. Yet even in difficult situations, God is working for our good. It's this truth that the author has in mind as he writes this passage of Hebrews. God, as a loving Father, may be disciplining us, sharpening and maturing our faith.

When people think of discipline, they often think only of corrective discipline or punishment. But discipline is far more. It is teaching. God is making disciples through his discipline. It is tempting to complain about discipline and to think it is a sign that God does not love us. Christians question how God can work for good through horrifying loss. Yet God was working for our good in the gruesome death of his Son. If ever we doubt God's love because of our circumstances, we can look to the cross and remind ourselves that God gave us his own Son so that we might in turn become sons of God.

Reflect and Discuss

1. Why is comparing the Christian life to a race such an apt analogy both for the author's audience and for Christians today? How does the analogy of a race apply to your life?

2. What three things are the people told to consider in verses 1-3 to help motivate them in their run? How does knowledge of the "large cloud of witnesses" encourage you? In what ways does Jesus encourage you?

3. Why does the author tell us to "lay aside every hindrance and the sin that so easily ensnares us"? What effects do sin and hindrances have on our spiritual races? How do they affect our endurance? Do you think these metaphors refer to the same thing? Why or why not?

4. What does active faithfulness look like? In what particular ways do you see Old Testament saints practicing active faithfulness? In what ways can you practice it in certain situations you experience?

5. What is the goal and finish line of the Christian race? In other words, why are we encouraged to endure? What did Christ receive for his endurance? How does considering Jesus motivate you to endure?

6. Why does God allow his people to endure persecution? What is the proper Christian response to it? List some of the various forms of persecution Christians experience.

7. Why might God discipline his church? What does the presence of God's discipline in someone's life indicate about that person? How should the Christian respond to evidence of God's discipline in his life? How might this help to mature faith?

8. Why can Christians trust that the Father's will is benevolent and perfect? What are some verses of Scripture that affirm the goodness of God's character and his plan, even in the midst of difficulty?

9. How does discipline as described in Proverbs and in this passage of Hebrews differ from our culture's concept of discipline? Contrast the purpose of the Lord's discipline with the way the world uses it.

Running to Finish the Race

HEBREWS 12:12-17

Main Idea: In order to finish the race of the Christian faith, we must clear all obstacles, encourage one another, and heed the warning of Scripture's negative examples.

I. **The Charge: Keep Running (12:12-13).**
II. **The Challenge: Live Holy Lives (12:14-17).**
   A. Pursue peace and holiness.
   B. Watch over one another.
   C. Avoid Esau's example.
   D. Heed the warning.

Those who study communication believe certain gestures are recognized in almost every culture. For instance, smiles and frowns universally communicate happiness or sadness. No one needs a translator to understand a look of resignation or a gesture of defiance. In this passage the author of Hebrews speaks about the Christian life with metaphorical language that makes use of universally understood gestures: drooping hands, weak knees, lame feet, and other imagery. These word pictures help us understand the Christian life as the exhausting struggle that it can be at times. And they also show us how to continue running this great race with endurance and perseverance.

The Charge: Keep Running

HEBREWS 12:12-13

We need to understand the context in order to grasp what the writer means when he says "strengthen your tired hands." At the beginning of the chapter he exhorts us to run the race by following the example of those who ran before us. The "therefore" at the beginning of verse 12 refers to the discipline he spoke about in verse 11. In other words, because the author knows that the Lord disciplines his church for its own joy, he encourages his people to persevere in trials and to be strong in the Lord.

The writer also exhorts God's people to "strengthen your . . . weakened knees." Weak knees are an almost universal illustration of fear. You don't have to be a Jew or a Gentile, or an ancient or a modern to get this. Thus, the author encourages this congregation to keep standing in the Lord despite difficult circumstances, presumably persecution. The race may be grueling, even deadly, but we do not run in vain.

The writer metaphorically speaks of our physical posture in order to address something of deeper spiritual significance. As Christians, we know that we were created for God's glory. We understand that God is sovereign and has a purpose for us. Even when he disciplines us, we must trust his goodness, knowing that it makes us more like Christ. Rather than being resigned to whatever fortune falls our way, we sincerely want what God desires for us. And so we have reason to strengthen our tired hands and weakened knees. We run for the joy set before us.

Although odd sounding at first, "make straight paths" is actually an immensely powerful expression when understood in its biblical context. The author is almost certainly drawing this idea from Isaiah 35, a chapter depicting Israel's return to Zion from exile (see also Isa 40:3-4). If you are going to run a race well, you will need a clear path, and to get a clear path, you will need to remove any obstacles. You don't want to leave any dangerous spots where you could twist an ankle or trip over a rock. Here the author is commanding these runners to clear their paths. These paths are moral ones that lead to righteousness. We need to free ourselves from the kinds of obstacles and dangers that are designed to trip us up. We must arrange our lives so that sin's opportunities to ensnare us are significantly reduced.

Should we fail to clear our paths, we will not find healing and will remain out of joint. It is what the second half of verse 13 teaches. It is common sense, but we have a hard time obeying this command. Rather than making our paths straight and running after Jesus, we avoid opportunities for accountability and entertain our sin just enough to keep it alive. The danger in this, of course, is that we are never healed, remain crippled in our sin, and eventually turn away from the Lord. Clearing our paths and following Jesus, on the other hand, will spiritually restore us.

The Challenge: Live Holy Lives
HEBREWS 12:14-17

Verses 14-16 string together a chain of moral imperatives that those running the Christian race live by. These imperatives give us a picture of holy, faithful running that stays the course to the very end. Conversely, the author also gives us a picture of unholy living in the person of Esau. We are told not to fall away as he did.

Pursue Peace and Holiness

The call to pursue peace is a very important Christian imperative. Notice verse 14 does not say, "achieve peace with everyone." It says we are to "pursue peace with everyone." We may not be able to achieve peace, but Christ's people are those who strive for it and are known for doing so. And notice we're called to do so "with everyone." We are not merely to seek peace with those in our own circles of concern, but with everyone with whom we engage. This exhortation echoes Paul's charge to the Christians in Rome: "If possible, as far as it depends on you, live at peace with everyone" (Rom 12:18). Seeking peace with everyone is part and parcel of the path of righteousness on which the author encourages his people to run.

In this same verse the author also exhorts his audience to pursue holiness. He warns that no one will see the Lord without it. Thus, holiness is required for the believer. Holiness is not a mark of unregenerate people, nor is it a mark of those who are falling away and failing to run the race of Christian faith. Here the author is using the term *holiness* to describe those who are pursuing the Lord. This does not mean those who run are perfect or sinless, but it does mean they are fighting sin and living faithfully. No one will see the Lord without this holiness, which makes the moral imperative to make straight paths for our feet eternally significant.

Watch Over One Another

The writer continues his chain of commands in verse 15. Believers should be vigilant that no one in the community of faith fails to receive the grace of God. While we may think of the grace of God in an evangelistic sense, this is not the author's focus here. He is speaking of the ongoing grace of God, which believers experience through the preaching of the Word and the Christian disciplines. In this context of the new covenant community, the readers were called to watch over one another—from the weakest brother to the strongest—so that all in their midst would grow in holiness and obtain the grace of God.

He also commands his people to see to it "that no root of bitterness springs up, causing trouble." Believers must be on guard against the poison of bitterness. Bitterness is a deadly contagion and a sign of serious spiritual trouble. It's an on-ramp to the way of sin, not to the way of righteousness, tearing apart the church as it spreads. We do not necessarily make a cognitive decision to become bitter, but we allow a wrong to fester just enough that it takes root in the heart. Thus, we must stop bitterness at the root, lest it spread to others in Christ's body and make us unclean.

In addition to remaining on guard against bitterness, we are also called to see to it "that there isn't any immoral . . . person." While other forms of immorality certainly exist, the Bible addresses sexual sin with particular candor. We live in a day that minimizes sexual sin, but the Bible maximizes its severity. Why? Because, as we read in 1 Corinthians 6:18, "Every other sin a person can commit is outside the body, but the person who is sexually immoral sins against his own body." Sexual immorality not only violates the law of God; it also defiles our own bodies, which are temples of the Holy Spirit (1 Cor 6:19-20).

Avoid Esau's Example

In the same breath, the author tells us not to be irreverent like Esau, who sold his birthright for a single meal. Is there a relationship between Esau and sexual immorality? Scripture gives us no indication that Esau was sexually immoral, so it does not seem that the combination is meant to point to Esau's sexual sin. Rather, the conjunction in the sentence— sexually immoral *or* irreverent like Esau—indicates the strong relationship between sexual immorality and irreverence. They are both markers of unfaithfulness to God.

Like those listed in Hebrews 11, the example of Esau is meant to encourage us to persevere in the faith. Yet, we are not encouraged to imitate his example; we are to avoid it at all costs, for his example was not one of faithfulness to God. Rather, Esau traded away his birthright in order to alleviate the physical discomfort of hunger (Gen 25:29-34). A single meal was more important to Esau than the birthright that belonged to him as Isaac's firstborn son. Trading it away to Jacob demonstrated his disinterest not just for his birthright, but for the holy things of God. In fact, Moses says that Esau's actions show that he "despised his birthright" (Gen 25:34). Thus, the author of Hebrews appropriately identifies Esau as irreverent, unfaithful, and unworthy of our emulation.

Why does the author regard the selling of a birthright as unholy? Esau's privileged position as Isaac's firstborn son designated him as the one who was to bear the responsibility of the family and carry his father's name and role after Isaac's death. Having such an honor and privilege was a direct result of God's sovereign choice. Therefore, what

Esau did was unthinkable. It was a crime not only against his family but also against Yahweh—the One who bestowed the birthright on Esau. He committed the offense willingly; he did not give it up by force. He let the appetite of his belly lead him into a serious offense against God.

Heed the Warning

This is not the end of Esau's story, though. After trading away his birthright for a bowl of stew, Esau longed to receive the blessing of the firstborn from his father. Jacob, however, deceiving Isaac, received it instead (Gen 27:27-30). When Esau learned of the blessing he had lost to his brother, he bitterly begged his father to bless him as well (Gen 27:34), but the original blessing could not be revoked.

Esau stands as an example of someone who regrets what he has done but does not truly repent of his wrongdoing. There is a crucial distinction between regret and repentance. God never rejects true repentance, but he has no interest in worldly regret (2 Cor 7:10). Esau does not respond in such a way that communicates genuine repentance over his offense. He simply regrets that he has lost his birthright and his blessing as the firstborn. It is not repentance that Esau seeks with tears, it's only what he's lost to Jacob: his father's blessing.

True repentance requires a hatred of sin. Tears alone do not signal repentance. There are many people who are brokenhearted over their sin, but they do not repent. They do not agree with God about what their sin is. They do not understand that their sin demonstrates a need for Jesus. They may show regret, but they are unwilling to repent. This is the warning the author presents to us in the person of Esau.

By drawing our attention to Esau, the writer presents us with two options: either we can follow the example of those who were faithful until the very end, or we can follow the example of Esau. We need the honesty and candor of Scripture not only for its positive examples but also for its negative examples. We must not follow the steps of Esau. We must heed the author's warning and run the race with faithfulness by truly seeking to turn from our rebellious ways.

Reflect and Discuss

1. What is the relationship between the Lord's discipline and the exhortation to strengthen our tired hands and our weak knees? How does verse 11 lead to the exhortation in verse 12? Why are Christians able to run with the kind of posture described in verse 12?

2. What obstacles are currently on your path, tripping you up in a spiritual sense? In what ways are you entertaining sin and not waging war against it? Do you have accountability and discipleship built into your life, helping you "make straight paths" for yourself?

3. What does pursuing peace have to do with the path of righteousness on which Christians run? What does the writer mean when he exhorts us to "pursue" peace with everyone? What does striving for peace look like inside the context of the local church?

4. How do Christians pursue holiness? If holiness is a divine gift, then in what sense can we legitimately strive for holiness? According to the way the author is using the term *holiness* in verse 14, would this be an accurate word to describe your life right now?

5. What does it mean to "fall short of the grace of God"? How should we understand this phrase? What role do we have in making sure that others obtain the grace of God?

6. Summarize a time when bitterness caused division in your church. How was it addressed? From where does such bitterness generally come? What are some practical ways that help us guard each other against bitterness?

7. Why do you think the author lists the command to make sure that no one is sexually immoral among these other imperatives? How is sexual immorality particularly destructive to our personal holiness? How is it related to Esau's irreverence? What do both demonstrate?

8. How does the poor example of Esau encourage you to endure? How does trading away his birthright demonstrate irreverence? What implications can you draw for your own life from his irreverence? How are you tempted to disregard the holy things of God in order to ease physical discomfort or temptation?

9. What is the difference between regret and repentance? Why is regret such an insufficient response to our sin? Why is it not enough to be heartbroken over our sin? Which biblical figures regretted their wrongdoing without repenting of it?

10. In addition to the positive and negative examples given in Hebrews and throughout Scripture, are there other people in your life whose examples of faithfulness or unfaithfulness teach you? How does the author use a portrait of unfaithfulness to warn his readers and encourage them to endure?

An Unshakable Kingdom

HEBREWS 12:18-24

Main Idea: Those who endure in the faith come to Zion, the mountain of God's new and better covenant mediated through Jesus Christ. His blood satisfies God's wrath and permits God's people to enter God's presence freely and confidently.

I. **Mount Sinai (12:18-21)**
   A. The scene at Sinai
   B. A dramatic scene change
II. **Mount Zion (12:22-24)**
   A. Reading eschatologically
   B. Joining the angels and the firstborn
   C. Hearing the better things of Jesus's blood

This passage is the climactic point the author has been building toward for the last eleven chapters. In Hebrews 13 the author makes closing application points and exhortations similar to the way Paul normally ends his letters, but the real culmination of the letter occurs in the final verses of chapter 12

Mount Sinai

HEBREWS 12:18-21

The word *for* requires the reader to look backward. It grounds what the author is about to say in what he has just finished saying in verses 12-17. This section, therefore, provides the reason why Christians can strengthen their tired hands and weakened knees and make straight paths for their feet. They can do these things because they have not come to Sinai. They have come to a better mountain: Mount Zion.

The Scene at Sinai

The reference to Sinai also requires the reader to look backward, this time all the way back to the Old Testament. The phrase "not come to what could be touched" points the reader back to the origin of the law at

Mount Sinai (Exod 19). Mount Sinai was the mountain Moses climbed to receive God's law on behalf of Israel. The Lord commanded Moses to warn the people of Israel not to go up the mountain or to touch it, lest they die (Exod 19:12). They could not touch the mountain because God's presence consecrated the place and set it apart from the sinful people. If an uninvited sinner touched the mountain when God was present, he or she would be put to death. When the Lord was present on the mountain, it was consumed by a thick smoke, earthquakes, thunder, and lighting (Exod 19:16). It was wrapped in smoke and trembled greatly because the Lord had descended on it in fire (19:18). Furthermore, the mountain resounded with a very loud trumpet blast, one that grew louder with every blow (19:16,19). All of this demonstrated the presence of God on the mountain. It represented his incomparable power, might, and sheer holiness. Thus, this mountain was a place of awe and terror for Israel. As they stood before it, they trembled in fear. This was the mountain to which the people of Israel had come.

Hebrews 12:19-20 continues expressing the terror related to the encounter and its effects on the people. When the Lord spoke from the midst of the smoke covering the mountain, the people begged for Moses to speak to them instead (Exod 20:18-19; Deut 5:24-27). The congregation was even commanded to stone to death any animal that touched the mountain (Exod 19:12-13). The severity of this command demonstrated the costliness of uncleanness in the midst of God's holy presence. The Israelites feared for their lives. The author of Hebrews uses the command to execute animals to show just how incomprehensibly terrifying God's presence on Sinai was for the people of Israel. It was so fearsome that even Moses was afraid.

A Dramatic Scene Change

Israel had come to this terrifying place; they had come to Mount Sinai. But this is not the mountain to which Christians have come. The word "not" in verse 18 is key to understanding the radical difference between our experience with God and Israel's experience with him. "Not" draws a stark contrast between the old and new covenants, the law and grace, and the promise and fulfillment.

The claim that Christians have come to Mount Zion would have shocked the original audience. Jews defined themselves and their history through Sinai. That mountain is where the Israelites met God, but it's not where Christians meet God in the new covenant. That's the point the author is trying to make by portraying the horror and dread the Israelites felt at the foot of Mount Sinai. He paints this terrifying picture of Sinai for his readers in order to make the contrast with the radiant, glorious, and gracious new covenant. The awful terror of Sinai, which is not the mount to which we have come, shows the radical mercy of Zion. At Zion God embraces us with his grace and administers to us a covenant where he does not merely write the law on tablets of stone but on the tablets of our hearts.

Mount Zion
HEBREWS 12:22-24

In the Old Testament we find that the earthly Zion was part of Jerusalem, captured by David (2 Sam 5:7). Mount Zion eventually was so identified with Jerusalem that it became synonymous with the city. Here, however, the author is not connecting Zion with the earthly Jerusalem; he's connecting it with the eschatological new Jerusalem. One of the reasons the author contrasts Zion with Sinai is to emphasize what Zion represents. As we have already noted, the Jews saw Zion as synonymous with Jerusalem. Zion was the city of promise and peace.

Furthermore, the distinction drawn between Sinai and Zion shows us that Christ perfectly fulfilled what Sinai represented. Christians do not come to Sinai, since Christ fulfilled the law of Sinai. Jesus did not nullify or invalidate the Old Testament law. Rather, he did what no sinful human could do: he perfectly obeyed and fulfilled the law. He fulfilled it in its letter and its spirit, which means that he obeyed it externally and internally, with his behavior and in his heart. Thus, because of Christ's work Sinai now stands as a mountain of fulfillment. And this fulfillment, of course, occurred on Zion, in Jerusalem, for Jesus accomplished his saving work and resurrection from the dead in the vicinity of Jerusalem. Thus, God's people no longer identify with the place that God's law was given, but with the place that God's law was fulfilled.

Reading Eschatologically

A proper reading of verses 22 and 23 requires that we interpret them through the lens of the already-not yet tension we find throughout the New Testament. The kingdom of God is inaugurated (already) though not consummated (not yet). In other words Christians can experience, in part, the fulfillment of God's promises even as they await the complete experience of those promises in the new creation. This is the tension we feel between this age and the age to come.

We have already seen the author speaking in terms of the already–not yet in Hebrews 2:8. The writer speaks in similar terms here in Hebrews 12:22-23. Coming to Zion hasn't been fully actualized in our experience, but it is a certain and promised reality. We've already come to the city of the living God in one sense, but that reality is not yet fully consummated. In other words, we've already come to Zion, but we're still waiting to get there.

Thinking in eschatological terms also helps us understand the word *city*. The word *city* is significant because it reveals an important point about God's kingdom. God reigns in his kingdom, but he doesn't just reign from any old place; he reigns from "the city of the living God." Speaking of the city reminds us that it will be the seat of the kingdom. Even as Jerusalem was the capital of Israel, so the heavenly Jerusalem will be the capital of God's kingdom. In coming to Zion, we have come to the chief city of God's kingdom and reign.

Joining the Angels and the Firstborn

Whom will we join there? We will join innumerable angels in festal gathering. This is something we can't possibly imagine. The city of the living God is filled with countless angels shining in the glory of God. Such a picture is indescribable, but it is nonetheless a picture of what awaits those who endure until the end.

Remember how Hebrews began. It opened with the author identifying Christ as the One superior to angels and the One with a name more excellent than theirs (1:4). But this doesn't mean that angels should be considered worthless in light of Christ. Angels are still superlative creatures in that they radiate the glory of God and testify to God's saving acts in Christ. In the heavenly Jerusalem, myriads of angels will joyfully gather to celebrate and worship the Lord. We've come to a city populated with tens of thousands of angels in festal gathering. We will join them in eternal citizenship and in the eternal worship of God.

Who are "the assembly of the firstborn whose names have been written in heaven"? In one sense, the author is referring to those he held up as examples of faith in Hebrews 11, those who trusted Christ even before his incarnation. But in another sense the assembly of the firstborn is much more than that. In Hebrews 12:1 the writer tells his readers that a great cloud of witnesses surrounds them. As we have already seen, those who were faithful to God and his promises even before Christ came make up this great cloud of witnesses. As we also saw, the author tells his people then—and believers today—that they are united in faith with those who have gone before them, with the firstborn enrolled in heaven. Because we are a part of the heavenly Jerusalem, we are a part of this congregation. We have already joined in eternal membership with the congregation of the firstborn who are enrolled in heaven. This is the church eternal and the church universal, and it is the church to which we have come.

Coming Before the Judge and to the Spirits of the Righteous

Verse 23 also tells us that we have come to God himself, the Judge of all. Just imagine the day in which all human beings in the history of humanity will be judged. For those who are righteously judged on account of their sin and never knew salvation in Christ, the day of judgment will be a day of unmitigated horror. Eternal hell stands on the other side of that day. But for those who have turned to Jesus Christ in faith and repentance and trust in his condemnation in their place, the day of judgment will be a day of unmitigated glory. Eternity with the only infinitely righteous, gracious, and merciful God stands on the other side of that day. The author of Hebrews talks about this day as if we're already there. We're already standing before God, the Judge of all. We're already standing before his throne.

Finally, the writer says that his readers have come to "the spirits of righteous people made perfect." This is speaking of all who come to Zion. There will be no one who is imperfect in heaven. No unrighteous or imperfect person will be in the heavenly assembly. We will not be righteous or perfect by our own accord. Our righteousness and perfection depends entirely on the imputed righteousness of Christ. His perfection is our perfection. His righteousness is our righteousness. There is no human righteousness in Zion. There is only Christ's righteousness.

Hearing the Better Things of Jesus's Blood

The author's list of things to which we've come climaxes with Jesus Christ. Now we've come to Jesus, the mediator of a new covenant, and to the sprinkled blood that says better things than the blood of Abel. Jesus's priestly work is the foundation of this city, so it is fitting that the writer caps this list by drawing our attention back to the blood of Jesus.

As we have already seen, the triumphant list of the faithful in Hebrews 11 begins with Abel (v. 4). God evidently ordered Abel's sacrifice of blood, and Abel obeyed. His obedience testified to his faith in God and his word, but his sacrifice of blood could not save him. The blood spilled through the animal sacrifices restrained the wrath of God for a time, but those sacrifices did not satisfy the wrath of God forever. The blood of Christ, however, accomplished what the animal sacrifices never could. His blood is sufficient to forgive sin and to save us from the judgment that sin deserves. Therefore, Jesus is the mediator of a new and better covenant. By his sacrifice and his sacrifice alone, we come to Zion and to the sprinkled blood that says better things than the blood of Abel. Christ's sprinkled blood says better things than Abel's because Jesus's blood saves. It completely washes away our sin and satisfies God's wrath once and for all.

This paragraph is the crescendo of the book of Hebrews. It reminds us in both poetic and prosaic terms that we are not going to that old mountain ever again. Sinai has been displaced and the old covenant has been fulfilled. We've come to a new mountain and a better covenant. We've come to Zion. God does not call us to a mountain we're not allowed to touch. He calls us to a Savior, the same Savior who told Thomas to place his finger in the holes of his hands and to place his hand on the wound in his side (John 20:27). In Christ, the old law has been annulled and a new one has been ratified. This new law does not condemn or judge us. Rather, by Christ's better blood, it guarantees for us an eternal inheritance and secures final forgiveness of sins. His blood brings us to Zion and into the glorious presence of the living God. These are better things indeed.

Reflect and Discuss

1. How does this passage relate to 12:12-17? How does the fact that you have *not* come to Sinai help you put into action the author's imperatives in verses 12-17? Think about each imperative in particular.
2. Why does the writer juxtapose Mount Sinai with Mount Zion?
3. How does the author use the command to stone an animal to draw out the severity of the scene at Sinai? How has Jesus displaced this command in the new covenant?
4. In your own words, explain why the use of the word *not* in verse 18 is so critical to understanding this passage and our relationship to God in the new covenant.

5. Why is Sinai no longer the mountain on which Christians define their experience with God? On what basis do Christians now come to Zion?

6. How should Christians think of the old covenant in light of Christ's fulfillment of it?

7. Explain why a proper reading of verses 22 and 23 requires reading through the lens of the already-not yet tension.

8. What is the significance in connecting Zion to the eschatological new Jerusalem? How does the author's usage of the word *city* play into this significance? What does it tell us about God's kingdom?

9. Why is Jesus's blood superior to the blood sacrifice offered by Abel? Why does the author compare the blood offered by Abel with the blood offered by Jesus?

10. How does the glorious picture of Zion in this passage help you endure in the faith? Why do you think the writer chose to use this picture to motivate his readers to endure until the end?

God's Impending Judgment

HEBREWS 12:25-29

Main Idea: God has spoken to us in the person and work of his Son, Jesus Christ. If we, like the Israelites, reject his merciful Word, we will not escape his coming judgment.

I. **He Who Speaks and Warns (12:25)**
   A. Do not reject his words.
   B. Those who reject will not escape.
II. **All That Remains (12:26-27)**
III. **An Unshakable Kingdom and Its Holy King (12:28-29)**

Certain passages in the Bible are particularly vivid, either in promise, judgment, or warning. Hebrews 12:25-29 is one of these vivid passages. It gives a stern word of caution. The warning advises against neglecting the gospel of Christ and refusing to hear God's Word. It is a sobering warning and one we must heed and take to heart.

He Who Speaks and Warns
HEBREWS 12:25

The author begins verse 25 similarly to 12:18. By placing the command in the negative rather than the positive, he gives greater emphasis to the following directive. The writer urges us to listen intently to the one who is speaking—that is, not to ignore God's Word. He goes on to explain the serious eternal consequences that arise by rejecting the one who is speaking.

Do Not Reject His Words

The idea of God speaking is essential to the entire passage and even the entire letter—indeed to all of Scripture. From the beginning of Hebrews, the author establishes God as a speaking God (1:1). In the Old Testament, God speaks directly to Israel. In Deuteronomy 4 God spoke through Moses to tell the children of Israel that he is their God. Thus, Israel belonged to God precisely because God spoke to them.

They were God's people because God told them so. Furthermore, Israel knew God existed because they heard his voice.

The verb *reject* is important to note. Our modern cultural context as well as general lack of attentiveness to the text often causes us to present the gospel in terms of consideration rather than command. This verse, though, helps us see that the gospel is never presented solely as an offer to be considered. It is presented as an ultimatum, as something to be either received or rejected. Presenting the gospel always produces a response. One either hears the gospel and believes it unto salvation or hears the gospel and rejects it unto eternal judgment.

Those Who Reject Will Not Escape

This passage also contrasts God speaking the old covenant to Israel with God now speaking to all peoples in all places through Jesus Christ. This is what the heaven-earth contrast insinuates. It is an argument from the lesser to the greater. If the consequences of disobedience under the old covenant given on earth through Moses were severe, imagine the consequences for rejecting the new covenant spoken from heaven through Christ! If those on earth did not escape God's judgment, how can those who turn away from him who speaks from heaven escape his judgment?

Again, the author's choice of words is significant. Why does he choose to use the word *escape*? Escape what? God's wrath against those who reject his Son. The Bible is straightforward about the certainty of God's holy wrath against sinners. Those who reject the word God has spoken through Jesus Christ will not escape his wrath. This is an essential part of the gospel, a part Christians should not be embarrassed to proclaim. Our rebellion against God merits his wrath. Praise God that he has placed that wrath on his Son for all those who repent and believe—for those who do not reject his word and do not turn away from his warning. If we reject Jesus, we will not escape wrath.

All That Remains
HEBREWS 12:26-27

The author continues drawing out the contrast between heaven and earth in verses 26 and 27. At first he considers what happened on Sinai when God shook the earth with his voice and caused an earthquake on

Sinai (Exod 19:18; Judg 5:5). Then the author quotes from Haggai 2:2-9. Here the Lord promises to shake both the heavens and the earth.

> *"Speak to Zerubbabel son of Shealtiel, governor of Judah, to the high priest Joshua son of Jehozadak, and to the remnant of the people: 'Who is left among you who saw this house in its former glory? How does it look to you now? Doesn't it seem to you like nothing by comparison? Even so, be strong, Zerubbabel—this is the Lord's declaration. Be strong, Joshua son of Jehozadak, high priest. Be strong, all you people of the land—this is the Lord's declaration. Work! For I am with you—the declaration of the Lord of Armies. This is the promise I made to you when you came out of Egypt, and my Spirit is present among you; don't be afraid.'"*
>
> *For the Lord of Armies says this: "Once more, in a little while, I am going to shake the heavens and the earth, the sea and the dry land. I will shake all the nations so that the treasures of all the nations will come, and I will fill this house with glory," says the Lord of Armies. "The silver and gold belong to me"—this is the declaration of the Lord of Armies. "The final glory of this house will be greater than the first," says the Lord of Armies. "I will provide peace in this place"—this is the declaration of the Lord of Armies.*

The Lord's word is crystal clear in Haggai 2. He is verbally ensuring the restoration of his temple. The Lord affirms that he owns all things and that his Spirit is in the midst of the people. He will do what is necessary to restore the temple to its former glory. He also claims that he will shake both the heavens and the earth and all nations, which means that he will judge the world.

The expression *yet once more* serves as a reminder that God's shaking has happened before and will happen again. God's judgment is looming. He shook the earth once at Sinai, and he will shake it again in such a way that encompasses all creation. Thus, the author picks up the words of Haggai in order to continue emphasizing the certainty of God's coming wrath and judgment of the world.

In verse 27 the writer seeks to explain his usage of the expression *yet once more*. The phrase signals the removal of the present world and pictures all its idols crushed, broken, and cast down. God will destroy all that man has made. All that remains will be that which belongs to the Lord. We should not put our hope in this present world, for nothing in it will continue. As the author of Hebrews will tell us in the next verse, let us indeed be grateful for receiving a kingdom that cannot be shaken.

An Unshakable Kingdom and Its Holy King
HEBREWS 12:28-29

The kingdom that remains is the kingdom of God's purchased people, who by virtue of their union in Christ will not be shaken. All other kingdoms, however, will ultimately face God's coming judgment. They will crumble and fall. For this, God's people should respond with reverent gratitude and worship.

What brings us together and causes us to worship every Lord's Day? Gratitude to God for giving us the gospel and a kingdom that cannot be shaken. While everything around us may look permanent now, it will pass away in an instant. Yet God's people will remain. Nothing can stop God's kingdom from triumphing over the kingdoms and rulers of this world. His kingdom and its citizens will prevail. It cannot be shaken. This is why the author exhorts his people to be grateful to God.

Additionally, he exhorts them to offer acceptable service to God. The idea behind acceptable service is the same one we find behind Romans 12:1, where Paul states we are to submit ourselves as a living sacrifice to God. All of life is worship and is to be a response to the One who redeemed us by the blood of the Lamb. When we present our whole selves to God in this kind of worship, it pleases the Lord. Acceptable service is about being a living sacrifice.

"Reverence and awe" must characterize true Christian worship. We should not flippantly and haphazardly approach the One who will shake the heavens and the earth. We worship him with reverence and awe. This simply means that we worship him with humility and holy fear, not with arrogance and carelessness. We worship him as those who know we do not deserve his mercy and grace. We worship with awe that we are citizens of his unshakable kingdom.

We live our entire lives with God's impending judgment in the future. Those who reject his Word will not escape this consuming fire. Only those in Christ will remain unshaken. This is the reason we worship with reverence and awe. Describing God as a consuming fire draws on the language Moses uses to describe God on Sinai (Exod 24:17; Deut 4:24). The gospel isn't merely fire insurance. The gospel is Christ's abundant mercy saving us from the holy wrath we rightfully deserve. Remembering that God is a consuming fire stokes our reverence and awe of him and reminds us of the severe and eternal consequences of failing to turn to him in faith and repentance. We must not fail as the Israelites did. We must persevere until the end.

Reflect and Discuss

1. How is God's speaking in the new covenant different from his speaking in the old covenant? How does the author use the heaven-earth contrast to draw out these distinctions?

2. The writer of Hebrews identifies God as a speaking God throughout his letter. Why is it important that we remember that our God speaks to his people? What does it mean to reject his words? How is the word he has spoken through Jesus Christ a message of both grace and judgment?

3. What is significant about the author's usage of the verbs *reject* and *escape*? What do these words tell us about the relationship between the gospel and God's wrath? About man's response to the gospel?

4. Many Christians and non-Christians have a difficult time comprehending God's wrath. Why must we talk about God's wrath when we talk about the gospel? Why is God's wrath an essential component to the gospel of Jesus Christ? Why must we take God's wrath against sin and sinners seriously?

5. Why does the author refer to Sinai and quote from Haggai 2? What truth is he driving home by making these references? What does God's shaking of the heavens and earth represent? What does the phrase "yet once more" signal?

6. How does the promise of God's impending judgment motivate you to live a holy life and to continue receiving his word today? How does it lead you to offer acceptable service to God and worship him?

7. Why does the author encourage his people to be grateful about receiving a kingdom that cannot be shaken? How does the promise of God's unshakable kingdom and its certain triumph encourage you to endure in the faith, even in the midst of today's increasing hostility toward Christians?

8. Why must reverence and awe characterize true Christian worship? What does it mean to worship God with reverence and awe? How does Romans 12:1 help us understand what it means to offer acceptable service?

9. How does the reminder that God is a consuming fire stoke your reverence and awe of him? How does it help you respond to him with obedience and faith?

Final Instructions: Love, Marriage, and Money

HEBREWS 13:1-6

Main Idea: Believers are to show brotherly love, to hold marriage in high honor, and to guard their hearts from the love of money.

I.   Love toward Saints: Enduring in Brotherly Affection (13:1)
II. Love toward Strangers: Showing Hospitality (13:2)
III. Love toward Prisoners: Remembering the Imprisoned and Mistreated (13:3)
IV. Hold Marriage in Honor (13:4)
V.   Hold Money Loosely (13:5-6)

I love reading letters. As a matter of fact, whenever I see a compendium of letters published by a major figure, I usually buy it. Reading letters reminds me that people used to write letters and that there was a time when personal and practical communication was accomplished by snail mail. This is the kind of communication we have in Hebrews 13.

In some ways the ending of Hebrews is similar to the ending of Romans. It's difficult to overestimate that letter's doctrinal and biblical engagement with the Old Testament as it lays out the gospel. Its ending, particularly chapter 16, reminds us that Romans isn't just a theological treatise; it's a letter to a congregation of actual people. Paul's conclusions demonstrate that he wrote his letters to actual people in real circumstances. Likewise, the author of Hebrews concludes his letter with personal and practical concerns in order to encourage people in the faith and exhort them to grow in holiness.

Before diving in, we should review what the author has just finished saying. Hebrews 12 concludes the great warning passage that began in chapter 10. The author explains what it means to be citizens of a heavenly kingdom, a kingdom that cannot be shaken. He closes the chapter by writing, "Therefore, since we are receiving a kingdom that cannot be shaken, let us be thankful. By it, we may serve God acceptably, with reverence and awe." In this last chapter the author tells us how to do that very thing.

Love toward Saints: Enduring in Brotherly Affection
HEBREWS 13:1

Hebrews 13:1 signals to us that a major shift between the old covenant and the new has occurred. In the old covenant, a sharp distinction existed between the chosen nation of Israel and all other peoples. This distinction was even on display within the temple itself. The temple was where God did business with *his people*. In order to enter the court of Israel, one had to be a Jew. And of course, not just any Jew could enter it—only one Jewish man could, the chief priest. For this reason, the word *brotherly* should stick out to us. It raises the question, Who is my brother? Our "brother" is anyone who is in Christ.

The word *brotherly* is revolutionary because it speaks to the relationship Christians have with one another. This love is a familial relationship unbelievers cannot understand. The world talks about the brotherhood of man and the fatherhood of God, but it doesn't really believe in God as Father, so it really has no concept of brotherhood. But Christians are joint heirs with Christ, and, by virtue of their union with him, are also sons and daughters of God. As such, we are brothers and sisters to one another. Faith in Christ makes us family. Thus, "let brotherly love continue" is a sweet exhortation. It insinuates that this distinct love is already there among the members of this congregation, so the plea is that it would continue.

Love toward Strangers: Showing Hospitality
HEBREWS 13:2

In verse 2 the author teaches that this brotherly love should even extend beyond the church. We should also show hospitality and love to strangers because, astoundingly, some of those strangers are angels. We often do not know with whom we're visiting. This is something we need to keep in mind, though it should not motivate our love. We simply do not know who we're really seeing when we notice a beggar on the side of the road, or a person in the hospital without a visitor, or someone in prison. The person we see might not be who we think we are seeing. In any case, we must show those in our paths hospitality for the glory of God.

Hospitality is an important Christian gift. Sadly, it's an often neglected one. Frankly, it's an aspect of our Christian calling about which we can learn much from our non-Christian friends. For instance,

Muslims and Mormons put an absolute premium on hospitality. I've yet to be in a Muslim home or institution where I was not offered rich hospitality. Nor have I met a Mormon who failed to go out of his or her way to show me a great measure of kindness. It's to our shame as Christians that we fail to be hospitable. We are called to show hospitality to everyone, even to strangers.

Love toward Prisoners: Remembering the Imprisoned and Mistreated
HEBREWS 13:3

Verse 3 addresses our responsibility to those in prison who are also part of the body of Christ. Here again, the church has often failed in its duty to care for the imprisoned. I'm personally thankful, among many other things, for Christians through the centuries who have given witness to Christ among prisoners. I'm thankful for their obedience to remember those who were in prison as though in prison with them. We ought to do the same. Some of my most meaningful moments in preaching have happened behind prison walls.

It's helpful to place this exhortation in the historical context of ancient jails. In the first century, prisons were not places one was sent to for any length of time. Prison was a place where one was held for trial or for debts. If you were in prison, you were most likely there because of your failure to repay a significant debt. Jesus's parables make this clear. You were more or less incarcerated until you could come up with enough money to buy your release. Otherwise, you would eventually be sold into slavery.

Hold Marriage in Honor
HEBREWS 13:4

Hebrews 13:4 comments on a very practical issue: marriage. The exhortation that marriage should be "honored by all" is essential because it demonstrates that Christ's people, where they are visible in the world, ought to be seen as a people who value marriage. Marriage isn't an issue at the bottom of the priority list for Christians, nor is it merely a secondary or tertiary issue. Instead, marriage is high on the list. "Marriage is to be honored by all" is a particularly comprehensive statement. It doesn't say, "Do not commit adultery." Rather, it's a positive statement.

Christians should give public, visible honor and private, personal honor to marriage as the monogamous union of a man and a woman.

The writer gives a second related instruction: "the marriage bed [is to be] kept undefiled." A great deal of commentary is not necessary for that statement. It's clear the author has sexual defilement in mind because of what he says next: "because God will judge the sexually immoral and adulterers." *Sexually immoral* is a broader category that encompasses adultery. Many Christians get issues of sexual morality right in terms of a checklist but wrong in terms of understanding. The Bible does not have a "yes" list and a "no" list when it comes to sexuality. There's no "allowed" list or "prohibited" list. Instead, the Bible teaches that sexual morality—in all of its aspects and manifestations—comes down to one central thing: sex belongs in marriage and nowhere else.

This is a radical statement to make in today's world, but it's deeply biblical. Scripture recognizes sex within marriage as something good and worthy of celebration. If we had a checklist on sexual morality, sex within marriage would be on the "yes" list. But everything else would be on the "no" list because every form of sex outside of marriage subverts and dishonors marriage. Any form of sex outside the marriage covenant, including adultery, is an affront to God's gift of marriage and is therefore deserving of God's judgment.

Hold Money Loosely
HEBREWS 13:5-6

The author's exhortation in Hebrews 13:5 is a call to live out the tenth commandment. Of the Ten Commandments, the tenth—do not covet—is perhaps the most difficult for us to fully comprehend, even though it tells us specifically what we should avoid coveting: our neighbor's wife, our neighbor's animals, or our neighbor's belongings. But today's entire commercial economy is built on a foundation that not only encourages us to have what we want, but to want what we don't have. We live in a society and operate within an economy of covetousness. As a result, it's a difficult thing to live free from want and free from a love of the money that can give us what we want. Nevertheless, this is exactly how Hebrews 13:5-6 tells us to live.

Verse 5 is not saying money is the problem. Instead, it warns against the *love* of money. Related to this first exhortation is the exhortation to be satisfied with what we have. In saying this, the author is not instructing his readers to stop working and simply live with what they have. Scripture comprehensively lays out the importance of thrift, labor, investment, and savings. God's Word gives us a rich economic tapestry, but this verse tells us to be content with what we have. Hebrews isn't giving us an economic philosophy; it's giving us a spiritual principle by which to live.

The second half of verse 5 and all of verse 6 tell us why we can be content with what we have. The source of our contentment is not the security and comfort we get from owning enough things; it's that we serve a God who takes care of us. We serve a God who will never leave or forsake us. God himself has promised.

In verse 6 the writer evaluates God's statement and applies it in a pointed way: "Therefore, we may boldly say, The Lord is my helper; I will not be afraid. What can man do to me?" This is an important Christian confession and reflects the same confidence in God's abiding character that the apostle Paul displays in Romans 8:31-39. It's good to ask ourselves these questions and to remember that nothing overly tragic can happen to us. We can lose everything we have, and it will be okay so long as we endure in the faith. I admit this is easy to say and a much harder thing to actually live out. But everything that *can* be taken away from us *will* be taken away from us one day. Nevertheless, we have everything we need in Christ, and we can be content because we serve a God who cares for us. The Lord is on our side.

Reflect and Discuss

1. Why is it important to remember that the book of Hebrews is a letter written to a congregation of individuals? How does thinking of Hebrews as a letter affect the way you approach this final chapter? What about the book as a whole?

2. What's unique about "brotherly love"? What does it teach us about the shift in the covenants? What makes brotherly love a distinctly Christian love?

3. How is showing hospitality a way of showing love? How can you show "brotherly love" or love toward strangers through hospitality?

4. Which people in your life have shown you particularly great hospitality? Why do you think some cultures (e.g., Muslim, Middle Eastern, Mormon, Hispanic) tend to be so hospitable? What can we learn from them?

5. Hebrews 13:3 commands us to *remember*. How is remembering a form of love? Who are some of the most often neglected and forgotten people in your life? What can you do to remind yourself of their situations so that you remember them in prayer or visit them?

6. That the author chooses to write specifically on marriage at the end of his letter demonstrates the importance of the subject in his mind. In what ways are you tempted—through your comments, thoughts, attitudes, or behaviors—to dishonor and defile marriage? In what ways does our culture promote the dishonor and defilement of marriage? Why does marriage matter to God?

7. Why is it important to present the biblical commands regarding marriage and sexuality in a positive form ("Do this") rather than always in a negative form ("Don't do this")?

8. List some practical ways to keep ourselves free from the love of money when we have a surplus of money. How can we keep the right perspective on money when we experience shortages?

9. What does it look like to be content with what you have? In what circumstances do you find it difficult to be content? How can we fight against our culture's constant enticements toward covetousness?

10. How does the gospel provide us with the motivation and the ability to keep ourselves from the love of money and to be content with what we have?

Final Instructions

HEBREWS 13:7-14

Main Idea: Christians must remember the unchanging faith of their leaders and safeguard it as they suffer with Jesus outside the camp.

I. **Remember Your Leaders**
II. **Remember Your Savior**
III. **Do Not Be Led Astray**
    A. Various kinds of strange teachings
    B. Strengthened by grace, not foods
IV. **Go Outside the Camp**
    A. A better altar and its better sacrifice
    B. Enduring for an eschatological city

To the casual observer, this final section of Hebrews might seem somewhat disjointed, in much the same way that those who read a military briefing from World War II today might find that account disjointed. In a military briefing, a commanding officer informs troops about the battle plan, provides tactical information, makes clarifications, and gives personal instruction. Troops receiving such a briefing would certainly see the instructions as coherent, but we, being so far removed from the original situation, would find it perplexing. This is why these concluding commands in Hebrews 13 might seem disconnected to us. Hebrews 13:7-14 is a commanding officer's last order of business with his troops. It was a word they needed to hear then, and it is a word we still need to hear now.

Remember Your Leaders

HEBREWS 13:7

As we've already seen, the letter to the Hebrews is filled with moral exhortations. This final section is no different. Here the author exhorts his people to remember their leaders. Specifically, he wants them to remember those who spoke the word of God. In the immediate context of the letter, this refers to those who taught them the gospel. If we broaden out, this refers to those who taught them the whole Bible.

The command to "remember" might seem peculiar to us at first. We would expect the author to encourage his readers to honor, respect, or greet their leaders, but why the call to "remember" them? It might have something to do with the martyrdom that was taking place at the time the letter was written. When the writer calls his readers to remember, it's very possible he is referring to leaders who had been killed for their faith.

The call to remember is a call to look back. The readers look back by considering the outcome of their leaders' way of life and by imitating their faith. This exhortation is common in the New Testament and similar to what Paul writes in 2 Timothy 3. Paul calls Timothy to avoid a wicked example and urges the young pastor to imitate Paul himself instead. He encourages Timothy to imitate his conduct, aim in life, faith, patience, love, and sufferings. This is the kind of instruction we see here.

Discipleship consists of living our lives before others in such a way that they learn from us—not only from what we teach but also from how we live. The leaders Hebrews 13:7 mentions testified to Christ by their manner of life. We should remember the teaching of our leaders, but we should also remember and practice their way of life. These leaders were faithful, and the letter's readers are called to imitate that faithfulness. We desperately need this kind of example today.

Remember Your Savior

HEBREWS 13:8

The unchanging nature of Christ is something Scripture makes abundantly clear. Jesus Christ truly is the same yesterday, today, and forever. We hear something similar about God in the Old Testament: "I am the Lord—I do not change" (Mal 3:6 TLB).

Though our outward circumstances are always changing, we do not have to worry about Christ changing. His disposition toward us is fixed for eternity. We do not have to worry about him waxing and waning in his saving power. Our leaders may die, but Jesus will still be faithful to his children. We can rest in the absolute confidence that he will never change.

Some commentators suggest that this concise, Christological hymn has nothing to do with its context. To them it appears out of place in the midst of these exhortations. In reality, though, verse 8 grounds the exhortations. Our faith and its teachings do not change. There is no such thing as new and improved Christianity. What we have is the faith "that was delivered to the saints once for all" (Jude 3). Though the letter's readers may have new leaders now and their circumstances will change, their Savior remains the same. He is the same yesterday, today, and forever. Therefore, we should remember the faithfulness of our leaders and not be led astray by anything contrary to the unchanging Christian message.

Do Not Be Led Astray
HEBREWS 13:9

Christianity, if rightly understood, is the same yesterday, today, and forever. This is because Jesus Christ does not change. And it is by his unchanging nature that we should be able to detect false teaching and not be led astray by it. This is what the author presses his people toward in verse 9.

Various Kinds of Strange Teachings

The author uses two noteworthy words to describe the kind of teaching we should avoid: *various* and *strange*. Theological variation in the gospel is not something to be embraced; it is something to be avoided. After all, there is only one faith, one gospel, and one Savior. Additionally, we should be able to recognize a teaching as strange when it runs contrary to the sound doctrine of Scripture. Strange is attractive because it is unusual, but it ultimately leads us astray. That is why the author gives us this exhortation.

Though these various kinds of strange teachings are not explicitly identified, the following verses suggest that the author has teachings that derive from the Old Testament law in mind. They most likely focus on food regulations, which were meant to distinguish the Israelites as God's holy people. Whatever they are, these teachings contradict the theological unity of the gospel message, so the readers are commanded to avoid them. The author warns his people that entertaining false teachings will lead them astray.

Strengthened by Grace, Not Foods

The author also reminds us that establishing or strengthening our hearts by grace, not through external food laws, is a good and wonderful thing.

At first, the contrast might seem confusing. We understand the dichotomy between grace and law, between gospel and law, but what about between grace and external food laws? The author obviously expected his audience to understand his comment. They heard his word as Jews who had become Christians.

One of the dangers of external laws like the Jewish dietary restrictions is that we tend to overemphasize them. We think we can be justified by keeping them. It seems that the Jewish Christians to whom this letter was addressed were focusing so much on Old Testament dietary laws that they forgot the greater and weightier things—salvation through grace by faith in Christ. They, like us today, desperately needed to hear the main message of Hebrews: the new covenant inaugurated by Jesus's blood is far superior to the old covenant.

Therefore, it does not matter how concerned we are with dietary rules, whether they are kosher or Atkins based. Christians live by grace, and our hearts are strengthened by grace. External matters cannot strengthen or save us. We are saved by the mercy of God, which has been demonstrated in the new covenant. This is exactly where the author takes us next.

Go Outside the Camp
HEBREWS 13:10-14

Rather than eating the right foods as per the old covenant, new covenant Christians feed on Christ, which is yet another contrast between the old and new covenants. We have seen this kind of contrast throughout the entire letter. So once again the author stops to reinforce one of his main points: Christ is the mediator of a new and better covenant enacted on new and better promises.

A Better Altar and Its Better Sacrifice

In verse 10 the writer compares the new covenant altar—the cross of Christ—with the old covenant altar. He points back to the tabernacle rather than to the temple, as he often does, to inform his readers that those who serve at the old altar have no right to eat at the new one. But believers do have a right to eat at this new and better altar, for they enjoy fellowship with God through the blood of Jesus Christ. Once again, the writer is demonstrating that Jesus is indeed a far better high priest, for his food and altar surpasses the food and altar of the old covenant.

The author then brings up the bodies of the animals that were sacrificed under the old covenant. Although we don't often think about what became of those carcasses, we know from Scripture that they were taken outside of the city and burned. It would have defiled the city if they'd been burned within its walls.

Like these old covenant sacrifices, "Jesus also suffered outside the gate." This parallel is most explicitly seen in John 19:17-20, as Jesus carries his cross to Golgotha, which was outside the gates of Jerusalem. We also know from the Gospels that he was buried outside the gates. This is truly an amazing correlation. But what makes Jesus's suffering outside the gates far superior to that of the Old Testament animals is what his suffering accomplishes: Jesus suffers outside the gates "so that he might sanctify the people by his own blood." His blood actually makes believers holy. This astonishing reality once again reveals that the old covenant sin offerings pointed to the better new covenant offering of Jesus Christ's blood.

Enduring for an Eschatological City

This reality also leads the author to draw implications for his people in verse 13. Since Jesus suffered outside the camp, his people must identify with him there. Following Jesus means joining him outside the camp. The writer's people were tempted to find their identity in Judaism and the old covenant. Instead of "bearing his disgrace" for the sake of Christ, they were looking for safety and security in something other than Jesus. Thus, the author is telling us that we must go outside the camp—even if it means we must suffer—in order to shine forth as his disciples.

Verse 14 tells us why and how Christians can suffer for the sake of Christ: because we anticipate an everlasting city. Our hope is not in the fading city of man, it's in the enduring city of God. We wait for an eschatological city, the heavenly Jerusalem. And it's this city for which we can endure persecution outside the camp with Jesus.

Reflect and Discuss

1. Do some of the verses in this last chapter of Hebrews seem disjointed to you? How does understanding the epistolary (letter-like) nature of the book help you understand any seemingly random instructions?

2. Hebrews 13:7 calls Christians to "remember" their leaders. What does that look like practically? How might we apply this command

today? What other instructions in this passage help us to apply the command to remember?

3. Who are some of the Hebrews 13:7 leaders in your life? How have they set an example for you in their faith and in their conduct? How are you conducting your own life so that others can learn from you?

4. What does it mean that Christ is unchanging? How does his unchanging nature relate to our relationship with him? How does this encourage you to go outside the camp with Jesus, even if that means suffering for his sake?

5. How is the statement about Jesus in verse 8 related to the commands given in verses 7 and 9? What implications does verse 8 have for us as we consider some supposed "Christian" leaders today and the content of their teaching?

6. With what various strange teachings does culture confront you? Do you ever feel tempted to entertain these teachings at all? Why or why not? How do these teachings differ from the one true and unchanging faith and message of Jesus?

7. What is the author of Hebrews trying to communicate when he encourages his readers not to be strengthened by foods? In what "external laws" are you tempted to find your own justification? What does grace have to do with establishing the heart?

8. How do verses 10-14 reiterate the main theme of the letter? Why don't those who serve at the old altar have any right to eat at the new altar? What does this say about the old covenant now that the new covenant has come?

9. What does it mean for something to go outside the gate? How did old covenant sacrifices suffer outside the gate? How does this point to Jesus? What does it mean for us to go outside the camp with Jesus? What role does going outside the camp with Jesus play in our discipleship and Christian witness?

10. What do you often finding yourself looking to for safety and security in rather than bearing disgrace for Christ? What relationship does the coming city of God have to our suffering? How does the reality of an everlasting city motivate you to endure in the faith?

A Fitting Conclusion

HEBREWS 13:15-25

Main Idea: The author of Hebrews brings his letter to a close with some final exhortations, a genuine prayer, and gospel encouragement for his readers.

I. Offer Up Pleasing Sacrifices (13:15-16)
II. Submit to Your Leaders (13:17)
III. Pray for Us (13:18-19)
IV. A Remarkable Benediction (13:20-21)
   A. The God of peace and the blood of the resurrected Shepherd
   B. Equipped to please
V. Final Words (13:22-25)

By this point, the author has made it abundantly clear that one of his primary concerns in writing his epistle is to show us the right way to read the Old Testament. This concern continues into the last section of the letter's final chapter. He begins by discussing worship using the patterns and language that would have been common to Jews in the first century. Having thoroughly addressed the matter, the author then concludes his letter with one last set of exhortations, a prayer, and a benediction of grace.

Offer Up Pleasing Sacrifices
HEBREWS 13:15-16

Because of Christ and the new covenant he enacted, we no longer offer animal sacrifices. Although God established animal sacrifices under the old covenant, God's wrath has now been fully satisfied in the atonement of Christ. Thus, animal sacrifices are no longer necessary. It is, however, for this very reason that the writer of Hebrews exhorts his readers to continually offer up pleasing sacrifices of praise to God in verses 15-16.

We are not to offer up a sacrifice of blood or of bulls or of rams; it is a sacrifice of praise and worship God now desires. This sacrifice comes "through" Christ. That preposition is incredibly important. We do not offer a sacrifice of praise in our own names or power; we do so through Jesus. He is the mediator. We only bring an acceptable sacrifice of praise to the Father if we offer it through his Son.

What does it look like to offer a sacrifice of praise? It looks like "fruit of [our] lips that confess his name." This harks back to what Paul says in Romans 10:9-10: offering up a sacrifice of praise to God requires that we publicly confess with our mouths our faith in the Lord Jesus Christ. Our lips are to echo what we believe in our hearts. A continual sacrifice of praise comes out of lips that confess and acknowledge that Jesus is our great high priest.

In verse 16 we are told *not* to neglect to do good. God is pleased with those who do what is right and meet the material needs of others in the church. Doing good and loving others by sharing what you have are described as sacrifices that please God. Sharing material needs was not a form of Communism; it was a gospel-driven desire and kindness to care for one another. Where we see the church, we should see a willingness to share. God is pleased with such simple acts of love.

Submit to Your Leaders
HEBREWS 13:17

Once again, the writer of Hebrews gives a call for Christ's people to listen to and receive the teaching of those who are commissioned to teach. They are not instructed to do so because their leaders are smarter, but because God knows what his people need—teachers. For this reason, the church rightly sets apart and commissions those who are called and given this gift. We are reminded, however, that they will be held to a higher accountability (Jas 3:1). In this passage the author of Hebrews does not simply instruct his readers to receive the words of their leaders, but to obey and submit to them.

He calls his readers to submit to what is taught—that is, to what the teacher teaches—not necessarily to the teacher. God has determined that his Word be conveyed by the human voice. Teachers are therefore just human instruments that set forth God's divine Word. This instruction is not some obscure statement of cultic authority. Insofar as the leaders teach in accordance with God's Word, they are to be obeyed and their teaching is to be taken seriously. Why? "They keep watch over your souls as those who will give an account."

Becoming a pastor, elder, or teacher in the church is no small thing. It involves the care of souls. Pastors and elders watch over the spiritual lives of their people and exercise their ministry before God, to whom they will give an account—an extremely sobering reality. We are to let our leaders shepherd us with joy and not with groaning, otherwise their labors of love are of no advantage to us. Grudgingly obeying our leaders does not sharpen our hearts; it hardens them.

Pray for Us
HEBREWS 13:18-19

The author's words in this section echo the closing address Paul gives in the book of Acts when he says, "I always strive to have a clear conscience" (Acts 24:16). Church leaders should pray and strive for this very thing. Our goal should be to have clear consciences as we faithfully lead Christ's church. We want to honor the Lord in all we say, do, and think. Like the author, we do not want to bring any reproach on the gospel. This is why we need the prayers of our people.

At this point in the epistle, we see how much of a letter this book really is. Letters naturally elicit the kind of intimate language that requires the first person pronoun. So far, we have not seen much of the first person because of the letter's formal nature. As the author begins to close the missive, however, the tone of the writing changes and the pronouns shift accordingly. He urges his readers, rather earnestly, to pray for him so that he might be restored to them sooner. He is a real live human being who is not there with his church but who wants to be.

A Remarkable Benediction
HEBREWS 13:20-21

We finally arrive at the benediction. This prayer might be one of the most beautiful prayers ever uttered by a Christian. It stands near the end of the letter as a declaration of absolute confidence in God. It is a prayer for the church from which the author is absent, but which he loves so dearly.

The God of Peace and the Blood of the Resurrected Shepherd

It is not a small thing to be able to say, "God of peace." God's disposition toward those who are in Christ is one of peace. Because of Jesus's work on our behalf, we now know God as the God of peace. We do not have to hope that God will respond to us with peace. In the Muslim system of thought, God's peace is something one hopes for but cannot presume upon. The reason for this is simple: Christ is missing from their theology. If it were up to us to achieve peace with God, we would always remain eternal enemies with him. Instead, we thank God that Christ has achieved that peace for us. Thus it is a wonderful thing to be able to say, "The God of peace."

This benediction also shows the centrality of Christ's resurrection. It is the foundation for our faith. Of all things the author could have brought up about Jesus, he chooses to emphasize his resurrection from the dead. This, among the many other reasons the author has pointed out throughout Hebrews, distinguishes Jesus from all other priests. Unlike every other high priest, Jesus is a high priest who *lives*.

The author also identifies Jesus as "the great Shepherd of the sheep." What an amazing title. Of the many titles given to Jesus, could there be a sweeter one? Sheep are aimless, vulnerable creatures; they desperately need someone to take care of them. Given that the letter's original recipients were Jews, they would have been well acquainted with the imagery of sheep. Therefore, they would have understood themselves to be Christ's sheep, his people. We are the sheep of Jesus's pasture. Such a designation encapsulates Christ's pastoral love for his people. His love runs so deep for his sheep that he gives his life up for us (John 10:11).

Even in this prayer, the author does not miss another opportunity to emphasize the superiority of the new eternal covenant God has made with his people. Jesus is the great Shepherd of the sheep precisely because he shed his blood on their behalf. And that blood establishes this eternal covenant with God. There is no need for another covenant to come. This is the "everlasting" covenant, the purpose for which God made the world: to demonstrate his glory in the salvation of sinners by the shed blood of the Lord Jesus Christ.

Equipped to Please

Verse 21 tells us what the author expects the Lord to do for these people by virtue of forgiven sins through the blood of Christ. He confidently asks God to equip them with everything good so that they can do his will and please him. We need God's help to do his will. We cannot accomplish it on our own. This is precisely why the author asks God to accomplish these things in his people.

Our aim as Christians should be to do "what is pleasing in his sight, through Jesus Christ." The only way we can please God is through Jesus. No one can please God without him. At the same time, the author asks his prayer to be fulfilled through Jesus Christ, whose great love for us leads us to glory in the Father forever and ever.

Final Words
HEBREWS 13:22-25

One would think the word *amen* that ends the benediction would also end the letter, but that is not the case. The author has a few more things to say and one last appeal to make. The writer intends for his letter to be both encouragement and exhortation. He does not write this church merely to inform them theologically. Though doing so is important, his main purpose is to exhort them to persevere in the faith, thus the appeal to bear with his word of exhortation. Dense as it may be, it is not a particularly long letter.

The writer also wants his readers to know the status of Timothy. This is the same Timothy we read about in 1 and 2 Timothy. He has been released from prison. We are not told why he had been incarcerated, but we can assume it was for the sake of the gospel. If he is able to join the author, the two will visit the readers together.

In the conclusion of the letter, we read the word *leader* for the third time in the chapter, which again emphasizes the responsibility and stewardship of those who teach. The recipients of this letter are also told that those from Italy send them greetings. This suggests that churches have cropped up throughout all of Italy, not just Rome, and those currently with the author send greetings to this church. This is another interesting statement reminding us that this church consisted of real human beings in a real historical time and place.

The writer of Hebrews closes his letter with "grace." There may be no more proper and precious way to end a letter like Hebrews than by asking God's unmerited favor on the recipients. The whole letter has really been about the grace established in the new covenant God has made with his people through the blood of Jesus Christ. We have been saved by grace, and we will endure until the end by grace. Grace be with all of us, indeed.

Reflect and Discuss

1. What does the author have in mind when he urges his readers to offer a *sacrifice of praise*? What does it look like for us to obey this instruction practically? What does the fruit of our lips have to do with this sacrifice of praise?

2. How might you meet the material needs of someone in your church? Why should local churches be marked by a gospel-driven desire to share and meet the needs of our brothers and sisters? In what other places in Scripture do you see this idea practiced and commanded?

3. How are our submission and obedience to our church leaders contingent on the substance of what they teach us? Why is it important to submit to our leaders with joy? Why is it to our detriment if our obedience and submission are given grudgingly?

4. How is the author's verse 18 petition for his readers to pray for him related to his desire? Why do church leaders and teachers especially need the prayers of their people? How does verse 18 encourage you to pray for your pastor?

5. What are some of the main elements/images of the Christian faith that you see in the writer's benediction? How does the author use these elements/images to rehearse the gospel for his readers in the benediction? How does this once again highlight the superiority of the new covenant?

6. How is the author's prayer in verse 21 connected to the exhortation he gave his readers in verse 16? Why is it impossible to please God through anything other than Jesus Christ?

7. What can you learn about godly prayers through the brief prayer preserved in this epistle? How can you apply what you've learned about prayer to your own prayer life?

8. How does the author choose to finish this letter? How did he begin it? Knowing the content of the letter, how is the subject at the end of the letter related to the subject at the beginning of the letter? Why is this a fitting way to end Hebrews?

WORKS CITED

Brown, John. *Hebrews.* Geneva Series of Commentaries. Reprint edition. Edinburgh: Banner of Truth Trust, 1961.

Bruce, F. F. *The Epistle to the Hebrews.* Revised edition. New International Commentary on the New Testament. Grand Rapids, MI: Eerdmans,1990.

Calvin, John. *Institutes of the Christian Religion.* Translated by Ford Lewis Battles. Edited by John T. McNeil. Philadelphia, PA: Westminster Press, 1960.

"Chicago Statement of Biblical Inerrancy." Dallas,TX: International Council on Biblical Inerrancy, 1978. http://library.dts.edu/Pages /TL/Special/ICBI_1.pdf

Ellingworth, Paul. *The Epistle to the Hebrews: A Commentary on the Greek Text.* New International Greek Testament Commentary. Grand Rapids, MI: Eerdmans,1993.

Geisler, Norman, and Frank Turek. *I Don't Have Enough Faith to Be an Atheist.* Wheaton, IL: Crossway, 2004.

Henry, Carl F. H. *God Who Speaks and Shows.* Vol. 3 of *God, Revelation and Authority.* Wheaton, IL: Crossway, 1999.

Horton, Michael. *Christless Christianity: The Alternative Gospel of the American Church.* Grand Rapids, MI: Baker, 2012.

Hughes, R. Kent. *Hebrews: An Anchor for the Soul.* Preaching the Word. Wheaton, IL: Crossway, 1993.

Lane, William L. *Hebrews 1–8 and Hebrews 9–13.* Word Biblical Commentary. Dallas, TX: Word, 1991.

Owen, John. *The Death of Death in the Death of Christ.* Carlisle, PA: Banner of Truth, 1959.

Phillips, Richard D. *Hebrews.* Reformed Expository Commentary: New Testament. Phillipsburg, NJ: P&R, 2006.

Schaeffer, Francis. *He Is There and He Is Not Silent.* Wheaton, IL: Tyndale House, 1972.

Schreiner, Thomas R. *Commentary on Hebrews*. Biblical Theology for Christian Proclamation. Edited by T. Desmond Alexander, Andreas J. Köstenberger, and Thomas R. Schreiner. Nashville, TN: B&H, 2015.

Warfield, B. B. *Inspiration and Authority of the Bible*. Phillipsburg, NJ: P&R Publishing, 1948.

SCRIPTURE INDEX

Genesis
1–2 *28*
1–3 *175*
1:26 *28*
3 *36, 91*
3:24 *128*
3:25 *20*
4 *172*
4:4 *172*
5:21-24 *173*
6:8 *177*
12 *175*
12:1-3 *102*
14 *99–100,
    103–4, 107,
    123*
14:17-20 *100*
14:17-24 *72*
15 *175, 182*
15:1-6 *188*
15:6 *171, 182*
15:18-21 *51*
17 *175*
17:16 *182*
17:17 *182*
21 *184*
21:1 *182*
22 *184*
22:1-2 *184*
22:3-4 *185*
22:5 *185–86*
22:10-14 *186*
22:16-17 *95*

22:17 *185*
25:29-34 *204*
25:34 *204*
27:27-29,39-40
    187
27:27-30 *205*
27:34 *205*
48:1-22 *188*
50:24-25 *188*

Exodus
1:22 *188*
13:21 *10*
16:31-34 *128*
19 *208*
19:12 *208*
19:12-13 *208*
19:16 *208*
19:16,19 *208*
19:18 *208, 216*
20:18-19 *208*
24:4-8 *137*
24:17 *217*
25:9,40 *122*
25:23-29 *128*
25–30 *127*
25:30 *128*
25–31, 35–40 *128*
25:31-40 *128*
26 *122, 124*
28 *104*
28:1 *72*
30:6 *128*

37:10-16 *128*
37:17-24 *128*
40:34-35 *10*

Leviticus
4 *104*
10:1 *127*
16 *129*
16:12-13 *128*
16:14 *156*
17:11 *138*

Numbers
12:7 *45*
17:1-13 *128*
22:28-30 *7*
25 *98*

Deuteronomy
4 *103, 214*
4:24 *217*
5:24-27 *208*
6:4-9 *71*
17:14-20 *104*
18:15 *45*
18:15-22 *189*
30:19 *26*
31:9-13 *71*
32:35-36 *164*
32:43 *19*
33:2 *26*

Joshua
1:7-8 *71*

2 *191*
6 *190*
6:22-25 *191*

Judges
5:5 *216*
6:36-40 *191*
8:24-27 *191*
11:30-31,34-40
 191
13–16 *191*

1 Samuel
2:17 *164*
15:22-23 *149*

2 Samuel
5:7 *209*
7 *19*
7:14 *19*
11 *191*

1 Kings
8:10-11 *10*
17:17-23 *191*

2 Kings
4:18-36 *191*

2 Chronicles
26:16-21 *99*

Psalms
2:7 *19, 72*
8 *29*
8:4-6 *28*
8:6 *28*
19:1-2 *9*
22 *33*
22:19-24 *33*
22:22 *33*
40 *148*

40:6-8 *148*
45:6-7 *19*
95 *51, 57–58, 63*
95:7-8 *52*
95:7-11 *50*
95:11 *57, 59*
102:25-27 *19*
104:4 *19*
106:6-43 *50*
110 *20, 73, 103–4,*
 107, 123, 150
110:1 *20*
110:4 *109–10*

Proverbs
3:11-12 *198*
7:1-3 *71*

Isaiah
5 *91*
6 *56, 99*
6:1 *99*
8 *33*
8:17-18 *33*
26:11 *162*
35 *202*
40:3-4 *202*
43:6-7 *32*
53 *149*
53:7 *190*
55:11 *61*

Jeremiah
10 *127*
31 *111, 153*
31:31-34 *123,*
 125, 151
31:34 *124*

Ezekiel
36:26 *52*

Habakkuk
2:3-4 *166*

Haggai
2 *216, 218*
2:2-9 *216*

Matthew
4 *66*
4:1-11 *35*
5:12 *166*
5:17 *8, 14*
5:28 *66*
12:31-32 *164*
13 *91, 93, 162*
13:10-15 *56*
13:13 *25*
13:22 *91*
16:18 *36*
18:20 *127*
24:24 *89*
27:14 *190*
27:51 *156*
28:10 *33*

Luke
2:9 *20*
2:10-11 *26*
22:20 *124*
24:13-49 *118*
24:25-27,44-47 *xiv*

John
1:1 *18*
1:1-3 *10*
1:14 *127*
3:16 *36, 59*
4:24 *127*
5:24 *89*
5:39,46 *xiv*
6:37 *158*

8:44 *35*
10:10 *35*
10:11 *234*
10:28 *158*
12:27 *75*
14:6-7 *10*
14:8-9 *57*
16:7 *164*
16:33 *165*
17 *75*
17:17 *25*
19:17-20 *229*
19:30 *123*
20:27 *212*

Acts
2:22-24 *142*
4:11 *46*
7:53 *26*
8:26-40 *190*
10:1-8 *26*
24:16 *233*

Romans
1:4 *18*
1:20 *9*
2:15 *109*
3 *67*
3:9-20 *133*
3:21 *13, 45*
3:21-26 *38, 146*
4:1-12 *171*
4:1-25 *57*
5:1 *133*
6:10 *141*
7 *195*
7:7 *109*
8:1 *133*
8:28 *21*

8:31-39 *223*
8:34 *12*
8:38-39 *174*
8:39 *89*
10:9-10 *232*
10:9,13 *156*
10:17 *25*
11:29 *89*
12:1 *133, 217–18*
12:18 *203*
15:4 *14*
16 *219*

1 Corinthians
1:6-8 *89*
3 *83*
3:1-2 *82*
3:17 *42*
6:18 *204*
6:19-20 *204*
7:5 *35*
11:14 *35*
14:3-5 *27*
15:14-15 *196*
15:20 *28, 37*
15:22-23 *37*
15:32 *178*
15:45-47 *28*
15:54-55 *37*

2 Corinthians
1:20 *189*
2:10-11 *35*
5:8 *36*
7:10 *205*

Galatians
3:19 *26*
3:29 *188*
4:4 *141*

Ephesians
1:3 *104*
2:1-7 *52*
2:19-20 *46*
2:20 *27*
2:21 *42*
4:8 *27*
4:11-12 *27*
6:11 *35*

Philippians
1:6 *52, 89*
2 *18, 120*
2:8 *33, 75*
3:20 *183*

Colossians
1:15-20 *16*
3:16 *52*

2 Thessalonians
3:3 *89*

2 Timothy
3 *226*
3:16 *14*
3:16-17 *5*
4:7 *195*

Hebrews
1 *11*
1:1 *7, 214*
1:1-2 *174*
1:1-3 *9, 15, 17*
1–2 *37, 41, 43*
1:2 *8–9, 18, 24, 27, 141*
1:3 *10*
1:4 *17–18, 210*
1:5 *18, 20*
1:5-6 *18*

1:7 *19*
1:7-12 *19*
1:8 *19*
1:8-9 *19*
1:8-11 *19*
1:10-12 *19*
1:13-14 *20*
1:14 *20*
2 *31, 41, 64, 68*
2:1 *25*
2:1-3 *24*
2:2 *24–26*
2:2-3 *25*
2:3-4 *27*
2:5 *28*
2:5-9 *28*
2:5-18 *95*
2:6-8 *28*
2:8 *28, 210*
2:9 *29, 31*
2:10 *31–32, 39, 75–76, 105*
2:10-13 *31*
2:10-18 *31*
2:11 *32–33*
2:12 *33*
2:13 *33*
2:14-15 *34, 36*
2:14-16 *34*
2:15 *36*
2:16 *37*
2:17 *39*
2:17-18 *37, 66*
2:18 *39*
3 *41, 55, 197*
3:1 *41*
3:1-4 *41*
3:2 *44*
3:4 *44, 46*

3:5 *45–46*
3:5-6 *44, 46*
3:6 *45–46*
3:7 *49, 57, 59, 151*
3:7-11 *49*
3:8 *50*
3:9 *50*
3:11 *51*
3:12 *51*
3:12-19 *51*
3:13 *51*
3:14 *52, 54*
3:15 *52*
3:15-18 *52*
3:16-18 *53*
3:19 *53*
4 *51, 55, 64, 70*
4:1-2 *55*
4:2 *56*
4:3 *57*
4:3-10 *57*
4:4 *57*
4:5 *57*
4:6-7 *57*
4:7 *59*
4:8 *58*
4:10 *58–59*
4:11 *60*
4:11-13 *60*
4:12 *50, 61*
4:12-13 *60*
4:13 *61*
4:14 *64–65, 69–70*
4:14–5:10 *79*
4:14-16 *69*
4:15 *33, 66, 69, 115*

4:16 *68–69*
5 *70, 98*
5:1 *70*
5:1-4 *70*
5:3 *71*
5:4 *72*
5:5-6 *72*
5:7-10 *74*
5:8 *75*
5:9 *75, 105*
5:11 *79, 93–94*
5:12 *80*
5:12-13 *80*
5:14 *83*
6 *91, 93*
6:1-3 *87*
6:1-8 *86, 93*
6:4-6 *89*
6:4-8 *89*
6:9-10 *92*
6:9-12 *93*
6:9-20 *93, 96*
6:12 *94*
6:13 *95*
6:13-18 *94*
6:18 *89*
6:19-20 *96*
7 *98, 103–4*
7:1 *99–100*
7:1-4 *99*
7:1-22 *113*
7:3 *101*
7:4 *101*
7:5 *102*
7:5-10 *102*
7:6 *102*
7:8-9 *103*
7–10 *112*
7:11-12 *106*

7:13-14 *107*
7:15-18 *108*
7:18 *109*
7:19 *110*
7:20-22 *110*
7:22 *110, 112*
7:23-25 *113*
7:25 *113–14, 156*
7:26-28 *115*
7:27 *141*
7:27-28 *5*
7:28 *105, 116*
8 *110*
8:1 *124*
8:1-5 *119*
8:2 *121*
8:3-5 *5, 121*
8:4-5 *121*
8:5 *121–22*
8:6-13 *122*
8:8 *120*
8:8-12 *123, 151*
8:9 *120*
8:13 *129*
9 *64, 140*
9:1 *127*
9:1-5 *127*
9:1-10 *134*
9:2-5 *128, 131*
9:5 *128*
9:6-10 *129*
9:8 *132, 151*
9:9 *131, 134*
9–10 *11, 39, 133*
9:10 *132*
9:11 *131*
9:11-12 *134, 146*
9:11-22 *133*
9:12 *134, 136, 141*

9:12,14,25-26 *164*
9:13-14 *135*
9:14 *135*
9:15 *136, 166*
9:16-22 *137*
9:18 *137*
9:22 *137, 140,*
    146, 148, 172
9:23 *141*
9:23-26 *140*
9:24 *141*
9:25-26 *141*
9:27 *142*
9:27-28 *142*
9:28 *142, 150*
10 *179, 219*
10:1 *146*
10:1-3 *5*
10:1-18 *154*
10:2 *147*
10:2-4 *147*
10:3 *148*
10:4 *89, 150*
10:5 *152*
10:5-7 *148*
10:5-10 *148*
10:8 *149*
10:9 *149*
10:10 *141, 149*
10:11 *150, 152*
10:11-14 *150*
10:12 *150*
10:14 *151, 153*
10:15 *49*
10:15-18 *151*
10:18 *152*
10:19 *154, 164*
10:19-22 *154*
10:19-25 *154*

10:20 *155*
10:22 *159*
10:23-25 *157*
10:24 *158*
10:24-25 *160*
10:26 *162*
10:26-27 *161*
10:26-39 *161*
10:27 *162*
10:28 *162*
10:28-31 *163*
10:29 *163–64,*
    169
10:30 *164, 168*
10:30-31 *168*
10:31 *169*
10:32 *169*
10:32-34 *165*
10:32-39 *169*
10:33-34 *165*
10:34 *165*
10:35 *166*
10:35-36 *187*
10:35-39 *166*
10:36 *166*
10:38 *167*
10:39 *167, 170*
10:24-25 *158*
11 *94, 167, 169,*
    170, 179,
    183, 192,
    194–95, 210,
    212
11:1 *176, 185,*
    189
11:1-2 *170*
11:1-10 *179*
11:2 *192*
11:3 *171*

11:3-4 171
11:4 171, 183,
    212
11:5 173
11:5-6 173
11:6 89, 173–74
11:7 175–76
11:8-10 177
11:9 178
11:11 182
11:11-12 181
11:12 183
11:13 183, 186
11:13-16 183
11:14-15 183
11:17-19 184
11:19 186
11:20-22 187
11:23-28 188
11:24 188
11:26 189
11:27 189
11:28 190
11:29 190
11:29-31 190
11:30 190
11:31 190
11:32-40 191
11:33-34 191
11:35-38 191
11:40 192
12 195, 207, 219
12:1 210
12:1-3 194, 200
12:2 196
12:3 197
12:4 198
12:4-11 198

12:5 198
12:11 201, 205
12:12 201, 205
12:12-13 201
12:12-17 207, 212
12:13 202
12:14 203, 206
12:14-16 202
12:14-17 202
12:15 203
12:18 208, 214
12:18-21 207
12:19-20 208
12:22-23 209–10,
    213
12:22-24 209
12:23 211
12:25 214
12:25-29 214
12:26-27 215
12:27 216
12:28-29 217
12:29 164, 176
13 207, 219
13:1 220
13:2 220
13:3 221, 224
13:4 221
13:5 222
13:5-6 222–23
13:6 223
13:7 225–26, 229
13:7-14 225
13:8 226, 230
13:9 227, 230
13:10 228
13:10-14 228, 230
13:13 229

13:15-16 231
13:16 232, 236
13:17 232
13:18 236
13:18-19 233
13:20-21 233
13:21 234, 236
13:22-25 235
13:23 5

James
3:1 xiii, 232

1 Peter
1:1 183
1:5 52, 195
2:5 46
2:5,9 42
2:11 183
5:8 35

2 Peter
1:10 91
1:21 49, 59
3:10 159

1 John
1:9 68
2:19 91, 162
5:13 156

Jude
3 227

Revelation
13:8 117
19:15 26
21:9-27 178